The Laughter of the Oppressed

The Laughter of the Oppressed

Ethical and Theological Resistance in
Wiesel, Morrison, and Endo

Jacqueline A. Bussie

*To my great teacher
Dr Jones love ~
Jacqueline a Bussie*

t & t clark

T & T Clark International, 80 Maiden Lane, New York, NY 10038

T & T Clark International, The Tower Building, 11 York Road, London SE1 7NX

T & T Clark International is a Continuum imprint.

Unless otherwise noted, the scripture quotations contained herein are from the New Revised Standard Version Bible, copyright © 1989 by the Division of Christian Education of the National Council of Churches of Christ in the U.S.A. Used by permission. All rights reserved.

Excerpts from *Gates of the Forest* by Elie Wiesel. English language translation copyright 1966 by Henry Holt and Company. Reprinted by permission of Henry Holt and Company.

From *Beloved* by Toni Morrison, copyright © 1987 by Toni Morrison. Used by permission of Alfred A. Knopf, a division of Random House, Inc.

From "Silence" by Shusaku Endo. Copyright © 1969 by Monumenta Nipponica. Reprinted by permission of Taplinger Publishing Co., Inc.

Library of Congress Cataloging-in-Publication Data

Bussie, Jacqueline Aileen.
  The laughter of the oppressed : ethical and theological resistance in Wiesel, Morrison, and Endo / by Jacqueline A. Bussie.
      p. cm.
  Includes bibliographical references and index.
  ISBN-13: 978-0-567-02677-4 (hardcover : alk. paper)
  ISBN-10: 0-567-02677-9 (hardcover : alk. paper)
  ISBN-13: 978-0-567-02678-1 (pbk. : alk. paper)
  ISBN-10: 0-567-02678-7 (pbk. : alk. paper)
  1. Laughter–Religious aspects–Christianity. 2. Laughter in literature.
  I. Title.

BT709.B87 2007
261.8—dc22

                                        2007020176

Contents

ACKNOWLEDGMENTS

I have found that in writing a book such as this you cannot help but accrue a tremendous amount of indebtedness and gratitude. First and foremost, I want to thank all of my former colleagues at the University of Virginia, where the seed of this book's idea was planted, watered, and encouraged to grow, especially by Gene Rogers, Esther Menn, Roberto Ransom, Peter Slade, Jonathan Malesic, and Paul Freedman. An unspeakable amount of gratitude goes above all to Larry Bouchard for his seven years of mentorship, constructive criticism, love of all things tragic and theological, and repeated lunches at Michael's Bistro (always his treat). A special thank you also goes to Charles Marsh for introducing me to Jürgen Moltmann at the Spring Institute of Lived Theology, 2005. I am grateful to U.Va. for an incredible education and for introducing me to the amazing intellects of these individuals who have so shaped my life, research, teaching, and writing.

Second, I want to express my gratitude to Tony Abbott, who is not only the most inspiring professor I ever had, but also the person who first introduced me to both theology and the field of religion and literature. Without Tony, I would not have become a university professor or writer, because it was in watching him do both things so well that I caught a first glimpse of my life's vocation. Third, I want to acknowledge my immense intellectual debt to everyone cited in this book, but especially my great spiritual teachers Professor Elie Wiesel, Dr. James Cone, and Dr. Jürgen Moltmann, who all generously took the time to read this manuscript and offer encouraging feedback in the early stages, though I was but a stranger to them.

Fourth, I want to thank all of my colleagues at Capital University for their continued support, especially Tom Christenson, Eva George, Joy Schroeder, Kurt Keljo, Brian Murphy, and Nichole Johnson. I also acknowledge my indebtedness to every student I have ever had the privilege of teaching at Capital, and in particular Terah Herman, who volunteered to be the first undergraduate reader of this manuscript. In like fashion, I acknowledge my indebtedness to all those whose laughter and supportive friendship enabled me to complete this book, with special gratitude extended to Julia Jones, Suzanne Hayes, Harry Heft, Nancy Smith, Jill Hunter Dale, Mike and Linda Biagini, Ann Younker, and everyone at Redeemer Lutheran. Fifth, I want to thank Trinity Lutheran Seminary, Skip Cornett, and all those at the Jewish Federation of Columbus who collaborate with me in Jewish-Christian dialogue.

Sixth, I must express in writing how grateful I am to the Trinity Press International Foundation for selecting this book as the 2006 Trinity Prize winner. It is not possible to adequately thank Ron Thiemann for encouraging me to apply for the prize, and for ever since then pushing me intellectually and theologically to greater heights than I ever thought possible. I thank the Harvard University Lutheran Academy of Scholars, where I first met Ron, for providing me a wonderful research opportunity in the summer of 2005. And finally, I am grateful to Continuum International Publishing and in particular Henry Carrigan, Jr., for being a wonderful first editor, and Gabriella Page-Fort, for seeing me through the rest of the editorial process.

I dedicate this work to my husband, Matthew Myers, to whom I owe nearly all of my life's laughter, and to my mother, Charlotte Bussie, to whom I owe everything.

1

Laughter "From Below"

Life does not cease to be funny when someone dies any more than it ceases to be serious when someone laughs.

—George Bernard Shaw, *The Doctor's Dilemma*

Truly it is not for us to pass our time in laughter.

—St. John Chrysostom, *On Priesthood*

There remains an experience of incomparable value. We have for once learned to see the great events of world history from below, from the perspective of the outcast, the suspect, the maltreated, the powerless, the oppressed, the reviled—in short, from the perspective of those who suffer.

—Dietrich Bonhoeffer, *Letters and Papers from Prison*

On November 26, 2005, four members of the Christian Peacemaker Team working in Iraq were abducted by members of the extremist group Swords of Righteousness. The kidnappers vowed on al-Jazeera television to kill the Christian peace activists unless the United States released all its Iraqi prisoners. On January 5, 2006, Greg Rollins, a member of the Christian Peacemaker Team in Iraq, made a surprising report to the faith-based magazine *Sojourners*: "The team in Iraq has found room to laugh in the middle of this seriousness. Sometimes we can't help it, it just happens."[1] Rollins begins his article entitled "Conquering Fear with Laughter" with the following commentary, "How do you laugh in the

1

middle of something as serious as an abduction? . . . If you try to add humor to the situation you run the risk of looking inconsiderate, uncaring, or thoughtless. At the same time if you don't laugh, you run the risk of drowning in severity." Rollins remarks that in the midst of the tragedy, the team had developed a running joke about the abductors, "We have a running joke on the team that those who took our colleagues must be men. We gave them our phone number, but they haven't called us." According to Rollins, this joke produced much raucous laughter among the Christian peacemakers, and reminded Rollins of a Palestinian in Hebron who had told CPT that if he didn't laugh about the torture he had endured in prison, he would have gone insane. Though of a different religion, culture, and ethnicity, Rollins and his colleagues share a striking similarity with the Palestinian: they too laugh at horror. Rollins continues the running joke, adding, "Someone on the team thought that the kidnappers aren't men, but must be women, women that CPT has wronged. That's why they're giving us the silent treatment."

As you read this page, at this very moment in time, someone in the world is laughing. Perhaps this person, watching the humorous antics of a child, laughs out of delight and amusement. Though such comic laughter is likely, Greg Rollins's testimony suggests that other more complex and intriguing possibilities exist. Perhaps instead this person, much like the members of the Christian Peacemaker Team, laughs in the midst of suffering and sorrow. Imagine for a moment the man or woman who laughs not at a comedy club but at, say, a funeral, or upon hearing horrible news. Almost all of us have had an experience of such "inappropriate" laughter—either our own or someone else's—but have we adequately explored the question of what such laughter at the horrible means? Have we sufficiently pondered the purpose of such laughter and its possible cross-cultural similarities? In particular, have people of faith turned an inquisitive ethical and theological eye toward this altogether different and unanticipated tragic laughter that occurs in the moments when we most expect tears? This book seeks to fill this inexplicable gap in contemporary theology and invites you to radically reconsider a phenomenon that everyone thinks they understand: the universal human behavior of laughter.

In these pages, I ask and answer several unusual questions, including what does it mean to laugh while one is suffering or disempowered? Why are people laughing who have no ostensible cause for laughter? And what is the ethical and theological significance, if any, of such laughter of the oppressed? Precisely because these questions sound so strange to us, I believe we should ask them. Even the mere association of the term "laughter" with "oppression" feels oxymoronic if not obscene. Juxtaposing the two terms evokes our immediate intellectual and spiritual discomfort, implying that most of us tacitly agree with the words of Cicero, "Neither great vice, such as that of crime, nor great misery is a subject for ridicule and laughter."[2] Most of us choose to shy away from the subject of tragic laughter, in spite of its universality. In our discomfort and neglect, we are not alone, but are arguably influenced by greater systems of Western thought, such as theology. The vast majority of traditional, Western theological and ethical thought, steeped in unexamined presuppositions, either ignores laughter or rejects it as nihilistic and irresponsible, especially if occurring within tragic circumstance.

An overview of Christian theology from the time of the church fathers through the contemporary period reveals an array of inchoate responses to the phenomenon of laughter, ranging mostly from ambivalence to antipathy. Positive assessments of laughter's potential function within theology prove to be virtually nonexistent, with the notable exception of Jürgen Moltmann.[3] As I was wading through these negative commentaries on laughter, I kept asking myself, why? Suddenly, I had a flash of insight: virtually all the voices I was hearing, from Augustine to Oecolampadius to Reinhold Niebuhr, were male. Not only that, they were white males in positions of power. (Moltmann, on the other hand, whom many consider the forefather of liberation theology, expends his theological energy on looking at the world from the perspective of the sufferer, hence his most influential book entitled, *The Crucified God*.) These authoritative male theologians did not explicitly state that they understood laughter as a threat to order and authority, but their philosophical predecessors, such as Plato, certainly had. I began to wonder if people with relative positions of power might find laughter intimidating because either consciously or unconsciously, they understood it as a threat to their own power or that of their group. I then asked, is it not likely that if people *with* authority perceive laughter as disempowering because it threatens their authority, persons *denied* authority would see laughter as empowering, for exactly the same reason? The voices of the marginalized, that is, those placing a positive valuation on laughter, however, would be lost to history, and by definition be absent from the authoritative theological annals. So could these men's limited and hegemonic cultural perspective unintentionally have led to one-sidedness in Christian theology's understanding of the complexity of laughter? Under the influence of these authoritative voices, have people of faith been looking at the phenomenon of laughter for all these centuries not only through a glass darkly, but also as if with one eye closed? Have we forgotten something?

In this book, I maintain that the dominant social location of these theologians and their secular theorist counterparts has led to a gap in inquiry, to a failure to consider laughter "from below." This book fills this regrettable gap within Western theological discourse by unmasking the potential and the historical reality of laughter as a theological and ethical resource. My reconsideration of laughter argues that laughter interrupts the system and state of oppression, and creatively attests to hope, resistance, and protest in the face of the shattering of language and traditional frameworks of thought and belief. Simply put, the laughter of the oppressed functions as an invaluable means of ethical and theological resistance.

Though that is the conclusion of my research, my work began with a simple question prompted by Dietrich Bonhoeffer's reflections on standing in solidarity with the oppressed: where is the theological consideration of laughter "from below," from the perspective of the outcast, the mistreated, the powerless, the oppressed, the reviled—in short, from the perspective of those who suffer? Christian theology has made no systematic inquiry into the laughter of those who suffer, not even into the laughter of its own believers. Similarly, though the importance of humor and laughter within Judaism is well known, we Christians have failed to explore the religious significance of the laughter of our Jewish brothers and sisters, and to ask in light of such an analysis if our own large-scale rejection of laughter on theological grounds is justified. And yet, might not this laughter of both Jewish and Christian persons of faith have something important to tell Christian theology? Might it not hold critical insights into the nature of faith, doubt, language, and the twin problems of evil and suffering? Surely academic theology would benefit by listening to what Kathryn Tanner refers to as everyday theologians—real people in the real world struggling to live lives of faith and integrity. In the course of writing this book, I discovered that these real people are laughing, yet regrettably theology has not asked them why.

For Christian theology, the laughter of the oppressed is uncharted terrain, terrain this book travels by listening to the laughter of "everyday theologians" that has been overlooked and unheard for centuries. This book asks both "why" the disempowered laugh and "where" the laughter of the marginalized can be heard and thus interpreted. My research reveals that the laughter of the disenfranchised can be found in its richest form in contemporary multicultural historical fiction, in particular the literature of the oppressed. Often when I explain this project on the laughter of the oppressed to colleagues and friends, they ask, why use novels? I answer this question here, as it is an important point of methodology.

Social scientist James C. Scott argues in his study of domination and resistance that "every subordinate group creates, out of its ordeal, a 'hidden transcript' that represents a critique of power spoken behind the back of the dominant."[4] Of necessity, then, a study of historically silenced voices of the oppressed cannot begin with history books, ecclesial theology, academic philosophy and theory, or other hegemonic resources that have tended throughout time to exclude the voices of the marginalized. Art, on the other hand, has often creatively functioned to capture the perspectives of the marginalized when the state or other systemic powers denied such persons mainstream political voice and expression. The voice of the disempowered and marginalized is, by definition, lost to the mainstream annals of history, drowned out as it is by the transcript of "authoritative" voices. Fortunately for us, however, some of the most acclaimed novelists of our time have recognized this scandal and undertaken the formidable task of "writing" wrongs, telling untold stories, and giving voice to the voiceless in their own works of historical fiction. Ear to the ground, listening to such authors, I have unearthed a "hidden transcript" of laughter and resistance which has for centuries empowered ordinary persons of faith.

This book therefore, begins its exploration of the laughter of the oppressed through an analysis of works of literature, with the understanding that the fiction of some of the greatest authors of our day is much more than mere fantasy and fabrication. Such critical works of fiction thereby make possible a theological rediscovery of the laughter of the disempowered by functioning as case studies and springboards for conversation with traditional history, theology, and philosophical theory. Bringing these pieces of everyday theology into dialogue with academic theology show us how academic theology and its understanding of laughter is enriched, ruptured, and reinterpreted by an engagement with everyday theology. This book creates a dialogue between theology and culture, and religion and literature, and reveals both to be rich dialectical engagements with surprising and revivifying ramifications.

For my discussion, therefore, I widen the theological lens to include the critically acclaimed and remarkably popular literary voices of Elie Wiesel, Shusako Endo, and Toni Morrison—all spokespersons for their respective traditions who write historical fiction exposing the depths of both oppressive experience and the life of faith. In the bestselling texts *Gates of the Forest, Silence,* and *Beloved,* these authors expose us to the laughter of Jews during the Holocaust, the laughter of the persecuted religious minority of Japanese Catholics, and the laughter of African Americans both slaves and free. Such multicultural literature provides us with much-needed case studies of the thought and theology(ies) of religious nonmajority traditions in the face of their respective historical encounters with oppression and radical evil. All the novels are tragic in content and replete with historical verisimilitude; thus I was shocked to discover that the characters' laughter resonates throughout the texts' pages. In short, reading Elie Wiesel, Shusaku Endo, and Toni Morrison awakened my consciousness to a laughter to which I had always been deaf.

It was not particularly reassuring to discover that I was not alone in my deafness. The virtual silence from contemporary religious and literary critics concerning the laughter in these tragic tales is so strange as to be baffling. Such silence suggests that our visceral discomfort with the conjunction of laughter and suffering continues to blindside us into an unfortunate failure to see either laughter's significance for religious thought or the "whole picture" of oppression. The mocking and derisive laughter and worldviews of Nazi torturers and white slave owners, for example, are well-known, but who among us has contemplated the significance of the laughter of the Holocaust victim or slave? Who even knew that they were laughing, prior to reading Wiesel and Morrison?

In my understanding, Wiesel's, Endo's, and Morrison's modern novels are akin in function to Jewish midrash—that is to say, they imaginatively fill in the gaps that the traditional texts leave empty, and in so doing, become an essential part of the original text and history. In other words, these new texts complete our otherwise incomplete interpretation of history, and without them, we hear only one side of the story. Though largely products of the imagination, these novels, like the midrash, grow out of, into, and beyond history as it is parochially conceived by tradition as the history only of the powerful and "important." In the end, these midrashic-style narratives, in dialogue with theological and ethical voices from within their traditions as well as beyond, play an invaluable role in helping us to construct a theology of laughter that is meaningful for twenty-first-century persons of faith. Along the journey, it is my hope that you make the same discovery I did: listening to the laughter of the oppressed teaches us much about what it means to be human, to live and to die, to believe and to doubt, to love and to lose.

Notes

1. Sojo-mail, January 12, 2006. See link at http://www.sojo.net/index.cfm?action= sojomail.display&issue=060112.

2. Quoted in John Morreal, ed., *The Philosophy of Laughter and Humor* (Albany, NY: SUNY Press, 1987), 17.

3. See for instance Moltmann's *Theology of Play*. Other exceptions include Conrad Hyers, *Holy Laughter* and *The Comic Vision of the Christian Faith: A Celebration of Life and Laughter*, and Harvey Cox, *The Feast of Fools: A Theological Essay on Festivity and Fantasy*.

4. James C. Scott, *Domination and the Arts of Resistance: Hidden Transcripts* (New Haven, CT: Yale University Press, 1990), xii.

2

Authoritative Voices Speak: Philosophers and Theologians Weigh in on Laughter

Human beings laugh and weep, and it is a matter for weeping that they laugh.
—St. Augustine, *Sermons*

By making our enemy small, inferior, despicable or comic, we achieve in a roundabout way the enjoyment of overcoming him—to which the third person . . . bears witness by his laughter.
—Sigmund Freud, *Jokes and Their Relation to the Unconscious*

Three reasons for theology's failure to recognize or interpret the *sui generis* character of the laughter of the oppressed emerge from the outset. First, both philosophy and theology appear to be on a mistaken quest for a one-size-fits-all theory of laughter. Contemporary philosopher John Morreal remarks, "In the first century the Roman Quintilian complained that no one had yet explained what laughter is, though many had tried. . . . The story is . . . the same today. We are still without an adequate general theory of laughter."[1] We answer Morreal that a general theory of laughter is impossible, because people laugh just as they do philosophy or theology—out of a particular social context. This valuable insight is the great contribution of liberation theologies, which all share in common an earnest endeavor to do theology "from below."

A second contributor to the failure to analyze the laughter of the marginalized is the fact that because theologians and philosophers alike tend to ignore laughter's social context, they share a mistaken tendency to conflate laughter with humor and comedy. Most theory therefore fails even to consider laughter in conjunction with horror or suffering, which leads to theoretical oversimplification and overgeneralization. Even Morreal, one of two contemporary philosophers to devote an entire text to laughter, constructs a "new" theory of laughter that argues that laughter cannot occur in tragedy, because only a "pleasant psychological shift" provokes laughter.[2] Theologian M. A. Screech summarizes a dominant strain of laughter theory from the time of Aristotle with the statement, "We laugh at what is defective . . . but not threatening or destructive."[3] Although laughter is generally associated only with comedy, this book interrupts this premature cognitive leap in order to inquire into the meaning of laughter that occurs *in tragedy*. By tragedy, I mean that aesthetic method of inquiry that interprets and criticizes various actions, characters, and worlds, and in which negativity and suffering are exposed and experienced as problems for thought.[4] In modern tragic fiction, as in classical tragedy, laughter abounds; for Christian theology to ignore its ubiquity in the works of some of the greatest writers of our time is hermeneutic irresponsibility.

A third reason for Christian theology's bias against laughter and in particular the laughter of the oppressed is quite possibly an inordinate influence from philosophy—a field also noticeably dominated by Western European men, and unsurprisingly filled with much vitriolic condemnation of laughter's purpose and suspect ethical role. As Morreal and others conclude, three main theoretical strains dominate the interpretive history of laughter, with most renowned philosophers falling under one of these rubrics. These three categories are superiority theories of laughter, incongruity theories, and psychological relief theories. An overview of these philosophical laughter theories merits our discussion prior to an analysis of Christian theology's interpretations of laughter, given the likely influence the former had upon the latter.

The superiority theory of laughter begins with Greek thought, with Plato and Aristotle. Plato is considered to have written the oldest extant theory of laughter in his Socratic dialogue *Philebus*. In this work Plato writes:

> Those who are weak and unable to retaliate when they are laughed at may rightly be called ridiculous. . . . To feel delight instead of pain when we see our friends in misfortune—that is wrong. . . . It is malice that is the source of the pleasure we feel at our friend's misfortune. . . . When we laugh at what is ridiculous in

our friends, our pleasure, in mixing with malice, mixes with pain, for we have agreed that malice is the pain of the soul. . . . On these occasions we both feel malice and laugh.[5]

Plato, then, theorizes that we laugh at those who are powerless, weak, and self-ignorant. Our laughter causes us to consider ourselves superior to them morally, socially, and psychologically. Laughter takes that which we perceive as inferior as object.

In the *Republic*, Plato expounds upon his original theory of laughter and adds:

Neither ought our guardians to be given to laughter. For a fit of laughter which has been indulged to excess almost always demands a violent reaction. . . . Persons of worth . . . must not be represented as overcome by laughter, and still less must a representation of the gods be allowed. . . . Therefore let us put an end to such tales, lest they engender laxity of morals among the young.[6]

Plato is the first theorist to conjoin laughter with ethical theory. Just as Plato censures Homeric depictions of the gods engaging in evil or vice, he condemns the portrayal of laughter of gods and heroes in literature, because he understands that these figures serve as ethical paradigms for the young. Laughter engenders intemperance, irrationality, and immoderate emotional responses, therefore laughter, which Plato believes can be cultivated, is a threat to both rationality and the governance of the state. Plato, with his vague reference to "violent reactions," reveals his belief that laughter can result in ethical rebellion and subversiveness toward authority. Plato is the first to recognize the truth that laughter threatens to undermine the status quo. However, for him this is a negative, rather than a positive.

Plato's student Aristotle aligns his thoughts regarding laughter with those of his teacher. Aristotle goes so far as to define humankind as *animal ridens*—the creature who laughs. Although the majority of Aristotle's thoughts on comedy are not available to us, one does find in the *Poetics* the following definition: "Comedy embraces the worse types of men . . . in the sense that the ridiculous is a species of ugliness or badness. For the ridiculous consists in some form of error or ugliness that is not painful or injurious."[7] The locus of laughter, then, for Aristotle is derision and a sentiment of superiority. Aristotle cautions against immoderate laughter as ethically unsuitable and even oftentimes cruel, "Most people take more fun than they should in amusement and joking. . . . A joke is a kind of abuse. . . . The buffoon, however, cannot resist any temptation to be funny, and spares neither himself or others if he can get a laugh."[8]

Cicero agrees with Aristotle when he writes:

> The seat and the province of the laughable, so to speak, lies in a kind of offensiveness and deformity, for the sayings that are laughed at the most are those which refer to something offensive in an inoffensive manner. . . . But very careful consideration must be given to how far the orator should carry laughter . . . for neither great vice, such as that of crime, nor great misery is a subject for ridicule and laughter.[9]

Both Cicero and Aristotle agree, therefore, that because laughter is a form of ridicule, certain subjects, like misery and crime, should be considered taboo as objects of laughter. Aristotelian theory precludes a discussion of laughter and tragedy, as the "good" is considered unfit as an object of laughter. Against Plato, Aristotle, and Cicero, Morrison, Wiesel, and Endo present suffering, death, apostasy, and oppression as evoking a laughter that is ethically responsible rather than reprehensible.

The superiority theory culminates in the work of Thomas Hobbes, who maintains that we laugh because of the "sudden glory" of the realization of our own relative superiority: "Whatsoever it be that moves laughter, it must be new and unexpected. . . . The passion of laughter is nothing else than sudden glory arising from some sudden conception of some eminency in ourselves, by comparison with the infirmity of others, or with our own formerly."[10] Laughter, in other words, degrades and derides. Friedrich Nietzsche agrees, as he prescribes that the overman, superior to the "herd," mockingly laughs at all traditional morality and authority. Nietzsche understands laughter to be an assertion of a radically autonomous will that only the elite possess, "You higher men, *learn* to laugh! . . . Whoever would kill most thoroughly laughs. Not by wrath does one kill but by laughter."[11] For Nietzsche, the overman uses laughter to establish sovereignty and creativity, and to annihilate the deleterious influences of tradition and religious and civil authority. The overman laughs at the sudden glory of his own eminence, "I bade them laugh at their great masters of virtue and saints and poets. . . . I laughed at all their past and all its rotting, decaying glory."[12]

The superiority theory, popular for centuries among intellectuals, proves revelatory not of the general nature of laughter as much as revelatory of the relative social dominance of its own proponents. All of these superiority theory philosophers describe laughter from only one particular social location, that of superiority and dominance. The superiority theory understands laughter to express scorn, derision, and ridicule toward its objects. But the superiority theory fails to account for the phenomena of the laughter of the oppressed, of the supposed "inferiors." Widespread uncritical acceptance of the superiority theory has precluded inquiry into the nature of the laughter of the "inferior" disenfranchised. While superiority theories provide many helpful insights, such as the association of laughter with power and autonomy, they can no longer claim the final word on the meaning of laughter. The superiority theory needs the following caveat: when the "weak" and oppressed laugh, their laughter *also* affirms autonomy and power, and thereby struggles to be heard over the laughter of the hegemony. The competing laughter of the oppressed serves as counterpoint to the dominant laughter, and destabilizes the oppressor's assertion of dominance.

The incongruity theory of laughter, on the other hand, originates with Immanuel Kant and Arthur Schopenhauer, and is of considerable importance for our discussion of the laughter of the oppressed. Kant states in his *Critique of Judgment*, "In everything that is to excite a lively convulsive laugh there must be something absurd (in which the understanding, therefore, can find no satisfaction). Laughter is an affectation arising from the sudden transformation of a strained expectation into nothing."[13] Laughter according to Kant then has two main characteristics: (1) laughter is a reaction to the absurd, to that which defies rational understanding, and (2) laughter arises out of the incongruity between our expectations and a reality that negates those expectations.

Schopenhauer adds to Kant by establishing the interrelationship between paradox and laughter, a theoretical move of great relevance in our analysis of the laughter of the oppressed. Writes Schopenhauer:

The source of the ludicrous is always the paradoxical. . . . Accordingly the phenomenon of laughter always signifies the sudden apprehension of an incongruity between such a conception and the real object thought under it, thus between the abstract and concrete object of perception. The greater and more unexpected, in the apprehension of the laugher, the incongruity is, the more violent will be his laughter.[14]

Schopenhauer here makes the important observation that laughter arises from an apprehended incongruity between thought and perception, between the real and the ideal.

Kierkegaard, fascinated with humor and irony, tends prematurely to collapse humor and laughter. However, he does make the interesting contribution that laughter springs from contradiction: "For wherever there is life, there is contradiction, and wherever there is contradiction, the comical is present. . . . Through being involved in a contradiction, that which is not in itself ridiculous may produce laughter."[15] George Santayana, Spanish philosopher and cultural critic, qualifies Kierkegaard and other superiority theorists by arguing that only "agreeable" incongruity and absurdity can evoke laughter, because human beings are by nature averse to paradox and contradiction, "We should stop laughing and begin to be annoyed if we tried to make sense out of our absurdity. . . . In humor, the painful suggestions are felt as such, and need to be overbalanced by agreeable elements."[16] Taken on their own terms, these incongruity theorists again lead us to ignore the fact that tragedy and oppression also involves incongruity, and therefore it too could evoke laughter.

Sigmund Freud, in his *Jokes and Their Relation to the Unconscious*, develops a psychological relief theory of laughter and humor. Freud argues that jokes can be about much more than mere comedy and entertainment, a thesis similar to this book's. Although it is only a small part of his work, Freud calls attention to the so-called "tendentious joke," which bears a hostile and subversive purpose. Freud defines a tendentious joke as one that functions to release repressed feelings of aggression, anger, and criticism toward people or institutions. A tendentious joke is a masked way of saying something forbidden, and getting away with it under the guise of humor. Reading Freud's description of tendentious jokes reminded me of the fool, who doubles as the voice of criticism, in William Shakespeare's plays. Freud himself offers the example of the popular joke, "A wife is like an umbrella—sooner or later one takes a cab," a saying that Freud interprets as a cathartic expression of anger at the institution of arranged marriages. Writes Freud:

> By making our enemy small, inferior, despicable or comic, we achieve in a roundabout way the enjoyment of overcoming him—to which the third person . . . bears witness by his laughter. Tendentious jokes are especially favored in order to make aggressiveness or criticism possible against persons in exalted positions who claim to exercise

authority. . . . Tendentious jokes are so highly suitable for attacks
on the great, the dignified and the mighty, who are protected by
internal inhibitions and external circumstances from direct dispar-
agement. . . . Here, as so often, a jest betrays something serious. . . .
In laughter, therefore, on our hypothesis, the conditions are present
under which a sum of psychical energy which has hitherto been
used for cathexis is allowed free discharge.[17]

For Freud tendentious laughter critiques authority and permits release
from repressed emotions of hostility and anger. While Freud here makes
a significant contribution, he does not make this idea bear fruit or consider the political and social ramifications of such laughter beyond the
moment of the uttered joke. Laughter "from below," far from being frivo-
lous and trifling, belies an utmost seriousness—a seriousness I argue has
social, ethical, political, and theological consequences. Expanding upon
Freud, I reimagine laughter as a mode of resistance to and interruption
of oppressive systems—a tendentious form of expression that paradoxically masks and reveals an aggressive social critique.

The modern philosopher and literary theorist Mikhail Bakhtin stands
out as an exception to our critique that theorists do not consider the
laughter of the oppressed. Perhaps Bakhtin, who himself wrote under
the Stalinist regime, takes the laughter "from below" into consideration
because he himself witnessed oppression firsthand. Bakhtin is really the
first to shift the theoretical focus of laughter from the empowered hegemonic elite to the disempowered folk masses. Bakhtin also is one of the
few modern theorists not to conflate laughter with comedy. Bakhtin's
text *Rabelais and His World* identifies both the political and social power
of peasant laughter and its locus in the popular cultural ritual of carnival.
Speaking of the laughter of the common people, Bakhtin argues:

Medieval laughter is directed at the same object as medieval seriousness. . . . One might say that it builds its own world versus the
official world, its own church versus the official church. . . . Next to
the universality of medieval laughter we must stress another striking peculiarity: its indissoluble and essential relation to freedom.
[Carnival] . . . was a temporary suspension of the entire official
system with all its prohibitions and hierarchic barriers.[18]

Bakhtin emphasizes the inversionary aspect of laughter, its creative potential to upset the status quo, overcome traditional fears and

prohibitions, and empower the disempowered. Bakhtin undeniably is influenced by the seminal work of French philosopher Henri Bergson, who underscores the "topsy-turvydom" of laughter and laughter's power as a social corrective, "[We] describe the laughable as causing something to appear mean that was formerly dignified. . . . In laughter we always find an unavowed intention to humiliate and consequently to correct our neighbor. . . . Laughter indicates a slight revolt on the surface of social life."[19]

However, Bakhtin goes beyond Bergson in two significant ways. First, for Bakhtin carnival laughter represents more than just a "slight revolt" in social life—that is, laughter's inversionary power creates genuine freedom and decentralizes power structures. The same cannot be said for Bergson, who conflates laughter with comedy and therefore understands laughter to occur only in conjunction with only trivial and unserious social issues. Second, Bergson, in stark contrast to Bakhtin, dissociates laughter and fear and disavows any authentic ethical significance to laughter:

> [Laughter] can only begin at the point where our neighbor's personality ceases to affect us. . . . It is the faults of others that make us laugh, provided we add that they make us laugh by reason of their unsociability rather than of their immorality. . . . Laughter is incompatible with emotion. Depict some fault, however trifling, in such a way as to arouse sympathy, fear, or pity; the mischief is done, it is impossible for us to laugh.[20]

In sum, Bakhtin goes beyond Bergson to inquire into the laughter of the disempowered and to identify their laughter with temporary (carnival) political, social, and ethical revolt. Bakhtin also distends Bergson by associating laughter with seriousness, fear, freedom, and emotion. But I want to push Bakhtin's ideas one step further, and associate laughter not only with seriousness, but with tragedy. Morrison's, Endo's, and Wiesel's tragic narratives qualify as situations Bergson deems "impossibly" compatible with laughter, yet laughter resounds throughout the texts' pages. Moving beyond both Bakhtin and Bergson, I argue for laughter's transformative power as a mode of social critique, theological critique, and means of resistance to oppressive systems—in short, as a phenomenon with lasting repercussions extending far beyond just the culturally accepted day of carnival.

Scholars have long acknowledged the influence of philosophy, particularly Greek philosophy, on theology, and the case of laughter appears to be no exception. Taking a cue from philosophy, condemnation of laughter in Christian circles begins with the early church fathers. The fathers were influenced by that predominant Platonic strain of Greek thought that equated laughter with ridicule. The superiority theory of laughter lurks below the surface of the early and medieval church's condemnation of laughter as its probable roots. The church, from Augustine on down through the Middle Ages, thus interprets laughter vis-à-vis Christianity, the church, and God, as a pernicious phenomenon that seeks to undermine ecclesiastical authority and doctrine. Augustine, for example, unequivocally denounces laughter in one of his sermons, "Human beings laugh and weep, and it is a matter for weeping that they laugh."[21] Augustine, in his *Confessions*, associates laughter with his childhood theft of pears, an incident recounted in order to describe his deleterious love of sin for sin's sake. He writes:

> It was all done for a giggle, as if our hearts were tickled to think we were deceiving those who would not think us capable of such behavior and would have profoundly disapproved. Why then did I derive pleasure from an act I would not have done on my own? Is it that nobody can easily laugh when alone? Certainly no one readily laughs when alone. . . . Alone I would not have done it.[22]

The early church appears unanimous in its compulsion to teach laughter as an evil to be avoided, in short, as a sin, or at least a conduit of sin and unbelief under the seductive guise of frivolity and pleasure. Hugh of St. Victor shockingly identifies laughter with pure evil when he writes, "*Notandum quod guadium tantum arguitur, risus vero omnino reporbatur, quia risus omnimode malus est; guadium non semper malum est, nisi quando de malo est* (Joy may be good or evil, depending on its source, but laughter is in every respect evil)."[23] Church father Basil deems laughter inappropriate for Christian righteousness and seriousness, "The Christian ought in all things to become superior to the righteousness existing under the law, and neither swear nor lie. He ought not to speak evil, to do violence. . . . He ought not to indulge in jesting; he ought not to laugh nor even to suffer laugh-makers."[24] Clement adds, "It is true that man is an animal who can laugh; but it is not true that he therefore should laugh at everything."[25] And Tertullian cautions, "Laugh at what you will, but let them [the demons] laugh with you!"[26] Summarizes one historian of religions, "From the beginning, the church stood in firm opposition to laughter. After all, lowly peasants just might learn to . . .

organize and launch their own scoffing attacks. Scornful laughter could turn every peasant into a self-styled vigilante."[27]

Laughter's censure as vice reaches its zenith with medieval monasticism. Tübingen historian Gerhard Schmitz writes that for medieval monastic thought, laughter "was not a positive value; on the contrary, it was a non-value. Weeping was valuable, laughter was contemptible."[28] St. Benedict, who established the code of conduct for Western monasticism, judges laughter to be a sign of unrighteousness and ungodliness. The Benedictine Rule states, "We absolutely condemn in all places any vulgarity and gossip and talk leading to laughter. . . . The tenth step of humility is that he is not given to ready laughter, for it is written: Only a fool raises his voice in laughter (Sir 21:23). The eleventh step of humility is that a monk speaks gently and without laughter."[29] The *Regula Magistri*, a monastic rulebook from the sixth century, advises, "Do what you do with seriousness, because the time of our monastic life is not a time of joy for laughing, but a time of penance."[30]

The church interprets laughter as inciting hubris, and not the humility and repentant spirit necessary for confession and salvation. Hildegard of Bingen argues that laughter manifests our state of depravity, and St. Ambrose concurs that laughter bespeaks pride, whereas tears bespeak penitence. Jerome concludes laughter should be held until Christ's Parousia, "As long as we are in the vale of tears we may not laugh, but must weep. So the Lord also says, 'Blessed are those who weep, for they shall laugh. We are in the vale of tears and this age is one of tears.'"[31] In the early church's view, laughter alienates humanity from God, while tears unite the human and divine. German theologian Josef Kuschel points out that in the Middle Ages as well there was no theology of laughter, but there was a theology of tears.[32]

St. John of Chrysostom, Bishop of Constantinople and perhaps the most outspoken church figure in his censure of laughter, develops this theology of tears. Chrysostom, in an essay entitled *On Priesthood*, warns, "Truly it is not for us to pass out time in laughter," and at another point excoriates the reader, "Christ was crucified and does thou laugh?"[33] Adds Chrysostom, "To laugh . . . does not seem an acknowledged sin, but it leads to acknowledged sin. . . . If then, thou wouldst take good counsel for thyself, avoid not merely foul words, and foul deeds . . . but unseasonable laughter, itself."[34] In the passage describing his theology of tears, Chrysostom also emerges as the first to appeal to the fact that Christ never laughed, a scriptural fact many critics of a theology of laughter have echoed since. Writes Chrysostom in a highly influential passage:

Nothing so unites and bonds to God as such tears. . . . If you also weep such tears, you have become a follower of your Lord. For he too wept. . . . And this indeed one may often see him do, but nowhere laugh nor smile even a little; no one at least of the evangelists mentions this. . . . For while you cannot escape punishment after the sentence at a temporal tribunal, however much you weep, here you have only to annul the sentence and obtain pardon. That is why Christ says so much to us about mourning, and blesses those who mourn, and calls those who laugh wretched. For this is not the theatre for laughter, neither did we come together for this intent, that we may give way to immoderate mirth, but that we may groan, and by this groaning inherit a kingdom.[35]

As proof texts for this theology of tears, Chrysostom presumably relies upon scriptural references such as James 4:9, "Lament and mourn and weep. Let your laughter be turned into mourning and your joy into dejection. Humble yourselves before the Lord, and he will exalt you," and Luke 6:21–25, "Blessed are you who weep now, for you will laugh. . . . Woe to you who are laughing now, for you will mourn and weep." Ecclesiastes 3:4 allocates a proper time to laughter, but elsewhere Qoheleth espouses a negative interpretation of laughter: "Sorrow is better than laughter. . . . For like the crackling of thorns under a pot, so is the laughter of fools" (Eccl 7:3, 6). These passages from both the Old and New Testaments doubtless served as the foundation of not only Chrysostom's opposition to laughter, but also the greater church's censure of the phenomenon.

It is fascinating to note that despite this pervasive theoretical opposition, however, in actual ecclesiastical practice laughter played an essential role for centuries in popular cultural and church festivals, including the medieval mystery plays the Feast of Fools (*festa stultorum*) and the Feast of the Ass. The Feast of Fools, celebrated on New Year's Day, was a parody mass in which the lower orders such as acolytes played the roles of priests and bishops. The "Lord of Misrule," the "Boy Bishop," and other participants dressed up in vestments that were torn or worn and proceeded to mock the sacred rituals of the regular mass.[36] During the Feast of the Ass, another parody mass reenacting Mary's travels to Egypt, a donkey was brought into the church and stationed at the altar. Correspondingly, the kyrie and the creeds ended with donkey brays from both priests and parishioners. After the mass, the clergy ran through the town reciting amusing and lewd verses, and performing humorous plays and shows.

Laughter was even evoked liturgically in the Easter mass of numerous German-speaking countries. To incite Easter laughter (*risus paschalis*) among the congregants, the minister exploited jokes, double entendres, humorous antics and stories, and even obscenities and sexual innuendo. The congregation understood their responsive laughter as an apposite celebration of the joy and triumph of the Easter resurrection of Christ. These common practices reveal that in spite of the theologians' protestations, laughter continued to play an essential role in the propagation of the Christian message and in the lives of most Christians.

The annual ritual of *risus paschalis* was virtually abolished in the sixteenth century, however, in large part due to outspoken, influential opposition from Basel reformer Oecolampadius (1482–1531). In the 1518 treatise *De Risu Paschalis*, Oecalmapadius denounces liturgical laughter and "the inappropriate jests at the Easter celebration with which they (the preachers) banish in every way the piety and gratitude towards God that we should increase. As though it were only permissible to receive with buffoonery the risen Christ who suffered death for us."[37] For Oecolampadius, solemnity alone is synonymous with the sublime, and laughter must be abolished from the liturgy, a position adopted by the church at large. Oecolampadius might be responding here to his contemporary, Martin Luther. Luther, who explicitly sought to interrupt the dominant consciousness of the church, is seen as the theologian who preeminently used laughter as his weapon, and sought to "expose the entire papacy to the laughter and derision of all creatures."[38] It is perhaps not unsurprising therefore that Oecolampadius, along with the church throughout much of its history, deemed laughter as threatening and blasphemous—some might argue the Reformation was built in part on such a foundation.

Closer to our own day, the well-respected Reinhold Niebuhr asserts in his essay "Humour and Faith" that we never laugh at "things that affect us essentially," or at "ultimate incongruities of existence which threaten the very meaning of our life."[39] In Niebuhr's understanding, faith and laughter emerge as contradictions, and laughter has no place within the ultimately sacred, "Laughter must be heard in the outer courts of religion; and the echoes of it should resound in the sanctuary; but there is no laughter in the holy of holies."[40] Niebuhr concludes that faith, not laughter, is "the only possible response" to threats to life's meaningfulness. Niebuhr with this stroke of his pen eliminates the possibility of laughter as a legitimate response of the faithful to situations of, for example, oppression and suffering. Here again, one of Christianity's most influential theologians exorcizes laughter from the "sincere" life of faith in a way that is untrue to the lived experience of many, in particular the faithful oppressed, who often laugh as they live in extremis.

The fact that Christ himself is never reported to have laughed, other than in the heretical Gnostic texts wherein Christ laughs derisively from the cross at his torturers, also historically has proven to be a powerful rebuttal to a theology of laughter. Nietzsche goes so far as to cite Christ's egregious refusal to laugh as justification of his own atheism, "What has so far been the greatest sin here on earth? Was it not the word of him who said, 'Woe unto those who laugh here'? Did he himself find no reasons on earth for laughing? Then he searched very badly. Even a child could find reasons here. He did not love enough, . . . he hated us and mocked us."[41] Theologians equally note that no witness testifies to Christ's ever having laughed. John of Salisbury in Polycratinus echoes Chrysostom in the twelfth century when he states regarding Christ, "No man has seen him laugh, but he has frequently wept."[42] Later commentator Gejerus notes, "In the Old Testament God laughed but never wept: in the New Testament he wept but never laughed."[43] A well-known dictum as old as the fourth century and popular well into the fifteenth avows, "*Ridere non devant habentes oculum ad judicium ultimum* (He cannot laugh who sees the divine judgment)."[44] Not only does Christ not laugh, Christ's scoffers laugh at him (Matt 9:24, Mark 5:40, Luke 8:53), further defaming the theological merit of laughter.

By no means, however, is the biblical witness to the phenomenon of laughter as unambiguous as those like Chrysostom claim. No theologian against risibility even mentions the intriguing verse, "Even in laughter the heart may ache"(Prov 14:13), a verse which legitimizes the very question of this work—the laughter of the suffering believer, the laughter of those whose hearts ache under tragic circumstance and oppression. A Jewish maxim also serves as counterpoint to Chrysostom and the like who ignore the phenomenon of divine laughter, "Man thinks, God laughs."[45] In the Hebrew scriptures, divine laughter occurs four times. In Psalm 2:4, rulers and kings plot against Yahweh, yet, "He who sits in heaven laughs; the Lord has them in derision." Psalm 37:12–13 reads, "The wicked plot against the righteous . . . but the Lord laughs at the wicked, for he sees that their day is coming." Psalm 59:5–8, "Spare none of those who treacherously plot evil. . . . You laugh at them, O Lord; you hold all the nations in derision." In Proverbs 1:26, Wisdom claims that to those who do not fear and obey Yahweh the Lord says, "I also will laugh at your calamity; I will mock when panic strikes you." In all these cases of divine laughter, much like in the superiority theory, the divine laughs out of a sense of judgment, derision, and condemnation at lowly human beings who with fool's bravura dare defy the divine will.

Moreover, according to the Hebrew scriptures, once Yahweh laughingly enacts justice, the righteous too will laugh at their foes, "The righteous will see . . . and will laugh at the evildoer, saying, 'See the one who would not take refuge in God!'" (PS 52:6–7) and laugh out of joy at redemption, "When the Lord restored the fortunes of Zion, then our mouth was full of laughter" (PS 126:1–2). Wisdom similarly laughs at future restoration in Proverbs 31:25: "She laughs at the time to come." All the righteous will one day join in redemptive laughter, "See, God will not reject a blameless person. . . . He will yet fill your mouth with laughter, and your lips with shouts of joy" (Job 8:20–21). Laughter is associated with the dissipation of fear on behalf of Yahweh's redeemed people, "At destruction and famine you shall laugh, and shall not fear" (Job 5:22), and also with the scorn expressed by Israel's enemies, "You make us the scorn of our neighbors, our enemies laugh among themselves" (PS 80:6). In scripture, therefore, human beings laugh too but ambiguously. God's people laugh, but so do their oppressors. On the one hand, in an echo of divine laughter, both Israel and her opponents laugh out of mockery and superiority over their respective foes. On the other hand, however, human beings laugh in a positive vein at the joy of receiving or even anticipating divine redemption and attentive love. Even in the Bible, laughter grows out of one's social context, as the oppressed or the oppressor.

Yet the most noted case of laughter in the Hebrew scriptures involves two human beings who laugh at Yahweh himself—Sarah and Abraham. In a priestly pericope in Genesis, God renames Sarai as Sarah, and tells Abraham that He will give him a son by Sarah, who will become the mother to nations. In response, "Abraham fell on his face and laughed, and said to himself, 'Can a child be born to a man who is a hundred years old?'" (Gen 17:17). As a result of this laughter, God deems the child's name to be Isaac, a Hebrew word meaning, "he laughs." In the next chapter, in the Jahwist version of events, it is Sarah who laughs when she overhears Yahweh's promise to Abraham that she will have a son, "Sarah was listening at the tent entrance behind him. Now Abraham and Sarah were old, advanced in age; it had ceased to be with Sarah after the manner of women. So Sarah laughed to herself, saying, 'After I have grown old, and my husband is old, shall I have pleasure?'" (Gen 18:10–12).

Yahweh is troubled, and even challenged by Sarah's laughter, which He interprets as manifest skepticism regarding the divine promise and capability, "The Lord said to Abraham, 'Why did Sarah laugh, and say, "Shall I indeed bear a child, now that I am old?" Is anything too wonderful for the Lord? At the set time I will return to you, in due season, and Sarah shall have a son'" (Gen 18:13–14). Hearing the Lord's obvious vexation, Sarah disavows her laughter, "But Sarah denied, saying, 'I did not laugh;' for she was afraid. He said, 'Oh yes, you did laugh'" (Gen 18:15). After Isaac's birth, however, Sarah reclaims her laughter, "Now Sarah said, 'God has brought laughter for me; everyone who hears will laugh with me'" (Gen 21:6).

Interestingly, the *midrash* tends to praise Abraham's laughter as a form of righteousness while condemning Sarah's laughter as manifestation of doubt and mistrust of the divine. An identical interpretation reappears consistently in Christian thought, as in M. A. Screech's book on laughter, "His (Abraham's) laughter was . . . taken to be not mocking or skeptical but joyful and trusting. . . . But Sarah lacked faith. She did not believe the divine promise, she did not trust in God. . . . If Abraham's laughter had been skeptical like Sarah's, God would have reprimanded him too."[46] Allowing my exploration of the laughter of the oppressed to lead me beyond the confines of traditional exegesis, I break with this (mis)reading and reinterpret Sarah and laughter as a scriptural paradigm for laughter-as-resistance, as an aggressive critique of Yahweh's patriarchy and long-delayed fulfillments of His own promises, which are the source of much suffering.[47]

This book's argument for a reinterpretation of the laughter of the oppressed as a mode of ethical and theological resistance begins in chapter three, with an analysis of Elie Wiesel's *Gates of the Forest. Gates of the Forest*, a Holocaust-related fiction written by a Holocaust survivor, is an appropriate point of departure for this essay, as the experience of the Holocaust crystallizes for twentieth-century Judeo-Christian thought the problem of linguistic rupture imposed by radical negativity. Within Holocaust studies, the Holocaust as event is often understood to have created a perhaps unprecedented crisis of representation. For ten years after Auschwitz, Wiesel himself kept a vow of self-imposed silence vis-à-vis the *Shoah*,[48] after which time he vowed instead to attempt to speak the unspeakable, to "communicate the incommunicable."[49] Wiesel's work therefore historically articulates core issues that are the paramount concerns of theology for the latter half of the twentieth century— namely, the problem of evil, oppression, ethical responsibility, and the fragmentariness of faith and theological expression amidst negativity and tragic suffering.

In the narrative of *Gates*, the Hasidic Jewish protagonist Gavriel reacts strangely to the Holocaust: he laughs, commenting, "I'm listening to the war and I'm laughing" (7). The term laugh(ter) occurs more frequently in *Gates of the Forest* (more than once per page) than in any of Wiesel's other novels, making the text ideal for our discussion of the laughter of the oppressed Jews. Oddly, though, criticism largely ignores the laughter in Wiesel, and the only text devoted to laughter in Wiesel is nontheological and tellingly remains untranslated from the original French.[50] Striving to fill this gap, I bring Wiesel's work into dialogue with Martin Buber, Fackenheim, Kenneth Surin, Susan Shapiro, and Hasidic thought, including that of Rebbe Nachman of Bratzlav, among others. In this chapter, we listen to the invaluable contributions Jewish post-*Shoah* thought makes to Christian theology. The goal of chapter two is to answer the questions: What can it mean that Wiesel conjoins laughter and Auschwitz? Why is Gavriel laughing? Why do Holocaust survivors and witnesses testify that camp prisoners and victims laughed? What is the meaning of Jewish laughter throughout history? What is the relationship between laughter and paradox?

In chapter three, we analyze Shusaku Endo's *Silence*. *Silence* depicts the tragic suffering and oppression of Japanese Christians and their priest, Father Rodrigues, in the 1600s, a time of ruthless persecution of Christians by the Japanese government. In the novel, Endo grapples with themes of theodicy that are remarkably similar to Wiesel's, but in the very different context of Japanese Christianity. Although the narrative's main themes are oppression, torture, death, fear, and betrayal, the text is replete with laughter; indeed, nearly every character in the text laughs. No character laughs more than the protaganist Father Rodrigues, who, though coerced into apostasy as he witnesses the brutal torture of his own followers, is often "seized with a fit of laughing."[51] As is the case regarding Wiesel's Gavriel, literary critics fail to interpret Rodrigues's incongruous laughter, as if an analysis of laughter would eclipse a discussion of the serious ethical and theological questions raised by the text. We, on the other hand, bring Endo's work and Asian Christian theologians like Kazoh Kitamori into dialogue with Western liberationist theologians such as Jürgen Moltmann and Dietrich Bonhoeffer. The goal of chapter three therefore is to answer the questions: What is the ethical and theological significance of the laughter of the disempowered and suffering apostate? What is the role of doubt within faith, and what is the relationship between doubt and laughter? Is there a relationship between laughter and kenosis? What is the relationship of a theology of cross to

Endo's work, and to laughter itself? How does Endo's work challenge us to reconceptualize the relationship between Christ and humanity, hope and tragedy, God and evil?

In chapter four, we discuss Toni Morrison's Pulitzer-prize-winning novel *Beloved*. *Beloved*, a narrative set during the American slave era that presents the story of Sethe, an African American slave woman who murders her own daughter in order to save her from a life of slavery. Uttering the terms "laughter" and "slavery" in the same breath makes us uncomfortable and ethically anxious, yet Morrison's story contains crucial narrative moments of incongruous laughter, laughter that at first glance is inexplicable. One slave, Sixo, laughs as he is burned alive. Another ex-slave and preacher Baby Suggs urges her community to laugh, saying in one of her sermons, "Let your mothers hear you laugh!" As is the case with Wiesel and Endo, however, critics neglect interpreting the laughter in Morrison. In this chapter, we engage Morrison's text with the theology(ies) and thought of James Cone, Dwight Hopkins, Patricia Hill Collins, Kelly Brown Douglas, Audre Lorde, and Cornel West, among others. We analyze the laughter of the three characters Baby Suggs, Sixo, and Paul D. The goal of chapter four is to answer the following questions: What is the ethical and theological significance of black laughter? Of slave laughter? Is laughter a conduit of protest? If so, how? Does laughter deconstruct white ideology? How is laughter an expression of the African American consciousness? Does laughter emancipate? Does it overcome the rupture of language caused by racism? Does laughter interrupt the banality of evil?

The goal of chapter five is to articulate a theology of laughter for Christian theology. The concluding chapter addresses the following questions: What fruit does our analysis of the laughter of the oppressed bring to bear on Christian theology as a whole? How might theology engage in self-critique in order to incorporate this understanding of laughter? What have we learned from our Jewish brothers and sisters about the limits of theology and theodicy? What characterizes a theology of laughter? A final goal of the chapter is to discuss how a theology of laughter challenges contemporary theology to reevaluate the possibility of theodicy, as well as rearticulate the relationships between God and humanity, God and evil, theology and language, oppression and resistance, doubt and faith, tragedy and hope.

Notes

1. John Morreal, *Taking Laughter Seriously* (Albany, NY: SUNY Press, 1983), 1.

2. After this work was completed, I discovered on the Internet a later essay (1997, posted 2001) of Morreal's that makes me wonder whether he has not changed or modified this thesis. The essay is entitled, "Humor in the Holocaust: Its Critical, Cohesive, and Coping Functions," and it is posted on the Holocaust Teaching Resource Center website, http://www.holocaust-trc.org/holocaust_humor.htm.

3. M. A. Screech, *Laughter at the Foot of the Cross* (New York: Penguin, 1997). 58.

4. Larry D. Bouchard, *Tragic Method and Tragic Theology* (University Park, PA: Penn State University Press, 1989), 5.

5. Quoted in Morreal, *Philosophy of Laughter and Humor,* 12–13.

6. Hazard Adams, ed., *Critical Theory Since Plato* (New York: Harcourt Brace, 1992), 23–25.

7. Quoted in Frances Gray, *Women and Laughter* (Charlottesville: University of Virginia Press, 1994), 24.

8. Quoted in Morreal, *Philosophy of Laughter and Humor,* 15.

9. Quoted in ibid., 17.

10. Quoted in ibid., 20.

11. Friedrich Nietzsche, *Thus Spoke Zarathustra* (New York: Penguin, 1954), 296, 315.

12. Ibid., 196.

13. Quoted in Morreal, *Philosophy of Laughter and Humor,* 47.

14. Quoted in ibid., 54–55.

15. Quoted in ibid., 83, 87.

16. Quoted in ibid., 96.

17. Sigmund Freud, *Jokes and Their Relation to the Unconscious* (New York: Norton, 1960), 122, 125, 128, 180.

18. Mikhail Bakhtin, *Rabelais and His World,* trans. Helene Iswolsky (Bloomington: Indiana University Press, 1984), 88–89.

19. Henri Bergson, *Laughter: An Essay on the Meaning of the Comic* (New York: Macmillan, 1913), 124, 136, 200.

20. Ibid.,134, 139.

21. Quoted in Josef Kuschel, *Laughter: A Theological Reflection* (New York: Continuum, 1994), 45.

22. Augustine, *Confessions,* trans. Henry Chadwick (Oxford: Oxford University Press, 1991), 33.

23. Quoted in Barry Sanders, *Sudden Glory: Laughter as Subversive History* (Boston: Beacon, 1995), 128–29.

24. Quoted in ibid., 128.

25. Quoted in Ingvild Soelid Gilhus, *Laughing Gods, Weeping Virgins: Laughter in the History of Religions* (New York: Routledge, 1997), 61.

26. Quoted in ibid., 57.

27. Quoted in Sanders, *Sudden Glory,* 70.

28. Quoted in Kuschel, *Laughter,* 44.

29. Timothy Fry, ed., *The Rule of St. Benedict in English* (Collegeville, MN: Liturgical Press, 1982), 31, 37.

30. Quoted in Sanders, *Sudden Glory,* 134.

31. Quoted in Kuschel, *Laughter,* 45.

32. Kuschel, *Laughter,* 48.

33. Sanders, *Sudden Glory,* 125, 132.

34. John Morreal, *Comedy, Tragedy, and Religion* (Albany, NY: SUNY Press, 1999), 118.

35. Quoted in Kuschel, *Laughter,* 46–47.

36. For a brief discussion of this mass, see Harvey Cox, *The Feast of Fools: A Theological Essay on Festivity and Fantasy* (New York: Harper and Row, 1969), 3.

37. Quoted in Kuschel, *Laughter,* 85.

38. Screech, *Laughter at the Foot,* 55. For an interesting discussion of Luther and his use of humor and laughter, see Hub Zwart, *Ethical Consensus and the Truth about Laughter: The Structure of Moral Transformations* (Kampen, The Netherlands: Kok Pharos Publishing House, 1996). Also Eric W. Gritsch, *Martin—God's Court Jester: Luther in Retrospect* (Philadelphia: Fortress Press, 1983).

39. Reinhold Niebuhr, "Humor and Faith," in *Holy Laughter,* ed. Conrad Hyers (New York: Seabury Press, 1969), 135.

40. Niebuhr, "Humor and Faith," 135.

41. Nietzsche, *Thus Spoke Zarathustra,* 293.

42. Quoted in Sanders, *Sudden Glory,* 136.

43. Quoted in Screech, *Laughter at the Foot,* 43.

44. Sanders, *Sudden Glory,* 132.

45. Ibid., 46.

46. Screech, *Laugher at the Foot,* xx–xxi.

47. I discuss this in more detail in a conference paper, "Sarah's Laughter: An Exegesis of YHWH's Patriarchy," presented at the International Society for Religion, Literature, and Culture's 12th Annual Conference in Sweden, October 2004.

48. *Shoah,* the Hebrew word for "catastrophe," is commonly used in Jewish literature to refer to the Jewish Holocaust of World War II.

49. Elie Wiesel, *Ethics and Memory* (New York: Walter de Gruyter, 1977), 13.

50. The text is Joe Friedemann, *Le Rire dans L'Univers Tragique d'Elie Wiesel* (Paris: Librairie A.-G. Nizet, 1981).

51. Shusaku Endo, *Silence,* trans. William Johnston (New York: Taplinger, 1969), 68.

3

"God's Mistake":
Holocaust Laughter in Elie Wiesel's
Gates of the Forest

When I was interviewed for Spielberg and they asked me what I thought was the reason I survived, they probably expected me to answer good fortune.... But I said that I thought it was laughter and humor.
—Holocaust survivor, in an Israeli humor and Holocaust research study (2000)

You don't know yet that a man can laugh while he suffers.
—Clara, in *Gates of the Forest*

Why was the most tragic of our ancestors named Isaac, a name which evokes and signifies laughter? Here is why. As the first survivor, he had to teach us, the future survivors of Jewish history, that it is possible to suffer and despair an entire lifetime and still not give up the art of laughter.
—Elie Wiesel, *Messengers of God*

Can laughter and the Holocaust go together? The very question reflects a recent sea change in Holocaust art and representation. In the years immediately following World War II, no reasonable person could have imagined a Holocaust comic book. Nor could anyone have fathomed the comedian Robin Williams as the star of a Holocaust film, or a so-called "Holocaust comedy" winning an Oscar as well as the Grand Prix at the Cannes Film Festival. All of these stylistic choices once upon a time were deemed grossly inappropriate; yet all three of these events have come to pass in recent years. Art Spiegelman's Holocaust comic *Maus* (1986) became a bestseller and has even inspired knock-offs such as Pascal Croci's graphic novel *Auschwitz*; Robin Williams starred as the comedic lead in the Holocaust "dramedy" *Jakob the Liar* (1999); and Roberto Benigni's controversial *Life Is Beautiful* walked away with the 1998 Academy Award for Best Foreign Film. But responsible people cannot get the nagging question out of their heads: *should* there be laughter in our representations of the Holocaust?

Writing in response to Maus's publication in the late 1980s, Holocaust scholar Terence Des Pres coins the term "Holocaust laughter" and ponders, "In literary treatment of the Holocaust, is laughter possible? Is the comic mode ruled out by the nature of the subject matter? Or is the general absence of humor the result of Holocaust etiquette?"[1] Des Pres argues that a set of unwritten rules governs Holocaust representation, and these rules include an appropriate solemnity toward the subject matter along with a "regime of truth" (absolute faithfulness to the facts of the event).

A preliminary question then becomes, does Holocaust laughter meet the "regime of truth" requirement? Did some victims of the Holocaust actually laugh? Des Pres answers with a cautious yes, Jews did laugh in places like the ghettoes, "where the community still felt intact." Though Des Pres seems to want to limit Holocaust laughter to the ghettoes, I push the envelope further and ask, is there laughter in Holocaust survivors' and victims' own representations (diaries, testimonies, artwork, etc.) of their experience not only in the ghettoes but also in the concentration camps? The surprising answer is yes. In an unprecedented research project done in Israel in the year 2000, Chaya Ostrower interviewed fifty-five Holocaust survivors and asked them to describe "humor in the Holocaust," with humor being defined as anything that made the person laugh or smile during the Holocaust.[2] Shockingly, all of the survivors testified that they experienced Jewish humor and laughter as playing a valuable role during the Holocaust, with a majority agreeing it functioned as defense mechanism. As exemplified in the above quote from the study, many of them perceived laughter and/or humor to have been essential to their survival of the camps such as Auschwitz. In a similar vein, Holocaust victim Etty Hillesum testified in one of her letters from within the walls of Westerbork concentration camp, "There was a moment when I felt in all seriousness that after this night it would be a sin to ever laugh again. But then I reminded myself that some of those who had gone away [on the transports] had been laughing, even if only a handful of them."[3] The question for us then becomes, why are these suffering people laughing? What does this Holocaust laughter mean? Are we as students, scholars, and as human beings ignoring the testimony of survivors' and victims' laughter because it is so difficult to understand and violates "Holocaust etiquette" as we understand it? I suggest that the key to answering these strange questions and understanding this strange phenomenon of Holocaust laughter lies, surprisingly, in the not-so-new writings of one of the most respected Holocaust witnesses, Nobel Peace Prize winner Elie Wiesel.

French poet Charles Baudelaire once wrote that a repetition of a particular word betrays the obsession and soul of an author. If true, laughter obsesses Wiesel. Laughter is everywhere in his works, both fiction and nonfiction. For the careful reader of Wiesel, an intimate yet counterintuitive relationship emerges between laughter and the tragedy of the Holocaust. The presence of this oxymoronic Holocaust laughter struck me most when I first read Wiesel's fictional narrative, *Gates of the Forest*, written in 1966. Laughter seemed to spring off every page, though nothing is ostensibly funny about the protagonist's loss of his entire family during the Holocaust. In *Gates of the Forest*'s original language of French, the word laughter (*rire*) and its derivatives occur a record 292 times for a mere 226 pages of text.[4] By contrast, crying and all related terms and derivatives such as tears, weep, and sob occur only ninety times. Indeed, the word laugh(ter) itself occurs 117 times in *Gates of the Forest*, more than in any other novel or text written by Wiesel (and perhaps more than in any other Holocaust novel ever written). *Gates of the Forest* is the ideal case study, therefore, for exploring the questions: How can Wiesel, Holocaust survivor and Hasidic Jew, propose the possibility of laughter as an apposite response to Auschwitz? What is Wiesel trying to share with us about what it means to be human and to suffer and to laugh? What is the ethical and theological purpose of the laughter of the oppressed in this Holocaust tale?

Above all, laughter in *Gates of the Forest* functions as a mode of ethical and theological resistance in the face of radically negating oppression that has ruptured both language and traditional frameworks of belief. But what are the Jews resisting? And how does laughter serve their desire to resist? My close reading of the narrative reveals that laughter of the oppressed functions in five main interrelated ways. First, laughter functions as a creative, extra-linguistic response to tragic suffering and the commonly acknowledged post-Holocaust rupture of language and crisis of representation. In this way, laughter also evokes the limits of Holocaust storytelling. Second, on the ethical level, laughter functions as an interruption of the system and state of oppression imposed on the Jews by the Nazis. In this way, Jewish laughter helps the sufferer resist internalization of the oppressors' values, including the oppressors' dehumanization of the oppressed. Third, laughter is a unique theodicean response to the problem of evil—a response that resists evil and acknowledges with Paul Ricoeur that evil cannot be thought. As a creative and protesting response to the twin problems of evil and suffering, laughter interrupts the banality of evil. Fourth, also on the theological level, laughter helps the suffering believer to resist metaphysical despair, absolute doubt, and the logical outcome of such despair—loss of faith. Laughter achieves this by capturing the paradox of faith, particularly Hasidic post-Holocaust faith, in a way that rational discourse cannot. And finally and fifth, laughter is a form of "mad midrash"—an attempt to hold together God and the world in the face of radical evil. I unpack the meaning of the laughter in Wiesel's work in each of these five ways through dialogue with other insightful minds who reflect on Jewish thought and tradition, including Martin Buber, Susan Shapiro, Emil Fackenheim, Kenneth Surin, and Hasidic thinkers such as Rebbe Nachman of Bratzlav.

Laughter as Ethical Resistance

Laughter as Response to Holocaust Crisis of Representation and Rupture of Language

In *Gates of the Forest*, the protagonist Gregor, a Hasidic Jew and lone survivor of his family, lives during the Holocaust. At the novel's beginning Gregor, who has sought refuge in a cave in a Transylvanian forest, is visited by a stranger. Gregor bestows his real name Gavriel, meaning "man of God," upon the stranger, and gives himself the new, non-Jewish name Gregor. But Gregor quickly discovers that the stranger, a fellow Hasid, exhibits a most unusual behavior: he laughs. Gregor describes his laughter as "not the laughter of one man but of a hundred, of seven times seven hundreds."[5] Previously paralyzed by fear and in hiding for over six days, Gregor is so stunned by Gavriel's incongruous laughter that he emerges from the cave and shouts at the stranger, "Stop! Stop laughing! . . . I'm alone and the war is still raging. It will go on and on, and I shall be more and more alone. Be quiet, will you? Listen to the war and you won't laugh any longer!" (7).

Gregor, like most of us, considers the rational, appropriate physiological responses to the war to be tears or cries of anguish, and so he quickly labels Gavriel's laughter obscene, cruel, and unfounded. Gavriel, however, subscribes to a strange logic that connects the war's tragedy with his own laughter as if in cause and effect, "I'm listening to the war and I'm laughing" (7). As Gregor talks to his new acquaintance, he discovers that contrary to human expectation, the deeper the darkness, the more strident Gavriel's laughter: "The sadder the stories, the more Gavriel laughed" (34). Gavriel affirms, "I've decided once and for all not to weep" (7).

Laughter for Gavriel, then, is a choice, an act of the will that not only disrupts our traditional conception of laughter as mere physiological response but also our parochial understanding of cathartic tears as the only appropriate ethical response to tragic circumstances. Because we usually understand laughter to manifest joy, pleasure, or amusement, the choice of laughter in tragic circumstances is inherently paradoxical. Wiesel expects that the reader will share Gregor's first response to Gavriel's unusual laughter, and at least initially, find it morally incomprehensible if not repulsive. Most of us reading *Gates* for the first time agree initially with Gregor's judgment that Gavriel must be a madman. However, Wiesel arguably commits the rest of the novel to overturning this naïve and preliminary understanding of laughter and its potential purpose. Wiesel ultimately presents us with a laughter that is, in the upside-down world of the Holocaust, ethically and theologically responsible rather than reprehensible. Gavriel emerges not a madman, but as the novel's hero. What is going on here?

In his nonfiction essays, Wiesel makes the case to his audience that the radical negativity of the *Shoah* irreparably ruptures language, rendering discursive thought lamentably inadequate. But how does Wiesel attest to this linguistic rupture in his fiction? In his novels, Wiesel uses the trope of laughter to awaken and heighten our consciousness of language's inexpediency in the face of Holocaust evil. In *Gates*, for example, the narrator explains in the midst of Gavriel's laughter that "at this hour . . . neither words nor wrath made any sense" (48). Similarly, in another of Wiesel's novels, *A Beggar in Jerusalem*, the protagonist Katriel states, "I don't like words! They destroy what they aim to describe, they alter what they try to emphasize. By enveloping the truth, they end up taking its place" (162).

In Wiesel's mind as a survivor, to speak of the sui generis event of the Holocaust is to betray it because words cannot begin to adequately circumscribe the experience; however, not to speak of the event is also a betrayal—a betrayal of the memory of the dead and the injustices perpetrated against them. Wiesel cites this as the double-bind of the post-Auschwitz world, "How can we speak of it; . . . how can we not speak of it?"[6] In Wiesel's personal struggle to deal with this double-bind, he appears to have struck a compromise. He took a ten-year vow of silence after the war, and only after a decade ventured to speak of what he had witnessed. Explains Wiesel:

> Language . . . has been . . . corrupted to a degree that it no longer serves as a vehicle to transmit knowledge or experience. It has become an obstacle rather than a mirror. As a writer hoping to communicate the incommunicable I feel it personally. It is not because I cannot explain that you won't understand; it is because you won't understand that I can't explain.[7]

Wiesel's interpretation of a post-Holocaust linguistic rupture does not stand alone. Within Holocaust studies, this crisis of representation is almost universally acknowledged. Numerous other Jewish thinkers, including Theodor Adorno, George Steiner, David Rousset, and Susan Shapiro, echo Wiesel's assertion of the irreducibility of the *Shoah* and its subsequent shattering of language. For Steiner, silence is the only possible answer to the Holocaust, because he understands the world of Auschwitz to lie outside speech because it lies outside reason. Rousset creates the term *l'univers concentrationnaire* to express the fact that Holocaust survivors "are set apart from the rest of the world by an experience impossible to communicate."[8] Adorno, well-known for having stated that there can be no poetry after Auschwitz, confesses likewise the failure of any discursive language vis-à-vis such radical negativity, "Rational cognition has one limit: its inability to cope with suffering."[9] He adds elsewhere, "No matter how hard we try for linguistic expression of such a history . . . there is a gap between words and the things they conjure. After Auschwitz there is no word tinged from on high, not even a theological one, that has any right unless it underwent a transformation."[10] All of these thinkers, along with Wiesel, agree with Susan Shapiro's well-stated summary of the post-Auschwitz linguistic problematic:

> How can one express or convey the experience of a radically negating event that shatters the very conventions of speech and discourse without employing those conventions and, thereby, already domesticating that radical negativity? How can one tell about an event that negates and shatters our assumptions about order (including . . . conceptions of God) . . . in discourse, the main function of which is the ordering of human experience? . . . One

hermeneutical strategy employed differently by various poets and novelists was to "not write with, but against words," so as to testify in this way to the impossibility of fully, actually telling.[11]

The challenge to Wiesel's own work therefore appears insurmountable: he must attempt in his writings about the Holocaust to *express the inexpressible.* To put it another way, Wiesel shares stories with us that he himself believes can never be told. Wiesel writes, yet he must evoke in his writing the limits of language, "All [I] can possibly hope to achieve is to communicate the impossibility of communication."[12] Wiesel does not want to be reduced to silence by radical negativity, but nor does he want to domesticate or negate the negativity with his written word. "Our words can only evoke the incomprehensible. . . . What we suffered has no place within language."[13] As is evidenced by Wiesel's prolificacy, however, Wiesel, unlike Steiner, cannot meet this challenge with mere silence. Wiesel chooses to write with words, yet on every page he seeks creative means to confess the inadequacy of his own instrument.

In *Gates of the Forest,* Wiesel's first creative means for dealing with communicating the incommunicable is his choice of the narrative form, perhaps to address Adorno's concern that conceptual, discursive language never exhausts the thing conceived without leaving a disturbing "remainder." Adorno feels that art, which can incorporate dissonance into its own form, may be the best medium we have to express historical suffering.[14] Agrees Wiesel, "Those experiences of which I try to speak have no answers, should have no answers. I'm afraid of anyone who comes in with a theory, a system, based on that experience. . . . I believe the experience was above and beyond theories and systems and philosophy. What remains is the question: How, what, and why?"[15] Wiesel chooses fiction because with such a medium he is not forced to make claims of conclusiveness, and is able to raise more questions than he answers.

In Wiesel's narrative quest to sustain the inexpressibility of the Holocaust in the face of this rupture of language, his second creative choice is his use of the trope of laughter to evoke the limits of his own storytelling.[16] The ubiquitous laughter in the novel testifies to the impossibility of fully telling. Laughter functions like a placeholder that in effect says to the reader: some of this story is so horrific that I cannot fully describe it nor will you fully understand what it was like to suffer it. Laughter helps Wiesel sustain a hermeneutics of rupture that he deems necessary to be true to the ruptured character of the Holocaust experience. (Similarly, Wiesel's characters are often mute; silence testifies as well to the lived problematic of the degradation of language.) Because language utterly fails Gavriel in his quest to describe his horrible situation, Gavriel at moments chooses to laugh rather than speak, "Sometimes Gavriel laughed without saying a word, and Gregor realized that the event was so heavy with horror, experienced or anticipated, that words could not really contain it" (34).

Gavriel's laughter, then, refuses to domesticate the negativity (à la Shapiro) by speaking of it. His laugher is a radical refusal to domesticate pain by painting pictures of it with paltry words. Language is crippled by the Holocaust, and in Gavriel Wiesel creates a character who teaches us this important point. Gavriel laughs to supplement the words he speaks because his story, like too many stories of severe human suffering, cannot be fully told. Laughter is both similar to and much more than its companion, silence. Wiesel states, "What matters is to struggle against silence with words, or through another form of silence."[17] In other words, although both silence and laughter are tacit acknowledgments of the language problematic invoked by the Holocaust (and in that way laughter, also an extra-linguistic form, can be understood as a "form of silence"), laughter is preferable as a more defiant and protesting stance. Although laughter is difficult to interpret, Wiesel suggests it says something, rather than saying nothing. Wiesel presents laughter as an explicit, supra-linguistic choice for human communication—a necessary interruption of the silence logically imposed by extreme emotional pain, and an expression of the tensions lived within an unlivable experience.

I had the incredible opportunity to meet Elie Wiesel at an intimate dinner gathering in the fall of 2003, at which time I asked him if it was a legitimate interpretation of the laughter in his works to say that it functioned as ethical and theological resistance because language was no longer up to the task. As you might expect if laughter does indeed testify to the fact that language fails, Wiesel was elusive, and did not answer my question (using language!). Instead, he smiled in seeming appreciation and asked me if I had read Friedemann, who has written the only book to date on laughter in Wiesel. When I said that I had, but that it was untranslated from the French, he then asked me if I had written on the topic as well, and I mentioned the chapter before you. Wiesel immediately then asked to read this chapter, and before the evening was through, had asked me several more times. Generously, he did read it, and gave me very positive feedback, though he never said if my interpretation was "right." I interpreted Wiesel's intense interest in this writing as a nod that I was headed in the right direction, at least with my understanding that laughter is extremely important in his work. And when I thought about it further, I realized that his nonanswer to my question was all the answer I needed. Wiesel's shift away from his intentions toward my (and other's) interpretations of the laughter is its own answer. The laughter is there so that we, the readers, will react to it and ask ourselves, what is going on here? If the laughter evokes a response from us, it has done its job. Wiesel cannot speak too much of the laughter or interpret it for us, because otherwise he negates its purpose, which is to make *us* consider the limits and ultimate failure of language in the face of Holocaust horror.

Laughter as Interruption of System and State of Nazi Oppression

In ethical terms, I understand Gavriel's laughter as a gesture of defiance against his oppressors, an interruption of the oppressors' objectives. What are the Nazi's objectives? The goal of any form of oppression is control and dominance of the oppressed group that is perceived as threatening or inferior. The Nazi objective was to dehumanize Jews to the point where they had internalized that dehumanization, thereby creating a people filled with self-hate who would be easier to control and destroy. At the beginning of *Gates of the Forest*, Gavriel has "lost" his name—the Jews have become numbers, tattoos on arms, statistics. Gavriel struggles against his lost humanity, and laughter is an important weapon in his ethical arsenal. With laughter, he jettisons the despair, tears, and self-loathing the Nazis strive relentlessly to inflict on him and his people. States Gavriel, "I've decided once and for all not to weep. . . . To weep is to play their game. I won't" (7). And when Gregor questions a rebbe regarding why the death of a *zaddik* is celebrated with dance and an "explosion of the Hasidim's joy" rather than tears, the rebbe's answer echoes Gavriel's, "To weep for his loss would give the Angel of Death too much satisfaction" (192–93). In the same way, Gregor's, Gavriel's, and their Jewish companions' consistent weeping would give their oppressors too much satisfaction. By no means do I want to suggest that there is no place for weeping and mourning, but only to propose what I hear Wiesel proposing: weeping should not have the last and only word. The oppressors of the Holocaust regime try desperately to impose tears and despair on their victims—a sobbing Jew is just the kind of Jew the Nazis want to see, as tears often signify submission, acceptance, pain, and sadness. In the story, Gavriel realizes that consistent weeping affirms rather than interrupts his oppressive state of being. He realizes that at some point, he must not give the Nazis exactly what they want and need in order to sustain their oppressive spiritual and psychological hold over the Jewish people. Gavriel's character suggests that choosing laughter, when circumstances dictate weeping, is to defy self-negation and the despair that welcomes death. It is to *choose* life over death-in-life, even though one may not physically live, which Wiesel suggests is a divine imperative, "God requires of man not that he live, but that he choose to live. What matters is to choose."[18]

If this interpretation of Gavriel's laughter as interruption of the despairing state of oppression as well as of the system itself were correct, then we would expect to find textual evidence that the Nazi characters in the novel react with alarm to such laughter. This is indeed the case. Gregor's encounter with one of his oppressors—Janos, a prison guard working for the Nazis—confirms Gavriel's own understanding of the ethical subversiveness of his laughter. Gregor tells Janos that he can recognize Gavriel by his consistent laughter. Gavriel's Jewish laughter deeply disturbs Janos, and, because he apprehends its subversive character, he vows to eradicate it:

"Laughs a lot, did you say?"

"Yes."

"Why? At whom?"

"At everything. At himself, perhaps."

"I thought Jews couldn't do anything but moan and groan."

"You don't know them, Janos. They laugh at you. They laugh, but you don't hear them. You're too busy making them cry," Gregor said, laughing.

Janos lost himself in thought for a minute . . .

"Don't worry. If I find him, he won't want to laugh again." (140)

In Wiesel's own words written in his nonfiction, Jewish life during and after the Holocaust is one continuous struggle to answer the question, "Why and how does one survive in a universe which negates you?"[19] The marginalized are by definition those who are forcibly silenced and denied language as a means of resisting their suffering. In a world where one is denied a voice, Wiesel suggests that the impossible laughter of the oppressed steps in as a threatening, subversive form of protest. Masked in the guise of frivolity, some laughter escapes the oppressors' watchful eye, but as in the case of Janos, some oppressors recognize the political danger in such critical laughter. The torturers have gone to great lengths in *l'univers concentrationnaire* to rob the Jews of any source that could provoke "normal" laughter—delight, joy, humor, and satisfaction. The laughter of the oppressed symbolizes a refusal to bend to the oppressive will.

In *Gates*, however, Gavriel is not the only one laughing; oppressors such as Janos laugh too. In accordance with the superiority theory of laughter, the oppressors use laughter in a scornful and derisive way, making the Jews the object of their mockery. Thus, Janos fears that if Gavriel laughs, Gavriel is laughing *at* him. Gavriel's laughter turns the psychological power structure on its head, exposing the power structure as absurd and imprisoning to both the oppressor and the oppressed in its chains. Under the status quo of the oppressive regime, Jews are to be mocked, humiliated, and dehumanized by their oppressors, and not the reverse. The laughter of the oppressors in *Gates* belies a terrifying, imperious Nietzschean will-to-power. The laughter of the oppressed, however, counters with a will-to-power that does not aim to destroy the selfhood or will of others, but strives just as ardently for the self-actualization of all. Gavriel's laughter aims to balance an egregiously imbalanced scale. The oppressed's laughter exposes the oppressors' laughter as an expression of will, not of necessity. It renders the oppressors' authority suspect.

Thus, it is not surprising to learn that Janos's real-life historical referent, Hitler, suffered from "a horror of being laughed at."[20] Wiesel remarks, "The dictator defines his own freedom in relation to the lack of freedom of others. . . . Every free man is his adversary, every free thought renders him impotent."[21] One of the Third Reich's first actions was to pass a censorship law that prohibited mockery of the Nazis, called the "Law against treacherous attacks on the state and party and for the protection of the party uniform." This law made even telling a joke against the Fuhrer or government an act of treason bearing the death penalty. People were put on trial just for naming their dog Adolf.[22] All of this suggests that perhaps even Hitler himself understood what Wiesel reveals through the character Gavriel: the laughter of the oppressed testifies to the existence of an autonomous self who not only exists but also makes choices independent of social authorities and thinks outside their ideological framework. Laughter is a form of free thought, which is in and of itself a negation of oppression.[23] To the oppressor, what could be more terrifying?

In *Gates of the Forest*, the Hasidic rebbe reminds Gregor that the Hasidic tradition cherishes song and dance precisely because they are supra-linguistic forms of resistance to oppression and its hidden enemies of fear and internalized inferiority:

> Who says that power comes from a shout, an outcry rather than from a prayer? From anger rather than compassion? . . . The man who goes singing to death is the brother of the man who goes to death fighting. A song on the lips is worth a dagger in the hand. I take this song and make it mine. But do you know what the song hides? A dagger, an outcry. . . . When you come to our celebrations you'll see how we dance and sign and rejoice. There is joy as well as fury in the *hasid's* dancing. (198)

Like song and dance, Gavriel's strange laugh masks a dagger and outcry against those who would bid his laughter cease. In actual history, too, during the Holocaust the Hasidic rebbes recognized and stressed to the people that self-negation, and its counterpart, despair, demanded the people's resistance:

> The Rebbe . . . urged his Hasidim to resist at all costs being dragged down to the level of their persecutors. "The intent is for man not to conceive of himself and void and corrupt, and thus reflect [the persecutor's] actions. Man must feel as a Jew, a Hasid, and a servant of God. . . . Severe suffering . . . is further compounded by a state of depression, resulting in insensitivity to one's own eminent stature. Thus, we must be strong, even during times of suffering, as would, indeed, a prince in captivity. Though he may be beaten, he is, nevertheless, a prince who is thus beaten."[24]

In one of Wiesel's other novels, *The Oath,* when the hero begins to laugh during a beating, the hero states, "Poor executioner, he does not know that his efforts are in vain, he doesn't know that his blows carry no more weight" (162).

The imperious social authorities define Gavriel as subhuman, but Gavriel persists in his internal belief that though he is beaten, he remains a prince. This paradoxical, protesting truth is the legacy he hopes to bequeath to Gregor, and part of the message Wiesel hopes to bequeath to us. The Jews' persistent belief in their own "princeliness" infuriates those within the corridors of power who try furiously to impose on the Jews their belief that they are merely beaten and deserve such a beating. Gavriel's laughter is emancipatory vis-à-vis the oppressive regime. As Joe Friedemann reminds us, laughter functions as a form of reciprocal aggression against the aggressors; laughter is "freedom made visible."[25] Laughter witnesses to sovereign, transcendent thought on the part of the Jews, rather then mere acceptance of forced disenfranchisement and self-devaluation. As such, laughter damages the status quo at its very roots.

Gavriel's laughter interrupts the emotional and psychological state of oppression by empowering him to transcend the debilitating state of fear bred by oppression. Gavriel's laugh is the "laugh of a man who has known total fear and is no longer afraid of anyone or anything" (18). Gavriel wants to teach Gregor to laugh because then he too can overcome the tyrannical fear of the oppressor, "At the end you won't be afraid, and then you'll learn to laugh as well" (200). Laughter thus sets an imperative chain of resistance in motion. Once released from the grip of fear over the psyche, the victimized become capable of greater and greater acts of resistance. Armed with laughter like a concealed dagger, Gavriel overcomes fear's paralysis and commits more dangerous and subversive acts of resistance. When Gavriel first encounters Gregor, Gregor is gripped by fear and unable to emerge from the cave in the forest. Gavriel's laughter, though, is the gate that leads Gregor out of the debilitating forest of fear and isolation into courageous solidarity with other Jews in the partisan resistance movement. In what is perhaps the ultimate act of resistance, Gavriel sacrifices himself to save a younger Jew, Gregor himself, who because of this selfless deed lives to survive the war. To save Gregor, Gavriel leaves the cave's shelter and deliberately delivers himself into the hands of the Hungarian police, "Then, in the face of the soldiers and the stupefied dogs, he burst suddenly into overwhelming laughter" (50). Empowered by his rebellious laughter, Gavriel emancipates himself from even the fear of death—a primary weapon used by oppressors to encourage not only physical but also psychological and spiritual submission: "'Don't you understand yet? Death has no hold on me.' He laughed, and Gregor could only shrug his shoulders, not understanding. . . . They can't do anything to me, how often must I tell you that?" (35, 50).

Gavriel's laughter, then, teaches us that the laughter of the oppressed *interrupts* not only the state of oppression (compliance,

despair) but also the system itself. Gavriel's laughter effectively destabilizes the oppressive system, perhaps only for a moment, but perhaps
permanently, as the expressive, defiant power of his laughter is forever
etched in the memories of survivors like Gregor. We must not forget that Gavriel's strange laughter is indeed that which gives Gregor
a reason for living out the war, "Was Gavriel, after all, crazy? If I live,
he said to himself, I'll give the rest of my life to finding out. This will
be the aim of my existence. I'll become him in order to understand
him better" (40). Gregor spends the remainder of the narrative looking for
Gavriel both literally and figuratively in what he terms *Operation Gavriel*.
Gregor wants to become Gavriel, that is, he wants to understand the cause
of his laughter and to learn how to laugh like him himself, "I really
ought to laugh . . . but I can't do it, not yet" (130). Gavriel wants to teach
Gregor to laugh because his laughter signifies his refusal to appropriate
the torturer's worldview. Moreover, it exposes the torturer's worldview
as absurd.

But is all of this a fictional construct—mere fantasy and wishful
thinking? For those of us living outside *l'univers concentrationnaire*,
laughter may appear to be mere "passive" resistance (as compared to
more "active" forms of physical resistance), or even to fall short of our
conventional understanding of resistance. Worse, it may seem to us that
mere laughter in the face of oppression fosters quietism. Perhaps Wiesel's
tale is just fiction after all. Many Hasidic scholars caution against dis-
tinguishing passive resistance from active or physical resistance in the
Holocaust context.[26] Wiesel himself admonishes, "Don't make facile distinctions. Don't divide them into resistance fighters and weaklings. Even
the heroes perished as victims; even victims were heroes. For it came
to pass in those days and in those places that a prayer on the lips was
equal to a weapon in the hand."[27] Wiesel cautions us not to underestimate either the radical circumstances of the Holocaust or the miracle of
protest in the midst of the whirlwind: "There may be times when we are
powerless to prevent injustice, but there must never be a time when we
fail to protest."[28] In *Gates of the Forest* the narrator similarly comments,
"One protests the best one can" (142).

What do other holocaust survivors, speaking candidly and not via
fiction, have to say about laughter as a form of protest? Can (and did)
the laughter of the oppressed really function in this way as a tool of survival and resistance? Chaya Ostrower's first-of-its-kind Israeli research
study about humor and the Holocaust provides us with a host of useful
survivor testimony that supports Wiesel's implicit narrative claim that

laughter was indeed a coping mechanism. A few examples suffice to make this point clear. One survivor testifies:

> Humor was one of the integral ingredients of mental persever-ance. This mental perseverance was the condition for a will to live, to put it in a nutshell. This I am telling you as a former prisoner. However little it was, however sporadic, however spontaneous, it was very important, very important. Humor and satire played a tremendous role, in my opinion. It was a cemetery all right and exactly for that reason, the fact that we wanted somehow to pre-serve our personality, they wanted to make robots out of us.[29]

Adds another survivor:

> There was a lot of humor about ourselves, about what we do . . . that is we made a joke out of every situation, we made fun, yes, why not, how can you live any other way? Look, if I say I'll die, I'll die, you'll die before you're dead, you should know there were many people who died . . . before their time was up because they did not know how to laugh. . . .[30]

Another asserts, "Look, without humor we would have all committed suicide. We made fun of everything. What I'm actually saying is that it helped us remain human, even under hard conditions."[31]

Much Holocaust laughter, Wiesel seems to suggest, has much to do with moments that are not "funny" or humorous per se, but rather tragic. Ostrower defines humor as anything that made survivors "laugh or smile during the Holocaust." The fact that her study con-flates laughter and humor too readily is in my mind one of the limita-tions of this otherwise ground-breaking study. What is interesting is that many of Ostrower's interviewees tacitly struggle with this prob-lem and distinction. One survivor thus talks about not just humor, but laughter *and* humor: "When I was interviewed for Spielberg and they asked me what I thought was the reason I survived, they probably expected me to answer good fortune. . . . But I said that I thought it was laughter and humor, not to take things the way we were living but to dress them up different."[32] Another survivor adds, "We were look-ing underground for things to laugh at, even when there weren't any." Still another man testifies:

The topic we laughed at the most . . . was that of the "Scheisse-kommando" the shit moving commando—pardon the expression. There was no sewage there or drainage, we would crap into holes in the ground and the Scheissekommando would come collect it and transfer it to where ever they would collect that stuff, and we would laugh. First of all, they smelled horrible, but they were considered as the richest, because they always dug up there lots of diamonds and gold and gold teeth. You see you can laugh and cry, laugh and cry.[33]

Ostrower concludes her study by saying that the use of humor during the Holocaust did not reduce for the survivors the objective horror and atrocity of the event, but instead reduced the horror subjectively, and therefore facilitated coping. These survivor testimonies provide an invaluable grounding for the profound historical significance of the Holocaust laughter in Wiesel's fiction.

Jewish laughter, therefore, in the Holocaust context should be considered as legitimate a form of protest as any other. One Hasidic thinker underscores the view that *any* form of resistance during the Holocaust, particularly the struggle for identity and dignity, is heroic, but notes that this fact is regretfully overlooked by scholars:

The characteristic Nazi strategy of the combined use of sudden terror, brutality, and deception . . . made any form of resistance extremely difficult. Meticulous research . . . reveals a pattern of Jewish heroism in the struggle for "survival with dignity." [Many thinkers do not] take cognizance of Jewish tactics that may indeed have been submissive, passive, or delaying in nature, aimed not at mere physical survival but at the type of continuity that would preserve and sustain Jewish identity and character. This type of resistance, though distinct from the physical kind, demanded an equal degree of dedication, raw defiance, and fortitude. . . . Resistance that sought to preserve spiritual authenticity, thus countering the objectives of that which was resisted, cannot be isolated from the heroic response pattern of the Jew during the Holocaust.[34]

In *Gates*, Gavriel emerges as a hero, just like every Holocaust survivor is a hero. Several key passages reify Wiesel's unwillingness to make facile distinctions between so-called "active" or "passive" resistance—either type of resister is equally a "conqueror," as they both share the same essential mode-of-being-in-the-world. The following dialogue between Gavriel and Gregor deliberately blurs any distinction between Gavriel, who survived the war laughing, and Yehuda, another friend of Gregor's who died taking part in an act of physical resistance against the enemy:

"You like Yehuda?" Gregor asked him [Gavriel].

"He died as a conquerer; that's why I love him."

"If you love him, then you are Gavriel. . . . Who knows? I might be Yehuda, mightn't I?" (209)

Differences between Leib, the leader of the resistance movement that Gregor joins after Gavriel saves his life, and Gavriel are similarly collapsed throughout the narrative, as Leib appears to be cut from the same archetypal mold as Gavriel. Of Leib, the narrator states, "To his comrades Leib was a Samson, triumphant over all ruses devised against him. He was not simply a Jew armed with anger, he was the wrath of all Jews, from the days of the temple's burning to their own day" (161). Analogously, the narrator says of Gavriel, "[His] was not the laughter of one man but of a hundred, of seven times seven hundreds" (7). Like Yehuda, both Gavriel and Leib are men who form a continuous chain of resistance within the tradition of Judaism. Their protest represents a movement greater than a personal cause—their resistance in the present hour plays an integral role in the perennial struggle against the persecution of Jews at all times and in all places. Gregor remarks that for the resistors in the forest, "Their Gavriel was Leib," that is, the person who inspires them to protest is Leib, just as Gavriel's laughter inspires Gregor to emulate him in protest (160). Although the form of Yehuda's, Gavriel's, and Leib's resistance differs, the *telos* of their behavior is the same: Jewish liberation from oppression in all its variegated forms—physical, systemic, spiritual, psychological, emotional. Wiesel thus depicts all three characters in our narrative as essentially sharing the same personhood, that of the hero. Gavriel laughs his way to heroism.

Laughter as Response to the Problem of Evil

Laughter as Collision of Narratives and "Both-And"

In the Holocaust, every person of faith, both past and present, comes face-to-face with the problem of the existence of radical evil in a world that is believed to be created and sustained by a loving, omnipotent, and just divine Creator. For such a believer, faith involves a collision of narratives, which is a helpful way of understanding how evil fractures belief in the lives of the suffering faithful. Writing on *Gates of the Forest*, philosopher Kenneth Surin observes that the narrative(s) of Jewish faith collides headlong with any narratives generated by Auschwitz:

> The narrative of faith collides with the narrative of its negation, but neither achieves an ascendancy over the other. At the level of belief, Auschwitz gives one reason both to believe and to disbelieve: the testimony of its witnesses speaks for both these seemingly irreconcilable moments, moments which must nevertheless be simultaneously affirmed. . . . To safeguard the possibility of truth it is necessary to hold the one moment as the necessary dialectical negation or counterpoise of the other. The testimony of affirmation needs to be "ruptured" by its counterpart testimony of negation, and vice versa.[35]

To paraphrase Surin in real terms, in the event of the Holocaust, the meaningful narrative of faith that Gavriel and the Jews as a people possess collides with the meaningless narrative of empirical radical evil and tragic-suffering. In order to attain truth, every theological affirmation uttered in light of Jewish tradition and scripture can and should be immediately countered with its negation—the evidence of empirical reality. It is part of Wiesel's task to respond in a religiously and historically responsible way to this problem imposed by evil. Wiesel captures this rupture in *Gates of the Forest* in several ways.

One strategy Wiesel uses is that his characters and narrator utter affirmations and then in the next breath negate these affirmations. In *Gates* we read, "Every death leaves a scar, and every time a child laugh it starts healing. . . . What then is man? Hope turned to dust. But whenever Gregor thinks of the remote village in Transylvania he knows that the opposite is equally true. What is man? Dust turned to hope" (87). Second, Wiesel figuratively portrays this collision of narratives by conceiving of God as on trial during and after the *Shoah*, with both the defense and the prosecution presenting their respective "narratives." As in any trial, the narratives negate one another. Can both sides be telling the truth? Can any judgment be reached? Gregor tells of a rabbi during the Holocaust who put God on trial:

"I intend to convict God of murder, for he is destroying his people. . . . The trial proceeded in due legal form, with witnesses for both sides with pleas and deliberations." Concludes Gregor paradoxically, as he grants the legitimacy of both the defense and the prosecution, "I tell you this: if their death has no meaning, then it's an insult, and if it does have a meaning, it's even more so." (197)

Wiesel reminds us that for every divine promise of blessing and life, one must also remember Hitler's curse and deliverance of death to little children; for every joy that comes in the morning, the darkness of the interminable night must not be forgotten. In the midst of this dialectic, Adorno avows:

If thinking is to be true—if it is to be true today, in any case—it must also be a thinking against itself. If thought is not measured by the extremity that eludes the concept, it is from the outset in the nature of the musical accompaniment with which the SS liked to drown out the screams of its victims. . . . One who believes in God cannot believe in God. . . . To a thinking that tries to remove the contradiction, untruth threatens here and there.[36]

Wiesel's text concurs with both Adorno and Surin on this point, as we read, "There was a trace of irony in his voice. It seemed to affirm and deny the conclusion: everything is true and everything is a lie. Men love and kill one another, God bids them pray and yet their prayers change nothing" (9). This paradox motif recurs when Gregor shouts accusingly at the rebbe, "After what happened to us, how can you believe in God?" The rebbe answers with a smile and the retort, "How can you *not* believe in God after what has happened?" (194). Belief stands counterpoised by disbelief, irreconcilable in Holocaust and post-Holocaust thought.

For Gavriel, the collision of coexistent yet irreconcilable narratives constitutes his very existence. The collision ignites the sparks of Gavriel's promethean laughter, a laughter born of conflict yet transcending it. Wiesel foreshadows this collision on the text's very first page when he writes:

Imagine a life and death struggle between two angels, the angel of love and the angel of wrath, the angel of promise and the angel of evil. Imagine that they both attain their ends, each one victorious.

Imagine the laugh that would rise above their corpses as if to say, your death has given me birth; I am the soul of your conflict, its fulfillment as well. (3)

The angel of promise (Gavriel's faith narrative) and the angel of evil (Gavriel's Holocaust narrative) are locked in combative embrace in Gavriel's psyche and spirit. However, just as Surin predicted, neither narrative achieves ascendancy over the other because each effectively negates the other. Wiesel makes the same assertion by stating metaphorically that if both angels are "victorious," this would mean that both narratives are equally dead, each canceling the other out and creating a "corpse." Caught in the collision of incommensurable narratives, Gavriel faces the supreme challenge of not only enduring but also *expressing* this inexpressible paradox. His faith remains, but in nuanced, broken, and ruptured form.

In order to be true to his own experience and to communicate the truth of this lived paradox to others, Gavriel must consistently confess that his testimony of affirmation and his testimony of negation coexist and reciprocally rupture one another. Gavriel must simultaneously honor both testimonies, without dissipating the dialectical tension that exists between the two narratives. As a character much like Wiesel himself who sustains his faith through the event of the Holocaust, Gavriel struggles within his own being to reconcile his faith and the tragedy. He must testify to both the reality of evil and the reality of faith, but which will win? To let either go from Gavriel's standpoint is, in Adorno's terms, to allow untruth to threaten here and there. Gavriel understands all too well the interminability of this struggle and the ensuing spiritual anguish of being unwilling to allow either narrative to "achieve ascendancy" or eclipse the reality of the other. In short, the problem: Gavriel believes fervently in two narratives—Sinai and Treblinka—that logic and rationality dictate negate one another. Nonetheless, Gavriel refuses to relinquish the equal yet opposite claim either narrative makes on his existence, faith, and worldview.

Language, precisely because it has been ruptured by this collision of narratives, does not and cannot safeguard the "possibility of truth" noted by Surin. This brings us to the third strategy Wiesel uses in *Gates* to testify to this conflict of narratives. Not language but *laughter*, which Surin fails even to mention, serves this function of testifying to "truth" for Gavriel. We have already established this rupture of language that leaves Gavriel in linguistic as well as spiritual crisis. As many Holocaust survivors have testified, a paradoxical belief in the truth of two antithetical narratives cannot be expressed in words. Laughter, however, *can* and *does* hold the affirmation of faith and its negation by tragedy together in one moment. Language cannot express the dialectic of presence and absence, horror and promise, faith and bewilderment in which Gavriel and his people are enmeshed, but his laughter functions in the text to sustain the tensive juxtaposition of both narratives. From the heart of the collision, Gavriel's laughter attests to the reality that both radical negativity and faith remain, challenged and ruptured by each other. Two contradictory narratives impel Gavriel to be both realist and idealist, to simultaneously both hope through faith and to abandon hope—a disjunction Wiesel wonderfully portrays in the following passage, "I no longer believe in the coming of the Messiah. . . . No, Gregor, there can be no more hope. . . . But until the last minute Gavriel did not give up hoping" (47).

The problem with discursive language and particularly theological language is this: they strive toward systematicness and clarity and thus reductively force thought into "either/or" distinctions. The Holocaust, however, enshrouds all thought in radical ambiguity, precluding facile either/or distinctions, "Unity of impression is precisely what the Holocaust experience cannot evoke."[37] Argues Wiesel, "Ambiguity is the name of our sickness, of everybody's sickness. What are we looking for in life, in existence, in history, in our own being? For the One to do away with ambiguity."[38] For now, however, ambiguity reigns, and Gavriel refuses to choose between the narrative of faith or the narrative of negativity, leaving him in an existential state that cannot be expressed in words. To communicate this absurd point of intersection, Gavriel laughs. Laughter attests to the absurdity of the contradiction and also to Gavriel's angry willingness to endure and resist its deleterious effects. Gavriel's laughter incorporates the paradox into itself by tacitly invoking language's inadequacy, and transcending paradox by defying silence. In short, laughter resists the "either/or" trap of discursive thought and instead embraces and incarnates the "both-and."

Gavriel's laughter, then, results because he desires to communicate an absurd contradiction created by the *Shoah* that words cannot grasp. Precisely because Gavriel refuses to relinquish either his belief in Yahweh's promises to his chosen people or his wartime horror experience, the Holocaust becomes for him a haunting, inescapable experience that resists thought.

To put it simply, Gavriel's laughter attests that *both* God is good *and* life is horror. Life is shit and life is beautiful, sometimes both at the very same time. Life is filled with beauty and with evil. Gavriel both believes in God and cannot believe. He both loves God and despises him. He is utterly skeptical, yet he dares to hope. Linguistically, this is all nonsense. Rationally, this is incoherent. Nonetheless, the "both-and" quality of Gavriel's fragmented faith represents the truth for Gavriel at the level of lived experience. Gavriel's laughter manifests his paradoxical, language-crippling struggle to hold both narratives of faith and negativity, neither of which can be willingly jettisoned, in relationship. A relationship of tension, no doubt, but a relationship nonetheless. The struggle to believe in both realities literally and figuratively tears Gavriel in two—at the beginning of the tale, Gavriel loses his name, and so the real Gavriel assumes the name Gregor and bestows his name upon the stranger. When I first read *Gates*, I wondered if the so-called Gavriel was not even real and just a figment of Gregor's imagination—a symbol that he felt as if he had been torn into two separate identities. The Gavriel/Gregor dichotomy throughout the tale symbolizes the collision of narratives every Holocaust survivor endures of their pre-Holocaust and post-Holocaust selves.

This both-and characteristic of the oppressed's experience, as well as their laughter, is not mere fiction. Most Holocaust survivor stories, including Wiesel's own autobiography *Night*, testify to this double consciousness. For example, Auschwitz survivor Charlotte Delbo describes herself as having an "Auschwitz double." She writes, "I live within a two-fold being."[39] Words, like thirst, have double meanings, "This word has split in two. *Thirst* has turned back into a word for commonplace use. But if I dream of the thirst I suffered in Birkenau, I once again see the person I was, haggard, halfway crazed, near to collapse; I physically feel that real thirst." Historian Deborah Lipstadt describes the Jewish double consciousness this way: "Jewish history and theology seem to be pulling us in two directions at one time: self-empowered and suspended over a void. Each seems mutually exclusive."[40] Witnesses like Etty Hillesum, Gerda Weismann Klein, and the survivor-interviewees in Ostrower's study report incidents of laughter among the camp prisoners and even among those being deported to their death. One of Ostrower's female survivors captures this both-and laughter in the following recountal of her own personal collision of narratives:

When they cut our hair in Auschwitz, that was something terrible. . . . After they cut my hair off . . . suddenly I saw some girlfriends of mine that I've known for a very long time. You couldn't recognize them, and then I started laughing. I don't know. Many cried. They cried after long hair and then I started laughing and they asked, "what, are you out of your mind, what are you laughing about?" I said: "This I never had before, a hairdo for free? Never in my whole life," . . . And I still remember, they looked at me as if I was crazy. I started asking them: "who did your hair?" I was used to Misha, he was my hairdresser back home.[41]

This survivor's empowered pre-Auschwitz life-story collides with her humiliating and powerless Auschwitz life-narrative, and in the face of this collision and the equally real pull of both narratives, she laughs. Laughter is a creative, extra-linguistic, and characteristically human response to the problem of evil.

Laughter as Interruption of Banality of Evil

Before we leave the problem of evil, I want to argue one final point: the laughter of the oppressed interrupts the banality of evil. As is well known, Hannah Arendt first used the controversial term "banality of evil" in her 1963 eyewitness report of the war criminal trial of German Nazi leader Adolf Eichmann. Oddly enough, Arendt begins the book *Eichmann in Jerusalem: A Report on the Banality of Evil* with an epigraph quote from Bertolt Brecht that mentions laughter: "O Germany—hearing the speeches that ring from your house, one laughs. But whoever sees you, reaches for his knife." Laughter is not the topic or even the theme of Arendt's book. But in choosing this epigraph, is Arendt suggesting that laughter would have been an appropriate response to the Nazi threat, or even to Adolf Eichmann, Nazi orchestrator of the deportation trains of death? Is she suggesting that a perceptive person who recognized the Nazis' real threat would have laughed, then reached for the knife in self-defense? Is laughter a sign of nonacceptance and resistance? Is laughter apathy's opposite? By bringing Arendt and Wiesel into conversation, I answer these latter two questions with a yes.

In Arendt's book, she makes the case that Adolf Eichmann displayed to twentieth-century eyes the banality of evil—"a phenomenon which stared one in the face at the trial."[42] A witness to the trial, Arendt was struck by the fact that Eichmann was not a typical villain in the style of Macbeth, but was instead a criminal "whose like was unknown in any court."[43] By this she means that Eichmann had no ostensible criminal motives but simply desired to carry out orders and do his job well. Eichmann stated that he "had no hatred for Jews" and "never harbored any ill feelings against his victims."[44] Eichmann's was a crime of thoughtlessness, something Arendt argues most of us neglect to consider in our understanding of evil, to our own detriment. Arendt uses the term banal because she concludes that Eichmann,

> merely, to put the matter colloquially, never realized what he was doing. . . . He was not stupid. It was sheer thoughtlessness—something by no means identical with stupidity—that predisposed him to become one of the greatest criminals of that period. And if this is "banal" and even funny, if with the best will in the world one cannot extract any diabolical or demonic profundity from Eichmann, that is still far from calling it commonplace.[45]

Many who read Arendt's report took offense, and continue to do so, because they understand her term banality to imply that Eichmann was not guilty because everyone has a little bit of Eichmann inside of themselves. These critics believe Arendt wants to exonerate Eichmann, but this is a misunderstanding of her work. Her conclusion is more this: Eichmann is guilty but so are we, the bystanders, all of us. We are all complicit. Arendt simply wants to underscore Eichmann's primary defense: he stated that the most powerful factor in soothing his own conscience was the simple fact that he never met anyone who was against the Final Solution.[46] Writes Arendt, "The whole of respectable society had in one way or another succumbed to Hitler, the moral maxims which determine social behavior and the religious commandments—'Thou shalt not kill!'—which guide conscience had virtually vanished."[47]

Another way of stating this is to say that no one around Eichmann found Nazi ideology and policy absurd, and Arendt finds in this fact an infinite well of regret. To use the Brecht quote, no one laughed at Nazi genocide and "called it out" as absurd, so to speak. Evil was, as Arendt says, banal. Banal is a word meaning lacking in originality or novelty. As a term it is often used to describe something that fails to arrest our attention or to stimulate a response. Banal's synonyms are ordinary, trite, and commonplace, but I would argue that Arendt is primarily using the term in the second sense to describe the fact that Nazi evil and terror failed to catch anyone's attention or draw a response. Evil only becomes a commonplace if we let it. If goodness was banal, that would be our ethical triumph. If evil is an everyday occurrence, this is never a result of necessity, but of moral laziness.

Arendt, then, uses the term banal not as a term of moral exoneration, but as a term of moral condemnation. If something is banal, that means we are apathetic toward it. But as Wiesel reminds us, if something is strange or absurd, we laugh at it. Anyone who has ever been laughed at knows that laughing at a person or group calls the attention of bystanders to the behavior of that person or group. Laughter draws attention to certain behaviors where they otherwise might have gone unnoticed or have evoked no reaction. In *Gates of the Forest*, Gavriel laughs at the Nazis, which ultimately empowers him to take up his knife against them in active resistance. Gavriel, we remember, laughs because he does not accept or internalize the Nazi oppressors' consciousness and devaluation of his people. He laughs because the Jewish narrative of the inherent value of all human lives collides with the Nazi myth that the lives of certain human beings, among them Jews, have no value whatsoever.

The following, then, is how laughter functions as interruption: *by labeling as absurd what everyone else has accepted as banal and commonplace.* Wiesel presents laughter as a potential antidote to apathy. Reading Wiesel in conversation with Arendt, one wonders: if more people had laughed at Hitler, would more people have felt empowered enough to actively resist him? Could protesting laughter, not only of the Jews but especially of all the bystanders, have thwarted his scheme of evil?

Laughter as Theological Resistance

We now turn our discussion to the religious meaning of the laughter of the oppressed in *Gates of the Forest*. It is my contention that within the context of Hasidism, which is Elie Wiesel's own tradition, laughter has four main functions. First, laughter embodies the Jewish spiritual virtues of *chutzpa* and *hithazkut,* both of which are religious forms of resistance. Second, laughter captures the paradox of post-Holocaust Hasidic faith, particularly Bratzlavian Hasidic faith, in a way which language cannot. Third, laughter is a mechanism for survival in emulation of the biblical Isaac. And fourth, to borrow Emil Fackenheim's term, laughter functions as a kind of "mad midrash."

Laughter as *Chutzpa* and *Hithazkut*

Gavriel's laughter represents *chutzpa*, a Jewish virtue. *Chutzpa* is a Hebrew word that means supreme confidence or daring. In Judaism, Israel is portrayed in constant dialectical relationship with the divine. Judaism understands God as a dynamic personality, who allows human beings to influence Him—*chutzpa* in a religious sense is this audacious human influence.[48] The Talmud describes *chutzpa* toward God as legitimate and useful. The best example of *chutzpa* as virtue comes from Abraham in the Hebrew scriptures. In the well-known Genesis story, Abraham influences God's actions regarding Sodom and Gomorrah, an event of which Wiesel writes, "Abraham was the first who dared query God. And God listened and answered. . . . God loves man to be clear-sighted and outspoken, not blindly obsequious. . . . Abraham won . . . and—so says the midrash—God loves to be defeated by his children."[49] Rotenberg explains:

> Thus from Abraham's daring (*chutzpa*) toward heaven in his famous attempt to bargain with God. . . . *Chutzpa* becomes a symbol for man's capacity to affect God and change his decrees and consequently man's future by his actions and justified complaints toward God. . . . Men may use *chutzpa* to challenge heaven into a questioning dialogue.[50]

In Hasidism, Wiesel's own branch of Judaism, humanity plays an integral role in fulfilling redemption and calling upon God to be God. Such is the true meaning of *chutzpa*.

While Abraham exhibited *chutzpa* through speech, however, Gavriel cannot protest through language because just as the problem of evil and suffering in the Holocaust ruptures human communication, it ruptures the dialogue of God and humanity as well. Laughter, however, as an alternative form of *chutzpa* for Gavriel, steps in to ensure the continuity of questioning dialogue and covenant. For this reason, in *Gates* Gavriel refers to laughter as God's mistake—through laughter human beings audaciously remind God of God's own promises. Gavriel explains:

> You mustn't forget laughter either. Do you know what laughter is? I'll tell you, it's God's mistake. When God made man in order to bend him to his wishes he carelessly gave him the gift of laughter. Little did he know that later that earthworm would use it as a weapon of vengeance. When he found out, there was nothing he could do; it was too late to take back the gift. And yet he tried his best. He drove man out of paradise, invented an infinite variety of sins and punishments, and made him conscious of his own nothingness, all in order to prevent him from laughing. . . . God made a mistake before man made his. (21)

According to Gavriel, then, laughter is paradoxically both gift and weapon. Gavriel portrays laughter as a "weapon of vengeance" not only against those who oppress but also against Godself. Gavriel's rebellious laughter protests to God about the misery and absurdity of God's creation. Wiesel notes that it is the mark of a Hasidic master to "complain to God about God."[51] Angry with Moshe the Beadle for not hastening redemption, Gavriel laughs and then screams in protest, "If this is God's will, then deny it! The time has come for you to impose your will upon His, to pin Him to the wall. . . . You'll be damned? So what" (48). Gavriel's risibility is weapon in that it angrily accuses God of injustice in the midst of tragic-suffering and expresses resistance to the absurd horror that appears to have overtaken God's creation. Proclaims Gavriel, "God likes those who stand up to him" (31).

Laughter is traditionally conceived as a manifestation of joy and hope, rather than a willful activity meant to invoke or create these states of being. In other words, laughter is usually seen as an effect, rather than a cause. In Hasidic tradition, however, exuberance, joy, and celebration are all "weapons to fight melancholy and despair."[52] To affirm life when even God himself seems to side with death is an act of incredible resistance and protest. Whereas in most discursive thought these states are mere either/or antitheses of one another and not commingling, in Hasidism we note that life-affirming behaviors are *antidotes* to despair and doubt, and not mere *antinomies*. Laughter is a "mistake" because it allows human beings to hold God accountable to God's creation; it allows us to criticize God and in particular, God's absence. Like the biblical Sarah, Gavriel with his laughter challenges God to faithfulness and fulfillment of God's incongruous promises. Also like Sarah's laughter, Gavriel's laughter emerges out of an incongruous collision of narratives and summons the divine to divine faithfulness. In short, Gavriel's laughter summons God to be God and actualize a much-awaited redemption. Furious about the nonarrival of the yearned-for Messiah, Gavriel laments, "I think of nothing else. That's the way we're made, I guess, to be blinded by presence and haunted by absence. I think of him all the time and I laugh" (48).

Gavriel's laughter also embodies a related Jewish virtue, *hithazkut*. In Hebrew, *hithazkut* means strengthening of spirit, morale, and the will-to-live. Interestingly, the antithesis of *hithazkut* is *ye'ush*, which means despair. The enemy Gavriel helps Gregor to fight is also that of *ye'ush*, for of course resistance is impossible when despair and resignation have overwhelmed the self. In the Jewish ghettoes signs were posted reading, "*Al ye'ush* [Let there not be despair]."[53] A spiritual and existential battle against doubt and despair rages in the life of those who suffer under radical negativity. It is not surprising, then, to find that violence and warfare are traditionally spiritualized in Judaism. Undoubtedly, World War II was not the only war going on during the Holocaust. On the contrary, a spiritual war was taking place in the soul of every Jew. Laughter is the character Gavriel's weapon in this war.

Hithazkut, a will-to-live, is an extraordinary form of resistance in a world that wills your death. Burgeoning *hithazkut* in a world where there is only ostensible cause for despair cannot help but have a paradoxical character. Says Rabbi Yisrael of Rizin, "As long as a Jew has any grasp on Judaism, despair is not possible for him. This may be compared to a pail which has fallen into the depths of a well. Because it is tied to a rope, one can pull it out of the depths."[54]

Laughter as Embodiment of the Paradox of Hasidic Faith

To this day, though Wiesel writes extensively on the brokenness of the covenant, the problem of doubt, and the temptation of atheism, he remains a Hasidic Jew. Wiesel, rather than jettison his own tradition, has found resources and themes within Hasidism that enable him to embrace and portray a religious mode-of-being as resistance. Four characteristics of Hasidism in particular contribute to our interpretation of the Hasidic laughter in *Gates of the Forest* as resistance.

First, Wiesel finds resources within Hasidism for coping with the Holocaust because Hasidism, like Holocaust thought, is born of the Jewish encounter with evil, persecution, and crisis. Since its inception, Hasidism has been a protest movement against oppression and its deleterious effects. "Hasidism is a movement out of despair, away from despair—a movement against despair. Only Hasidism? Judaism too. Who is a Jew? A Jew is he—or she—whose song cannot be muted, nor can his or her joy be killed by the enemy, ever."[55]

The era before and during the Baal Shem Tov's lifetime (1700–1760) was a cruel time of persecution and oppression for Eastern European Jews, who predominantly felt powerless, marginalized, and abandoned by God. Humanity's self-evident propensity for evil made many Jews feel hopeless about the human condition. Wiesel explains:

Hasidism was accomplishing something vital and necessary for Jewish continuity: it was offering hope to the hopeless and a sense of belonging to those who needed it . . . the uprooted, isolated, impoverished, and uneducated villagers who, due to conditions not of their own making, lived on the edge of history. . . . God is not indifferent and man is not his enemy—that was the substance of the Hasidic message. It was a message against despair, against resignation. . . . It taught him that hope must be derived from his own history and joy from within his own condition. Hasidism's concern for the wretched, for the victimized and forgotten Jew . . . responded to a need, hence their [its] inevitable success.[56]

Hasidism for Wiesel responds also to a need to grapple with the post-*Shoah* crisis of faith and representation. Given the analogy of the oppressed plight of Holocaust Jews and eighteenth-century Jews, Wiesel finds the Hasidic tradition peculiarly suited to respond to the Holocaust. But Wiesel makes a clear distinction between a response and an explanation or a theodicy—neither of which Hasidism or Wiesel offers.

Second, Wiesel also seems to respect his tradition because it tacitly acknowledges the inexpediency of language, which as we have seen is a primary concern of Wiesel's. Hasidism therefore provides Wiesel with a theological warrant for turning to supra-linguistic resources for coping with the post-*Shoah* crisis of representation. As is well-known, Hasidism understands redemption to be possible at every moment and through every human action, no matter how seemingly mundane. As we have encountered in *Gates of the Forest*, Hasidism radically reinterprets secular activities such as song and dance as modes of worship and dialogue with the divine. To these supra-linguistic modes of human-divine dialogue, Wiesel adds a third: laughter. Wiesel's text suggests that even Gavriel's laughter can be seen as containing potential cosmic significance in the ongoing struggle against evil in pursuit of redemption.

Third, Wiesel's work posits the implicit notion that Hasidism is the only real possibility for post-Holocaust faith because Hasidism is born of paradox, in that it acknowledges both the presence and absence of God. The Hasidic faith is itself paradox; as one thinker explains, "The Hasid is one whose rebellion is found in his fidelity."[57] Hasidism teaches that in the primordial time, divine sparks of creative fire fell into all created things and beings on the earth and are now in exile, awaiting their redemption and reunification with God. Martin Buber explains that God (*Shekina*) dwells in the world, providing it with its sacramental possibility, but God is also, by virtue of His indwelling, in exile. Hasidism, then, makes the paradoxical claim that the divine glory and omnipresence dwell in conditions of ostensible divine absence—namely, in human brokenness and suffering. The *Shekina* makes redemption possible, but not without human assistance. An axiom that appears regularly in Hasidic thought reads, "*Uveubdah deletata* (With action below), *it'ar le'elah* (one has an effect above)."[58] Wiesel asserts unequivocally, "This is one of the most appealing characteristics of Hasidism: everything is offered, yet everything remains to be done. Though powers may be given by God, it is for man to take them from him."[59] In the struggle against evil for redemption, Hasidism emphasizes a radical and intimate reciprocity within the divine-human relationship. The rebbe in *Gates* reflects this attitude.

Fourth and finally, Wiesel elects to remain within the Hasidic tradition because he understands its thought as encapsulating an irreconcilable collision of narratives—namely, the narrative of redemption with the narrative of evil, and the narrative of divine promise with the narrative of history. In other words, Hasidism can incorporate a collision of narratives event like the Holocaust into its thought. Hasidism, like Wiesel himself, interprets the world as plagued with ambiguity and contradiction. Buber explains that Hasidism simultaneously asserts the reality of both the fall (the world's need for redemption) and redemption, and shared divine and human responsibility for that redemption. Accordingly, every Hasid has the incredible responsibility to strive toward the hallowing of the world, to struggle to redeem the divine sparks from their shells of evil and reunite the *Shekina* with God. In this context, we can better understand Wiesel's assertion, "*We* can bring the Messiah, not God. Only man can bring the Messiah. Only man can bring redemption *to* God. But the name of the Messiah, the beginning of the process, is rooted *in* God."[60]

Hasidic faith, then, is inherently paradoxical in its worldview. Writes Buber, "Central to Hasidism is faithfully to endure the contradiction and thus to redeem the contradiction itself."[61] Wiesel similarly confesses, "Hasidism does not fear contradictions: Hasidism teaches humility and pride, the fear of God and the love of God, the at once sacred and puerile dimensions of life. . . . Contradictions are an intrinsic part of man."[62] Buber goes on to add:

> We are sent into the world of contradiction; if we soar up away from it into the spheres where this world seems translucent to us, we foresake our mission. It would be contrary to the faith and humor of our existence (Hasidism is both faithful and humorous) to suppose that there is a level of being into which we need only to lift ourselves in order to get "behind" the problematic. The absurd is given to me that I may endure and sustain it with my life; this,

the enduring and sustaining of the absurd, is the meaning which I can experience.[63]

Buber suggests here that the Hasidic tradition has resources for addressing Adorno's post-Holocaust injunction against understandings of mere negation of negativity as tantamount to redemption. In the works of both Wiesel and Adorno, if meaning is to be found and redemption is to be authentic, the present reality of negativity cannot merely be overlooked or forgotten. In other words, suffering must be remembered, in order for salvation to maintain any real theological value. Negativity on the scale of the Holocaust cannot be conceived as merely "undone" without committing a severe injustice against those victimized by it. Heaven, or the eternal afterlife with God, cannot be a mere forgetting of the past.

Wiesel's work suggests that we must vigilantly guard against facile notions of redemption that become obscene in the face of radical suffering. Redemption cannot be authentic if there is no real cause for it. The tension within redemption is precisely this: a tragic and oftentimes absurd absence of redemption precedes, and therefore necessitates redemption. Any theology of redemption that does not incorporate this tension, this tragic element, into its very essence cannot, for Wiesel, be a genuine theology of redemption, as it cannot speak to the experience of those who have undergone radical suffering.

In the end, Wiesel can sustain a relationship to Hasidism because it addresses the question that is paramount in his mind post-*Shoah*: namely, how can one theologically speak of redemption in a world that is so obviously still unredeemed? Silence is undoubtedly one answer, yet for Wiesel ultimately an unacceptable one, "To refuse to speak . . . would be to acknowledge the ultimate triumph of despair."[64] Buber mentions that Hasidism is "humorous" although he makes no further mention of laughter or humor's function within the tradition. I propose, however, that laughter is a way in which Wiesel's character Gavriel conveys a nonobscene hope in the possibility of redemption in an unredeemed world.[65]

Wiesel portrays the laughter of the oppressed in *Gates* as an imaginative method of sustaining the broken, paradoxical, and contradictory character of post-Holocaust faith. Gavriel expresses through laughter that there is no way behind the problematic—the situation in which Jews find themselves during World War II is absurd. Gavriel endures and sustains the absurd and evidence of this struggle is his laughter. Gavriel's laughter is born of the paradox and unresolved contradictions that defy language's ability to circumscribe them. The Holocaust renders faith problematic unto itself, leaving it contradictory and paradoxical. Wiesel recognizes an element of the absurd in post-Holocaust faith, in accordance with the Kantian definition of the absurd as that in which the understanding can find no satisfaction. But Hasidism incorporates this absurdity into its theology by affirming that the world is indeed a curious admixture of presence and exile, hope and anguish, negativity and promise. Hence the Seer of Lublin's aphorism: "A Hasid, like a child, should cry and laugh at the same time."[66]

For Wiesel, understanding the Holocaust is an impossibility. Therefore, post-Holocaust faith shares in the absurd because in confronting the Holocaust, Jewish theology encounters a radical dissonance between the scriptural divine promises for the Jews as Yahweh's chosen people and the tragic-suffering and catastrophe that historically befell the elect during the *Shoah*. Emil Fackenheim best encapsulates the incommensurate conditions forevermore burdening Yahweh's people in his statement, "At Treblinka, Jews were singled out for death as inexorably as at Sinai they had once been singled out for life."[67] If post-Holocaust art and theology even attempt to ignore or get behind this problematic, they condemn themselves to inadequacy and irrelevance. Here we need only call to mind Irving Greenberg's touchstone for post-Holocaust theological statements: nothing can be said that is not credible in the presence of burning children. Nearly all of Wiesel's work, however, grounded as it is in Hasidic tradition, grapples with this ontological dissonance inherent in post-Holocaust faith and theological thought. Indeed, it might be no exaggeration to say that Wiesel's literary texts emerge out of the ontological dissonance Wiesel experiences as a Holocaust survivor who remains a Hasidic Jew and man of faith—a relentless dissonance that compels him to write.

Laughter as Mode of Survival in Emulation of the Biblical Isaac

Interestingly enough, Wiesel finds scriptural warrant for his view of laughter-as-resistance, and in so doing, suggests that scriptural tradition can weave even the Holocaust into its rich but ragged tapestry. For Wiesel, the quintessential survivor in Jewish history is surprisingly Isaac, who at first glance might not appear heroic: "Why was the most tragic of our ancestors named Isaac, a name which evokes and signifies laughter? Here is why. As the first survivor, he had to teach us, the future survivors of Jewish history, that it is possible to suffer and despair an entire lifetime and still not give up the art of laughter."[68] Isaac therefore is a paradigm for the Jewish people because he survived the first holocaust—*ola*, meaning burnt offering—requested by God of Abraham, and all Jews alive today have also survived the Holocaust of World War II. Isaac's dilemma, that of reconciling his faith in a benevolent, omnipotent God with the world's negativity that negates God's benevolence and omnipotence, is therefore a universal dilemma facing all post-Holocaust Jews. Wiesel concludes in a more recent interview, "In my own way, I speak of Isaac constantly, in all my writings. In fact, I speak of almost nothing else."[69] Gavriel is just such an Isaac character; when he introduces himself to Gregor, Gregor asks why he laughs and Gavriel responds, "I thought I was the only one left, the last survivor. That gave me the right to laugh didn't it?" (8).

But why does Wiesel uphold Isaac as the model of Jewish faith? Isaac's narrative, like the narratives of the *Shoah*, is tragic and theologically bewildering, yet he is laughter's incarnation—the very name Isaac means "he who laughs." When Yahweh tells Sarah that she will bear a child in her old age, the incongruous collision of the divine promise with empirical reality gives birth to Sarah's laughter, laughter made incarnate in her son Isaac. Wiesel unfortunately does not often address the laughter in his works, and he does not explain forthrightly what he means by Isaac's defiant "art of laughter." In one radio interview, however, Wiesel elaborates on his interpretation of Isaac and his laughter:

> I find that laughter belongs to Jewish history. It takes part in Jewish mystery. Example: Isaac, the second patriarch, is after all called Isaac. Why Isaac, he who will laugh? Why does he laugh? The most tragic figure in Jewish history after all is Isaac, the son of Abraham, almost killed by his father, for his Father. I believe therein lies the secret of Jewish existence, because Isaac for me is the first survivor, the first survivor of the first Holocaust. Now, normally Isaac, after this horrible experience, should have become numb, bitter, angry, should have committed suicide, should have sent to the devil all his brothers, all his prayers, all his dreams. However, he was a dreamer, a poet. What does this mean? It means this: of course Isaac, the survivor of the Holocaust, always remembers having seen his father, knife in hand, and the voice of God ordering his father to commence killing his son. . . . And in spite of everything, Isaac, in spite of everything, was capable of laughter. It's that laughter that I try in my books, my tales, to capture, and to transmit.[70]

In these rare comments on Isaac we discover a hermeneutical key that helps unmask the meaning of laughter in Wiesel's writing. For Wiesel goes on to characterize Isaac and his laughter as "representing defiance," an exegetical move that lends credence to our interpretation of Gavriel's laughter as a form of hope that empowers him for survival.[71] Wiesel clearly links laughter and resistance in the heroic figure of Isaac, as surely as we have argued that Gavriel's laughter embodies protesting hope and defiance of oppression. Many biblical hermeneuts would find an assertion of Isaac's defiance somewhat baffling, however, since Isaac quickly acquiesces to Abraham's binding of him to the sacrificial pyre. Yet Wiesel suggests that it is Isaac's living incarnation of laughter that makes him the model for post-Holocaust faith. The many critics who conjecture that Wiesel would find Job to be the most heroic biblical figure should note that Wiesel considers Job's final acceptance of the divine will to be a "hasty abdication," commenting, "I was offended by his [Job's] surrender in the text. . . . He should've continued to protest."[72] Isaac's very survival and laughter, on the other hand, represents a victorious protest for Wiesel. We might even say that Job, unlike Isaac, failed to learn the art of laughter, a form of defiance that occurs within faith and signifies dialogue with the divine, and not mere subservience. As Gavriel says, "God likes those who stand up to him" (31).

Gavriel and Isaac's laughter is not sheer rebellion, nor is it sheer resignation—it occurs within the dialectical questioning that is the life of faith. Wiesel feels that as long as it is on behalf of humanity, Jewish tradition permits human beings to say anything to God. I want to suggest that Gavriel and Isaac's laughter posits the following theological questions: Are radical evil and God's radical love for humanity compossible? How and why can they coexist? What does it mean for us if doubt and faith, suffering and joy, despair and hope, absence and presence not only coexist but intertwine? Gavriel's (and Isaac's) laughter interrupts these dualisms to assert the more ambiguous character of reality and theological truth.

Such laughter thus testifies to the reality of God and the reality of suffering as persistent mysteries, as unanswered questions. Such laughter witnesses to the reality that the life of faith is inherently paradoxical and ambiguous. It resists understanding suffering as a reality that necessitates abandoning one's faith. The paradox again cannot be fully expressed in language, nor can it be comprehensively thought—it can only be laughed at and lived through. Laughter can be conceived of then as a form of apophatic expression. That is, it speaks volumes by testifying to the fact that some things cannot be said.

Gavriel then, as Hasidic hero, follows the paradigm of the Jewish biblical patriarch Isaac. In both the Holocaust and the near-sacrifice of Isaac, the God of mercy, compassion, and covenant seems hauntingly absent, and macabre ambiguities shatter thought and disfigure language. Gavriel is "haunted by absence," and in both situations humanity appears radically estranged from the divine. With laughter, Gavriel and Isaac both attempt to invoke God and God's justice and bid Him to cease existing as stranger. Isaac's laughter springs, like Gavriel's, from the paradox of the "both-and" collision of incommensurable narratives: Isaac remembers the triumphant narrative of promise and descendants that is Abraham's and therefore his own, yet surely he can equally recall, as Wiesel explicitly states, his own father with knife in hand, ready to slaughter that very son at God's command. In protest at absurd injustice and in hope that the former narrative of faith must also remain mysteriously true, Isaac embodies laughter, enabling later survivors of the Holocaust, like Gavriel, and perhaps even Wiesel himself, to echo his defiant laughter.

Laughter as Incarnation of Paradox of Bratzlavian Faith

Although I have dealt elsewhere with the subject of the striking similarities between the eighteenth-century Rebbe Nachman of Bratzlav and Wiesel, I would like to make brief mention of them here. Wiesel acknowledges his indebtedness to Nachman, "I remember reading these [Rebbe Nachman's] stories as a child and, spellbound, thinking that I had understood them. Now I reread them, and though I am still under their spell, I no longer understand them. . . . I shall not live his adventures, though I may sometimes claim those of his heroes and their victims as my own."[73] Gavriel is likely one such hero inspired by the real-life Nachman.

Hasidic followers know Rebbe Nachman to be a man who fluctuated between intense doubt and depression on the one hand and extreme joy on the other; the rebbe considered such a dialectic to be a sign of a living, authentic faith. Rebbe Nachman thus understood the Hasidic faith to embody paradox. For this reason, the great teacher often spoke in parables, and even spoke of having "no words" to express the complexity of his paradoxical faith. Rebbe Nachman seemed to place a special spiritual value on laughter, as one popular saying about him says, "He [Rebbe Nachman] thought that he would take his wife and go live in some far-off place, hidden from the public. Sometimes he would go out to the market to have a look at the world—and to laugh at it" (Hayyey II 2:19).

Additionally, Hasidic tales describe Rebbe Nachman of Bratzlav as strangely masquerading as a madman in the public square. Doubt, paradox, linguistic rupture, playing the madman—it is obvious that Wiesel draws literary and spiritual inspiration from the person of Rebbe Nachman. Therefore better understanding Bratzlavian Hasidic thought can give us insight into the meaning of the laughter of the oppressed in Wiesel.

Rebbe Nachman of Bratzlav, acting the clown in public, created a hermeneutical stir in his own day and in ours. Wiesel does not write about Rebbe Nachman's theory or teachings, but he tellingly interprets the Rebbe's ostensibly mad *laughter*. Other than Wiesel's statements on Isaac, Wiesel's interpretation of the Rebbe's laughter is arguably the passage in all of his work that best describes his own understanding of the function of laughter, a subject on which he is typically reticent. Wiesel writes:

> Why was the Rebbe posing as a madman? . . . I lean toward an explanation that places the accent on his laughter. . . . Laughter that springs from lucid and desperate awareness, a mirthless laughter, a laughter of protest against the absurdities of existence, a laughter of revolt against a universe where man, whatever he may do, is condemned in advance. A laughter of compassion for man who cannot escape the ambiguity of his condition and his faith. To blindly submit to God, without questioning the meaning of this submission, would be to diminish Him. To want to understand Him would be to reduce His intentions, His vision to the level of ours. How then can a man take himself seriously? Revolt is not a solution, neither is submission. Remains laughter, metaphysical laughter.[74]

Gavriel's laughter can be understood as metaphysical laughter like Rebbe Nachman of Bratlav's, as laughter of protest, revolt, compassion, and questioning complaint that arises out of a desperate and lucid awareness of the ambiguities of faith and human existence. It is a laughter that sustains the divine-human dialogue by invoking God's hearing and attention to the absurdities we must endure. It is not merely revolt, which would concede victory to the narrative of tragic suffering and rational empiricism, nor is it mere submission, which would overlook negativity with the lens of blind faith. And as Buber says, "True faith . . . is not "blind," it sees the reality and does not deceive itself; only it listens as well to what is *above* this reality, what commissions and empowers it to *change* reality."[75] Gavriel's faith is broken but not blind, and his laughter reflects a faith that forever refuses to relinquish the mad possibilities of hope, change, and redemption.

In the words of one Hasidic thinker, the peculiarity of Bratzlavian theosophy is that it, like Wiesel's thought vis-à-vis the Holocuast, resists either/or, "The coexisting . . . I and thou . . . embrace but do not eliminate each other. . . . [This is] life as a hypothesis [and] . . . living in contradiction and paradox between coexisting polar elements that are not remolded through an either/or battle into a new synthetical state."[76] In Rebbe Nachman's vision, a "questioning hypothesis" or *kushya* (which in Hebrew means literally "difficulty" or "challenging complaint") characterizes the relationship between both man and God and empiricism and the human imagination. Rabbi Nachman states, "That is the way it ought to be . . . that there should be *kushyot* concerning the Almighty."[77] In other words, questioning God is a sign of faithfulness. Wiesel seems to agree that faith is an open question characterized by challenging complaint, "Is there hope despite everything, despite ourselves? Despair, perhaps? Or faith? All that is left is the question."[78] We can interpret Gavriel's laughter as giving voice to both the paradox of living in a *kushya* state of faith and this resistance to either/or thinking.

Bratzlavian Hasidism allows paradox to remain paradox and has a hermeneutic of suspicion with regard to answers and totalizing explanations. It comes as no surprise, therefore, that Wiesel seems to have appropriated it into his fiction. Wiesel states in the aptly titled *Hope against Hope*:

> I deliberately use paradoxical language when it comes to the question of faith after Auschwitz. . . . The paradox in this is that despite everything and in defiance of everything we must have faith. Even if we find no faith we must raise it up in the hope that one day we will understand why, and that one day we will be able to give a reason for believing.[79]

In anti-Hegelian fashion, Wiesel's character Gavriel refuses the artificial either/or dichotomies of faith and doubt, hope and despair. Wiesel demonstrates this narratively by the juxtaposition of contradictory affirmations. At one point Gregor whispers into the night, "There's no hope," and Gavriel answers, "We'll get along without it"; yet only a few pages later the narrator describes Gavriel, "Every one of his words reflected hope and certainty. 'The future's my domain,' he said" (32, 40). Wiesel has asserted elsewhere that "after Auschwitz, hope itself is filled with anguish."[80]

Gavriel's laughter, then, is highly creative because it eliminates neither the narrative of morning nor the narrative of mourning, but holds both narratives in a state of dialectical questioning. In the valuable words of one Hasidic scholar:

> Creative thinking would therefore refer to the ability... to envision how the sunny morning emerges from the dark evening without having to eliminate either one of the conditions.... Consequently it is intuition and faith that imbue us with the strength to climb on the giant shoulders of logical rationalism in order to see the steps of the redeeming Messiah through the clouds of catastrophe.[81]

In this way, Gavriel's laughter pits faith against pure rationalism. Wiesel asserts that "victory does not prevent suffering from having existed.... The mystery of good is no less disturbing than the mystery of evil. But one does not cancel out the other. Man alone is capable of uniting them in remembering."[82] In his very being, Gavriel unites victory and suffering, catastrophe and redemption, hope and the painful need for hope's invention. Gavriel remembers both good and evil, but does not seek to reconcile them. Indeed, Gavriel embodies the life as dialectical hypothesis described by Rotenberg—a life lived under the coexistence of opposites that are, in fact, both true. With his very existence, Gavriel, much like Wiesel himself, performs a radical exegesis of the Holocaust. As one might expect, Gavriel personifies a paradox in that he never ceases to say his daily prayers, yet he repeatedly defies God, admonishing Gavriel, "Strike against heaven if it is necessary, and it is necessary" (46).

It is considered one of Rebbe Nachman's greatest contributions to Hasidism that he recasts doubt not as weakness, but spiritual virtue—a sign of a faith that is genuine. In Nachman, faith and doubt constitute a dialectic; Gavriel's laughter arguably captures this dialectic. For Wiesel, living post-Holocaust, it is especially important to understand Jewish faith as incorporating doubt. Laughter is an appropriate resource for post-*Shoah* communication because it makes room for doubt as it underscores and does not mitigate ambiguity. Though the narrative of negativity evokes doubt, Gavriel chooses to hold this narrative in dialogue with his faith narrative. For Gavriel and his fellow Jews, faith and doubt survive in tensive coexistence as surely as Sinai and Treblinka survive united in memory. Wiesel comments, "This tragedy defies and exceeds all answers. If anyone claims to have found an answer; it can only be a false one. So much mourning, so much agony, so many deaths on one side, and a single answer on the other? One cannot understand Auschwitz either without God or with God."[83] Faith in God, then, is at all times a struggle, as it is constantly endangered by the empirical reality that contradicts faith and induces doubt. The text *Gates of the Forest* ends with Gregor telling his wife Clara in words that echo Gavriel and his laughter's message, "Let's resume the struggle. . . . It is because it is too late that we are commanded to hope" (225).

Gavriel's laughter therefore reveals the anemia of language and rational thought in the Holocaust world. It manifests the reality that in the situation of tragic-suffering, faith that is not defeated by the tragedy manages to hold both the narrative of promise and presence in dialectical tension with the equally real narrative of brokenness and absence. Although Gavriel's position may appear logically inconsistent, his laughter nonetheless implies that hope and tragedy, faith and doubt do not mutually exclude one another but survive and even enrich one another. By laughing, Gavriel is not refraining from expression, but is, as Buber remarks of Hasidic song and dance, "only renouncing all conceptual utterances about that which is not given to concepts."[84] Gavriel's laughter, the laughter of the person of faith who suffers radical negativity, interrupts the dualism of faith and doubt and prevents a recurrence to this debilitating false dichotomy.

Yet just as Rebbe Nachman's contemporaries considered him mad, most of the characters surrounding Wiesel's laughing heroes (and probably most of Wiesel's readers) consider Gavriel insane. In response to such mistaken interpretations, the character Clara (Gregor's girlfriend/wife) makes the important commentary, "You don't know yet that a man can laugh while he suffers" (174). Gregor also ponders, "Was Gavriel, after all, crazy. . . . I'll give the rest of my life to finding out" (40).

Madmen are messengers in Wiesel's texts, and they are heroic because they communicate an impossible message of ambiguity and paradox, one that most people do not want to hear or cannot bear. Gavriel's laughter transmits a message shrouded in ambiguity as it remembers simultaneously both suffering and the promise of redemption. Yet Gavriel's message clings to faith and does not adopt an attitude of apathy toward the divine. In such tragic circumstances, Gavriel's faith, though disfigured, remains heroic and miraculous. Wiesel comments, "In our epoch, I would say, there is nothing so whole as broken faith. Faith must be tested. But . . . without faith we could not survive."[85] In this sense, any believer and true person of God (and Gavriel means "man of God") who resists despair and doubts total eclipse of faith is likely to appear mad in the eyes of the world.

Laughter at horror looks like madness, but only to those who do not understand that such laughter can be a weapon against the genuine madness of despair and nihilism, and to those who do not grasp Wiesel's claim that "laughter itself is a miracle, the most astonishing miracle of all."[86] Such a person of faith, as we have already said, asserts illogical absurdities that are rationally incoherent both-and paradoxes that defy either/or cognitive thought. Wiesel's heroic characters are thus "mad" and on some level, so are Wiesel and all other post-Holocaust believers; Wiesel writes of himself, "I wouldn't say that I am not mad. . . . I'm obsessed not with Death but with the Dead. . . . At the same time I am obsessed with Life. Mystical madness is important. One has to be mad today . . . to say certain things and believe that they could make a difference."[87] To believe, as the Hasidim do, that a laugh, a tear, or a dance can change the world or stimulate its redemption will doubtless always appear as madness to many. Such is the legacy of Rebbe Nachman.

Laughter as Resistance to Despair and Loss of Faith

This brings us to the final way in which Gavriel's laughter functions theologically—as a form of resistance to the despair and loss of faith logically imposed on him by negativity and its contradictions. Faced with the theological contradiction posed by simultaneously remembering both Sinai and Treblinka, Gavriel laughs rather than to throw away Sinai.

The paradox of extreme suffering paralyzes its victims primarily by silencing them into despair and acquiescence of an inconceivable fate. Paradox befuddles our thought, thus its logical result is silence. The juxtaposition of Gavriel's faith tradition with present historical circumstance is so absurd and illogical as to induce despairing silence. The juxtaposition ruptures God-language. Vis-à-vis the Holocaust, language itself becomes paradox; in the words of Paul Celan, language "remained available. But it had to find sustenance in its inability to explain."[88] Adds Langer, "Speech proved lethal and silence laden with terror while the victim trembled helplessly between the two."[89] Trapped within the paradox of Sinai and Treblinka, Gavriel understands that speech is grossly inadequate, and silence grants a second victory to the oppressors as it robs him of self-expression of his faith and belief. He chooses not to tremble, but to transcend paradox. Gavriel discovers in laughter a third possibility, an extra-linguistic means of witnessing to a faith that is substantively changed yet not annihilated.

Faith and doubt, hope and tragedy are not mutually exclusive: this is Gavriel's message for Gregor and all the other Jews who are suffering. This is also Wiesel's message to all his readers. Wiesel states the paradoxical collision of narratives survivors experience in this way, "Because I remember I despair. Because I remember, I have the duty to reject despair."[90]

Laughter is not only weapon, but also divine gift. The narrative *Gates of the Forest* suggests that perhaps the most tragic aspect of the Holocaust is that it renders human beings strangers, not only to themselves and to one another, but also to God. The rebbe, who dances "with a vigor that might have seemed desperate," explains that the purpose of his furious dancing is to "so forcefully . . . invoke God that . . . God himself will cease to exist as a stranger" (193). Perhaps Gavriel's laughter is gift because it too seeks to invoke God's presence. Perhaps Gavriel, like the biblical Sarah, hopes to attract divine attention and counteract divine forgetfulness by incongruous laughter. Their laughter says, "God, you say that you remember me, but my very life testifies against you."

Even defiance is a form of communication, however. Everyone knows that a relationship is not really over until both sides stop talking altogether. Gavriel's laughter indicates his wish to continue the divine-human dialogue; his laughter is the opposite of indifference or apathy. Thus Gavriel protests *to* God. For Wiesel and the Hasidic viewpoint, indifference signals the end of relationship and dialogue and is therefore a more shattering response than hate or even anger, "The opposite of love is not hate but indifference."[91] Wiesel's commentary on prayer helps us to unpack laughter's similar dialogical, giftlike character, "Maybe our prayers will be against God, . . . [they are still] existentially and dialectically affirmative. For the fact that I pray means there is someone there to listen, that what I am saying is not uttered to a great void. But what I do say, I say with anger."[92] Likewise, Gavriel laughs with anger and addresses not a void but God, thereby granting continuity, albeit tenuous and turbulent, to the covenant relationship. His laughter is an unanswered question, or what we might term "protesting-hope," a challenge to divine justice and compassion hurled toward heaven, containing within itself the hope of being heard.

Wiesel points out that even the Hebrew word for prayer—*tefillah*—is a cognate of the Hebrew term for struggle—*naftolin*. Indeed, within Judaism, a fundamental metaphor for conceiving of the nature of the divine-human relationship is the biblical image of Jacob/Israel wrestling with the angel/God—an image that reveals that the divine-human rapport is characterized by a dialectical struggle for relatedness. Gavriel's struggle and protesting laughter, then, comes from within faith, and like Wiesel's own, is not to be understood as a rejection of faith, "I'm asking the questions from within faith, not from outside faith. If I didn't believe what would be the problem? But if you do believe, then you have painful questions."[93] Adds Wiesel, "The revolt of the believer is not that of the renegade; the two do not speak in the name of the same anguish."[94] As we have already made clear, Gavriel must endure a collision of narratives only because he is unwilling to relinquish the narrative of divine promise and presence. While on the one hand to allow the narrative of horror to engulf him would be to give in to despair, on the other hand clinging to both narratives creates its own particularly difficult situation of existential paradox and spiritual ambiguity. Wiesel's character Gavriel also remains a Hasid, a man of faith, and thus he can be compared to Job of whom Wiesel writes, "Did he ever lose his faith? If so, he rediscovered it within his rebellion. He demonstrated that faith is essentially a rebellion."[95]

Because so much in the world negates faith, Gavriel recognizes that faith has an in-spite-of character, as it appears to defy all worldly evidence that speaks against its validity. Gavriel recognizes that faith is a struggle. States Gavriel, "No one has a right not to believe in miracles just because it's a time of war or to make fun of those who believe in them, because their faith is in itself a miracle" (170). Wiesel insists that this tension and ambiguity within faith must remain unresolved in order for faith to be authentic. The narrative of faith and the narrative of anguish and nothingness are dialectically related and as such one cannot be spoken of without the other. The path of least resistance would be to let one of the narratives go—namely, to allow negativity to swallow faith. From Wiesel's perspective, relinquishing faith altogether is the easier choice of least resistance; to let it go eliminates incongruity and paradox. However, in a world where Jewishness is condemned, the relinquishment of faith is tantamount to acquiescence to the oppressor's imperious will. For Wiesel, therefore, jettisoning faith is not a feasible option. Wiesel believes that in accordance with Hasidic tradition, heroes are those who endure the ambiguous collision of narratives in the hopes of one day redeeming it. Wiesel praises the spiritual leadership of the Rebbe Barukh for this reason:

He grasped the awesome weight of questions.... The beauty of Rebbe
Barukh is that he could speak of faith as not opposed to anguish but
as being part of it. "Faith and the abyss are next to one another," he
told his disciple. "I would even say: one within the other."[96]

Laughter as "Mad Midrash"

We conclude by noting that perhaps the most apposite genre for Wiesel's
fiction, and particularly *Gates of the Forest*, is Emil Fackenheim's illustra-
tive term "mad midrash." Midrash is a form of exegesis, an imaginative
inquiry into the holes found not only within scripture but also within
contemporary human experience. Fackenheim considers post-Holocaust
existence to be plagued with the overwhelming theological question: how
can a Jew say or believe anything religious from this point on? Fackenheim writes:

> To affirm a bond between God and the world is always problem-
> atical. Midrash, however, is aware of this fact. Radically consid-
> ered, a bond between a God who is truly God and a world that is
> truly world may well be considered as not merely problematical
> but nothing short of paradoxical. For its part, however, Midrash
> does not shrink from paradox, but confronts it, and in the very act
> of confrontation reaffirms the bond.[97]

Gavriel laughs, therefore, because he confronts the paradox of affirming a bond between God and the world. His laughter, moreover, unabash-
edly reaffirms that such a bond exists despite all evidence to the contrary.
Fackenheim describes mad midrash as a form of absolute protest that is
ultimately serious in its determination to restore the world and sustain a
"seemingly impossible fusion," a holding fast to both God and the world.
The parallel is obvious: Gavriel's laughter too holds fast to the impossible fusion of both the narrative of faith and the narrative(s) of suffering. By laughing, Gavriel affirms the fusion of God and the Holocaust,
inexhaustible life and inexplicable death. To put it simply, Gavriel with
his very life undertakes a radical exegesis of the Holocaust. His ensuing
laughter is itself a form of mad midrash. Gavriel's life is midrashic existence according to Fackenheim's description:

> Philosophical reflection may find it necessary to choose between
> a God who is divine only if he is omnibenevolent and omnipo-

tent, and a world that is truly world only because it contains elements contradicting these divine attributes, namely, evil and human freedom. Midrash recognizes the tension yet refuses to choose. . . . Midrash does not grope for concepts in order to solve problems and dissolve paradox. The Midrashic word is story. It remains story because it both points to and articulates a life lived with problem and paradox—the problems and paradox of a divine-human relation. This life is midrashic existence. Midrashic existence acts as though all depended on man and prays as though all depended on God. . . . Climactically, Midrashic existence endures the strain between these extremes without palliatives or relief.[98]

Yet ironically, Fackenheim fails to note that laughter, particularly the laughter of the oppressed Jew that is perceived as madness, is perhaps the most signaling characteristic of midrashic existence. On the contrary, Fackenheim in this very essay on midrashic existence decries laughter as Nietzschean, as an irresponsible response to the Holocaust universe. Fackenheim cites the SS man who "laughed only at . . . the smashing of the non-Aryan baby's skull," and the post-Holocaust man who laughs at the "crimes of the murderers, the anguish of the victims," and concludes, "With this laughter, his [man's] self-destruction is complete."[99] While the laughter of the executioners surely exists and must be condemned absolutely, it is a strikingly ironic omission that Fackenheim, who mentions *Gates of the Forest* explicitly, completely overlooks in the text the altogether different laughter of Gavriel that in fact incarnates the very midrashic madness Fackenheim envisions.

I conclude then, by asserting that Gavriel's laughter is mad midrash that is essential to post-Holocaust theological and ethical thought and resistance. With each laugh, Gavriel, like his ancestors Isaac, Abraham, and Sarah, affirms that the existence of the faithful is indeed a curious admixture of hope and anguish, violence and blessing, exile and presence, negativity and promise. Until such time as this contradiction is redeemed, the laughter of the oppressed faithful continues to testify to the dialectical tension captured by the axiom, "Hope without remembrance leads to illusions, just as remembrance without hope can result in resignation."[100]

Notes

1. Terrence Des Pres, *Writing Into the World: Essays: 1973–1987* (New York: Viking, 1991), 278.

2. Chaya Ostrower, "Humor as a Defense Mechanism in the Holocaust" (PhD diss., Tel-Aviv University, 2000). Ostrower notes that her project is the first time in Israel that survivors were asked about humor, and she adds that it was "a subject that was taboo until now." Detailed abstract used for citations throughout this chapter found at http://remember.org/humor/abstractn.html.

3. Carol Rittner and John K. Roth, eds., *Different Voices: Women and the Holocaust* (St. Paul, MN: Paragon, 1993), 48.

4. All statistics taken from Friedemann, *Le Rire dans l'Univers Tragique d'Elie Wiesel*.

5. Elie Wiesel, *Gates of the Forest* (New York: Schocken Books, 1966), 7. All future references cited parenthetically.

6. Alvin H. Rosenfeld and Irving Greenberg, eds., *Confronting the Holocaust* (Bloomington: Indiana University Press, 1978), xii.

7. Wiesel, *Ethics and Memory*, 13.

8. Lawrence Langer, *The Holocaust and the Literary Imagination* (New Haven, CT: Yale University Press, 1975), 33.

9. Theodor Adorno, *Aesthetic Theory*, ed. Gretal Adorno and Rolf Tiedemann, trans. C. Lenhardt (Boston: Routledge and Kegan Paul, 1984), 27.

10. Theodor Adorno, *Negative Dialectics*, trans. E. B. Ashton (New York: Continuum, 1966), 53, 367.

11. Susan Shapiro, "Hearing the Testimony of Radical Negation," *Concilium* 175 (1984): 3–10.

12. Elie Wiesel, "The Holocaust as Literary Inspiration," in *Dimensions of the Holocaust*, ed. Lacey Baldwin Smith (Evanston, IL: Northwestern University Press, 1978), 18.

13. Elie Wiesel, *From the Kingdom of Memory* (New York: Summit, 1990), 33.

14. Adorno, *Negative Dialectics*, 5.

15. Harry James Cargas, *Harry James Cargas in Conversation with Elie Wiesel* (New York: Paulist Press, 1976), 106.

16. For an in-depth discussion of the relationship between laughter and Holocaust storytelling and Rebbe Nachman of Bratzlav and Elie Wiesel, see my chapter, "Laughter and the Limits of Holocaust Storytelling: Elie Wiesel's Gates of the Forest" in *Elie Wiesel and the Art of Storytelling*, ed. Rosemary Horowitz (Jefferson, NC: McFarland Press, 2006).

17. Wiesel, *From the Kingdom of Memory*, 21.

18. Ibid., 74.

19. Rosenfeld and Greenberg, *Confronting the Holocaust*, 84.

20. Robert Waite, *The Psychopathic God: Adolf Hitler* (New York: Basic Books, 1977), 13.

21. Wiesel, *From the Kingdom of Memory*, 220.

22. John Morreal, "Humor in the Holocaust," 3.

23. Adorno is right when he describes thought itself as an act of negation or resistance to that which is forced upon it. Adorno, *Negative Dialectics,* 19.

24. Pesach Schindler, *Hasidic Responses to the Holocaust* (Hoboken, NJ: KTAV Publishing, 1990), 72–73.

25. Friedemann, *Le Rire dans l'Univers Tragique d'Elie Wiesel,* 48. It is important to state here that my book is not a mere repetition of Friedemann. Friedemann presents an analysis of laughter in nearly all of Wiesel's novels, including a chapter on the laughter of the executioners. Although my arguments do contain some overlap with Friedemann's interpretation of the ethical significance of laughter, I depart significantly from Friedemann's interpretation of Gavriel's laughter as disengagement and detachment from reality, as sign of metaphysical revolt and radical doubt. I interpret Gavriel's laughter instead as manifesting a supreme engagement with reality. I also discuss the theological significance of Gavriel's laughter and its religious context of Hasidism; Friedemann does not.

26. Schindler, *Hasidic Responses,* 97.

27. Elie Wiesel and Albert H. Friedlander, *The Six Days of Destruction: Meditations Toward Hope* (New York: Paulist Press, 1988), 52.

28. Wiesel, *From the Kingdom of Memory,* 248.

29. Ostrower, "Humor as a Defense," 8.

30. Ibid., 4.

31. Ibid., 5.

32. Ibid.

33. Ibid., 6–7.

34. Schindler, *Hasidic Responses,* 107–8.

35. Kenneth Surin, "Taking Suffering Seriously," in *The Problem of Evil: Selected Readings,* ed. Michael Peterson (Notre Dame, IN: Notre Dame University Press, 1992), 344.

36. Adorno, *Negative Dialectics,* 365, 401–2.

37. Lawrence Langer, *The Holocaust and the Literary Imagination* (New Haven, CT: Yale, 1975), 12.

38. Cargas, *In Conversation with Elie Wiesel,* 18.

39. Rittner and Roth, *Different Voices,* 331.

40. Ibid., 353.

41. Ostrower, "Humor as a Defense," 4.

42. Hannah Arendt, *Eichmann in Jerusalem: A Report on the Banality of Evil* (New York: Penguin, 1994), 287.

43. Ibid., 298.

44. Ibid., 30.

45. Ibid., 287–88.

46. Ibid., 116.

47. Ibid., 295.

48. Mordechai Rotenberg, *Dialogue with Deviance: The Hasidic Ethic and the Theory of Social Contraction* (Lanham, MD: University Press of America, 1993), 14.

49. Elie Wiesel, *Messengers of God: Biblical Portraits and Legends,* trans. Marion Wiesel (New York: Random House, 1976), 71, 91, 93.

50. Rotenberg, *Dialogue with Deviance,* 14, 183.

51. Elie Wiesel, *Souls on Fire: Portraits and Legends of Hasidic Masters,* trans. Marion Wiesel (New York: Random House, 1972), 176.

52. Elie Wiesel, *Four Hasidic Masters and Their Struggle with Melancholy* (Notre Dame, IN: University of Notre Dame Press, 1978), 90.

53. Schindler, *Hasidic Responses,* 72–73.

54. Ibid., 88.

55. Wiesel, *Four Hasidic Masters,* 95.

56. Wiesel, *Four Hasidic Masters,* 13, 15.

57. Michael Berenbaum, *The Vision of the Void, Theological Reflections on the Works of Elie Wiesel* (Middletown, CT: Wesleyan, 1979), 57.

58. Schindler, *Hasidic Responses,* 167.

59. Wiesel, *Souls on Fire,* 25.

60. Cargas, *In Conversation with Elie Wiesel,* 17.

61. Martin Buber, *The Origin and Meaning of Hasidism,* ed. and trans. Maurice Friedman (New York: Harper and Row, 1960), 178.

62. Wiesel, *Souls on Fire,* 9.

63. Buber, *Origin and Meaning,* 178–79.

64. Wiesel, *From the Kingdom of Memory,* 188.

65. While these four resources Wiesel discovers within Hasidism help us to understand Jewish laughter as a mode-of-resistance, it bears mentioning that Wiesel does not simply adopt Hasidism as much as he transforms and radicalizes it, considering even Hasidism itself as ruptured by the Holocaust. Hasidism is the best possible choice in Wiesel's view, though even Hasidism too possesses only fragmentary knowledge. Wiesel parts ways with Hasidism, and Judaism, on several points. First, many Jews and Hasidim would not agree with Wiesel's radical claim that the Holocaust ruptured the covenant (thus the argument between Gregor and the Rebbe in *Gates of the Forest*). And second, although Judaism has a strong tradition of arguing with God, perhaps stronger than any other Western religion, Wiesel radicalizes even this and in his novels such as *Gates,* puts God on trial, accusing God of indifference if not injustice. Some might argue, therefore, that Wiesel adopts an extreme position, one he, though perhaps not all Jews, considers legitimate within Judaism.

66. Wiesel, *Four Hasidic Masters,* 91.

67. Emil Fackenheim, "Midrashic Existence after the Holocaust: Reflections Occasioned by the Work of Elie Wiesel," in Rosenfield and Greenberg, *Confronting the Holocaust,* 99.

68. Wiesel, *Messengers of God,* 97.

69. Elie Wiesel and Michael de Saint Cheron, *Evil and Exile* (Notre Dame, IN: Notre Dame University Press, 1990), 172.

70. Quoted in Friedemann, *Le Rire dans l'Univers Tragique d'Elie Wiesel,* 28. Translation mine.

71. Wiesel, *Messengers of God,* 96.

72. Ibid., 234.

73. Wiesel, *Souls on Fire,* 180.

74. Ibid., 198–99.

75. Buber, *Origin and Meaning*, 66.

76. Rotenberg, *Dialogue with Deviance*, 182.

77. Ibid., 183.

78. Wiesel, *From the Kingdom of Memory*, 35.

79. Ekkehard Schuster and Reinhold Boscher-Kimmig, *Hope Against Hope: Johann Baptist Metz and Elie Wiesel Speak Out on the Holocaust*, trans. J. Matthew Ashley (New York: Paulist Press, 1962), 95.

80. Wiesel, *From the Kingdom of Memory*, 196.

81. Rotenberg, *Dialogue with Deviance*, 177–78, 173.

82. Elie Wiesel, *A Beggar in Jerusalem* (New York: Avon, 1970), 254.

83. Wiesel, *From the Kingdom of Memory*, 183.

84. Buber, *Origins and Meaning*, 230.

85. Wiesel and de Saint Cheron, *Evil and Exile*, 11.

86. Wiesel, *Beggar in Jerusalem*, 43.

87. Cargas, *In Conversation with Elie Wiesel*, 2, 3.

88. Langer, *Holocaust and the Literary Imagination*, 9.

89. Ibid.

90. Wiesel, *From the Kingdom of Memory*, 248.

91. Ibid., 174.

92. David Patterson, *In Dialogue and Dilemma with Elie Wiesel* (Wakefield, NH: Longwood, 1991), 83.

93. Elie Wiesel, *A Journey of Faith* (New York: Donald I. Fine, 1990), 2.

94. Wiesel, *Souls on Fire*, 111.

95. Wiesel, *From the Kingdom of Memory*, 248.

96. Wiesel, *Four Hasidic Masters*, 58

97. Fackenheim, "Midrashic Existence," 108.

98. Ibid., 108-9.

99. Ibid., 115.

100. Jürgen Moltmann, *The Crucified God: The Cross of Christ as the Foundation and Criticism of Christian Theology* (Minneapolis: Fortress Press, 1993), ix.

4

Believing Apostates:
Laughter in Shusaku Endo's *Silence*

I bear no grudge against you! I am only laughing at man's fate. My faith in you is different from what it was; but I love you still.
　　　　　　—Father Rodrigues to God after his apostasy, in Shusaku Endo's *Silence*

Christ suffered so that we may laugh again. He died that we may live as liberated human beings.
　　　　　　—Jürgen Moltmann, *Theology of Play*

Man is a splendid and beautiful being and, at the same time, man is a terrible being as we recognized in Auschwitz—God knows well this monstrous dual quality of man.
　　　　　　—Shusaku Endo, *Endo Shusaku: A Literature of Reconciliation*

How do Christians respond to oppression? Can Christian thought and laughter complement one another in ways we might never have imagined? The internationally best-selling Japanese novel *Silence*, a moving case study of oppressed Christians in Japan, helps us to answer these questions. *Silence*, a work of historical fiction written by Shusaku Endo, is a tragic tale about torture, doubt, fear, betrayal, martyrdom, and death. The narrative explores the all-too-common oppression and persecution that religious believers in a minority tradition have experienced throughout history. Careful readers are surprised, therefore, to discover that almost every character in *Silence* laughs in the midst of this tragic context—the peasants, Kichijiro, the torturers, Inoue, the interpreter, and even the protagonist Father Rodrigues. The text is replete with the laughter of the disempowered, that is, those whose laughter strikes us as counterintuitive.

Of particular interest for our purposes are the forced apostate peasant Kichijiro and the Catholic priest Rodrigues, who is also persecuted into apostasy and made a lifelong prisoner of the Japanese government. Ironically, Rodrigues and Kichijioro laugh more than any other characters in the book. Their laughter remains uninterpreted within the text, however, just as it remains uninterpreted in the literary criticism of the novel. While Endo, via Rodrigues, repeatedly interprets the laughter of his oppressors as derisive and mocking, Rodrigues's and the peasant Kichijiro's laughter linger, unanalyzed and strange, within the text. I ask, therefore, what is the ethical and theological significance of the laughter of the disempowered and suffering apostate? In this chapter, by engaging *Silence* with contemporary Christian thought and theology, I answer that the laughter of the oppressed functions in some startling and significant ways. Laughter emerges (1) as an imaginative supra-linguistic response to problem of evil and its concomitant rupture of language, (2) as an expression of some of the paradoxical and difficult theological concepts of the Christian faith such as *simul justus et peccator*, faith and doubt as dialectic, and theodicy's need for a tragic theology, (3) as a form of kenosis in imitation of Christ's own kenosis, and (4) as a manifestation of and supplement to a genuine theology of the cross. In my understanding, laughter in Endo functions much as it does in Wiesel: as a form of ethical and theological resistance. In the course of our discussion, therefore, some intriguing similarities between Judaism and various strands of Christian thought will be brought to light.[1]

Shusaku Endo's *Silence*, often referred to as the Japanese version of Graham Greene's *The Power and the Glory*, fictionally plumbs the psychological, spiritual, and emotional depths of a priest who is based on a historical person. The protagonist of *Silence*, Father Rodrigues, is based on Giuseppe Chiara, a Portuguese priest who traveled to Japan in the early 1600s in an effort to continue an underground missionary apostolate and, presumably, to make amends for his former teacher Christovao Ferreira, the first missionary on record to apostatize under Japanese persecution. Between the years 1614 (the date of the Edict of Expulsion) and 1640, approximately six thousand Christians were martyred under the Tokugawa Shogun, a feudal military dictatorship that ruled Japan from 1603–1868. Historical records reveal that Chiara too apostatized, and died forty years later, stating paradoxically to those who would listen that he was still a Christian. When Endo began to study the Catholic Church's history of Christian missions in Japan, he quickly realized that this history was a litany of courageous martyrdoms.[2]

Endo, however, discerned a gap within the "official" history that he subsequently sought to fill. Endo in *Silence*, much like Toni Morrison in *Beloved*, seeks to imaginatively recapture and tell a story that was never told. He gives voice to those denied a voice, and describes the difficulty of being a Christian in Japan, where Christians even today are a religious minority. States Endo, "If [the Christians of this era] were to be divided into the weak and the strong, I would be among the former. . . . History knows their sufferings: I believed it was the task of the novelist to listen to their sufferings."[3] Endo realized that because the church keeps no real record of apostates, other than to write them off as mere renegades after their apostasy, Christians of today have no access or understanding of their psychology, emotions, or spiritual anguish. As a novelist, Endo made a similar discovery to Wiesel's: the stories of the oppressed go untold in the annals of authoritative history.

Rather than follow ecclesiastical authority by casting hasty judgment on the apostate's course of action, Endo in his work instead sympathetically portrays the complexity of the apostate's situation—"the unrecorded despair and ignominy endured by those who, for whatever reason, ultimately succumbed to torture, both physical and psychological, and went through the ritual of *efumi* (treading on the crucifix), that most public act of apostasy."[4] Comments Endo in an interview, "If I had been confronted with the decisions faced by [the Nazi collaborator in *White Man* . . . or by Rodrigues in *Silence*], who am I to say I would not have responded as they did?"[5] Endo says that the novel *Silence* grew out of this line of questioning, and that the story centers around the following questions that he asked himself upon seeing a *fumie* in a Nagasaki museum: "1) If I had lived in that period of history, would I have stepped on the *fumie*? 2) What did those who stepped on the *fumie* feel? 3) What kind of people trod on the *fumie*?"[6] Endo explores these questions through the narrative development of the character Rodrigues, who comes to sympathize with those very apostates that as a church leader he had once condemned.

Laughter as Creative Response to the Problem of Evil

When Rodrigues embarks for Japan, he is unequivocally optimistic about his "great mission," and he comments, "Never have I felt so deeply how meaningful is the life of a priest. These Japanese Christians are like a ship lost in a storm without a chart" (26, 31). Rodrigues finds meaning and purpose in his perceived vocation as the peasants' "chart." In his first letter, Rodrigues writes that he contemplates the face of Christ and finds it to be one of "encouragement," a face that instructs him to "Feed my lambs." Rodrigues remarks, "It is a face filled with vigor and strength. I feel great love for that face. I am fascinated by the face of Christ just like a man fascinated by the face of his Beloved" (21). Rodrigues feels watched over by Christ, and considers himself to be Christ's beloved. At this stage, Rodrigues believes unquestioningly in divine Providence. Commenting on Santa Marta, the unfortunate missionary who is unable to continue on to Japan because of illness, Rodrigues writes with cavalier flourish, "Alas, I feel no inclination to write about Santa Marta. God did not grant to our poor companion the joy of being restored to health. But everything that God does is for the best" (21).

I want to argue that with this very first letter, however, Endo sets up the overarching problematic for the entire text. With this set-up, Endo leads the reader to ask, what will happen to Rodrigues if and when he no longer feels like the beloved of Christ, and instead feels betrayed and abandoned by Him? What will happen to Rodrigues's faith if his unequivocal belief in divine justice and providence is personally challenged—that is, if it seems everything God does is *not* for the best? What would it mean for Rodrigues if loving Christ means not being able to feed His lambs? What will happen to Rodrigues's faith if his mission has a more ambiguous outcome and is *not* "great," that is, not successful? All of these disappointments are exactly what befall Rodrigues, and his encounter with radical evil evokes each of these questions that he must personally answer. The question thus becomes, how does Rodrigues respond, and how does his faith withstand evil's assault? What role does laughter play in helping him respond to the problem of evil?

Laughter as Result of Collision of Narratives and Rupture of Language

As we recall, Kenneth Surin helps us recognize that the problem of evil presents a peculiar dilemma to the person of faith—that is, the narrative of faith collides with the narrative of negativity, resulting in existential paradox. Although Surin speaks only of the Holocaust, his words apply to Rodrigues's situation too:

> The narrative of faith collides with the narrative of its negation, but neither achieves an ascendancy over the other. . . . The testimony of its witnesses speaks for both these seemingly irreconcilable

moments, moments which must nevertheless be simultaneously affirmed. To safeguard the possibility of truth it is necessary to hold the one moment as the necessary dialectical negation or counterpoise of the other. The testimony of affirmation needs to be "ruptured" by its counterpart testimony of negation, and vice versa.[7]

In *Silence* as in *Gates of the Forest*, Rodrigues's faith eventually runs headlong into the theological problem of evil. This paradox of the collision of faith with its negation results in linguistic rupture and inescapable theological tension. I contend that as Rodrigues develops as a character, he laughs precisely at those crucial moments when he can no longer ignore the messy collision of negativity and faith. Indeed, his laughter expresses his acknowledgment of the incommensurability of these narratives, and a revision of his previous theology to include a more tragic theology.

Although usually overlooked, Endo foreshadows this collision of narratives at two crucial junctures in the text's first pages. The first occurs through a jarring series of juxtapositions. Rodrigues, having just completed the preliminary leg of his journey to Japan, writes, "I feel like shouting out that it is a miracle. Is it true that I am in Macao? Am I not perhaps in a dream? I cannot believe this whole thing. On the wall is a great big cockroach" (21). The cockroach, ever a literary symbol of filth and darkness since Kafka's unforgettable tale of Gregor Samsa, perches on Rodrigues's wall as an ugly, ominous threat. Although Rodrigues observes the cockroach, its presence does not invoke any interpretation; indeed, Rodrigues seems ignorant of this incongruity, merely passing over it and abruptly shifting in the very next line back to dichotomous thinking, "Go into the world and preach the gospel to every creature. He who believes and is baptized will be saved; he that does not believe will be condemned" (22). Rodrigues's world is either/or: either you are saved, or you are condemned.

Rodrigues thinks everything is miraculous salvation and light for those like himself who believe, but the cockroach's omnipresence from the start makes us uneasy. The bug's presence on the stark wall calls into question Rodrigues's unequivocal beliefs and unambiguous attitude toward his mission. Rodrigues's comment "I cannot believe this whole thing" foreshadows his own eventual uneasiness, however, and the eventual collapse of his own impossible-to-sustain unambiguous, dichotomous worldview. In short, the ignored cockroach leads us to ask, does Rodrigues ignore the existence of filth, that is, evil, and how does (or will) Rodrigues's theology address the problem of evil when forced to confront it? To think in terms of both-and, the cockroach's omnipresence also leads us to ask, does Rodrigues likewise ignore the presence of God when it appears in an unlikely, perhaps even ugly, form or incarnation, namely that of Christ?

A second early proof text of a collision of narratives occurs at another place in Rodrigues's first letter: "The rain makes this wretched town even more wretched. The whole place was shrouded in ashen gray, while the Chinese, huddled in little houses that looked like dog-kennels, left the dirty streets. . . . As I look at such streets I think (I wonder why?) of the mystery of human life—and then I grow sad" (16). Rodrigues in the novel's beginning thinks in terms of black and white, either/or categories—that is, one is weak or strong, faithful or apostate, coward or martyr. In the above lines, however, Rodrigues significantly remarks upon the ashen-gray wretchedness, the dirt and the dog-kennels that characterize the existence of those around him, which no doubt collide with his own experience of relative comfort and wealth. But he immediately represses these seeming acknowledgments of God-forsakenness, and any subsequent doubt and questions regarding divine omnibenevolence and omnipotence that would naturally accompany such observations. In Rodrigues's role as authoritative priest, he adopts the party line, so to speak.

At this point, Rodrigues's own sadness and theological questioning merely puzzle him; he wonders why looking at the streets of an impoverished town should upset him, as if a person of faith should not be disturbed by such matters. Here, Rodrigues chooses not to answer his own question regarding the suffering and poverty of others, and instead classifies these issues under "the mystery of human life." Theodicists who seek to justify the ways of God to humanity often resort to this argument of inscrutability, claiming that mere human beings cannot know God's plan and that all suffering has a "purpose." But both Gavriel and ultimately Rodrigues find this appeal weak, facile, and unsatisfactory in the face of their negating historical experiences. Although Christian theology has often resorted to such cavalier comments with regard to people's suffering, both Wiesel and Endo suggest that these explanations not only fail to satisfy, they are often hurtful and alienating. Post-Holocaust Jewish thought has made this poignant criticism time and after time, and Christian theology could do more to heed it faithfully.

When we first encounter the early Rodrigues, he, unlike many of the peasants, does not acknowledge tragedy or feel any compelling need for Christian theology to address the twin problems of evil and tragedy. Upon arriving in Japan, Rodrigues expresses his unequivocal optimism,

"My feeling is that we will not be captured. . . . In our little hut I have a feeling of eternal safety. I don't know why this should be" (35). Shortly thereafter, Rodrigues adds, "Never before had I felt so deeply the sheer joy of being alive. . . . The conviction grows deeper and deeper in my heart that all is well and that God will protect us" (36). On another occasion, Rodrigues declares as he serves the peasants of Tomogi, "Feelings of joy and happiness suddenly filled my breast: the feeling that my life was of value and that it was accomplishing something. I am of some use to the people of this country" (45). He adds, "Lord, everything that you have created is good. How beautiful are your dwellings" (71). Words such as these come easily to the lips of those who have never experienced severe oppression.

Rodrigues's last remark in this unequivocally positive vein comes just prior to the seizure and execution of Mokichi and Ichizo by the authorities—notably the first tangible event of persecution and martyrdom that Rodrigues witnesses. Rodrigues asserts, "I am completely at peace. Our hut is full of light, I can hear the cock crow from the foot of the hill" (47). As a literary device and obvious biblical allusion to the betrayal of Christ, the symbol of a cock crowing prefigures treachery and impending conflict. As in the case of the cockroach, this troubling juxtaposition is not lost on the reader, but appears entirely lost on the priest Rodrigues, who juxtaposes "light" and "peace" with the cock crow in the same sentence, as if there were no immediate incongruity between them. For a man who constantly compares his own narrative to that of Christ's, such an omission indicates a certain blindness and lack of self-awareness on Rodrigues's part. As readers, we should be on guard and conscious of Rodrigues's hermeneutical failings; therefore, we should not unquestioningly accept Rodrigues narration (and hence interpretation) of events. To be sure, at the moment Rodrigues writes these confident words, an informant has already betrayed the Tomogi Christians and alerted the local samurai to their presence, and actions have been taken that will lead to the eventual death of Mokichi and Ichizo.

The brutal murder of the peasants is Rodrigues's encounter with inexplicable, world-shattering radical evil. As such, their innocent death marks a turning point in Rodrigues's theology, as his subsequent laughter reflects. As Rodrigues witnesses the brutal death of these martyrs who refuse to renounce their faith, his facile either/or theological distinctions begin to show the first signs of erosion. In reading Rodrigues's description of the comparison between the martyrdom of his imagination and genuine martyrdom, we are reminded of Dostoevsky's admonition in *The Brothers Karamazov*: "Love in action is a harsh and fearful thing compared with love in dreams."[8] Writes Rodrigues:

> I had long read about martyrdom in the lives of the saints—how the souls of the martyrs had gone home to heaven, . . . how the angels had blown trumpets. This was the splendid martyrdom in my dreams. But the martyrdom of the Japanese Christians I now describe to you was no such glorious thing. What a miserable and painful business it was! The rain falls unceasingly on the sea. And the sea which killed them surges on uncannily—in silence. . . . I know what you will say: "Their death was not meaningless. . . . Mokichi and Ichizo are with the Lord. . . . They now enjoy everlasting happiness." I also am convinced of all this. And yet, why does this feeling of grief remain in my heart? Why does the song of the exhausted Mokichi, bound to the stake, gnaw constantly at my heart. . . . I myself do not quite understand . . . the silence of God . . . the feelings that while men raise their voices in anguish God remains with folded arms, silent. . . . Yet what had happened to our glorious dream? Yet one priest remaining in this country has the same significance as a single candle burning in the catacombs. (60–61)

Rodrigues's choppy and repetitive use of the words "yet," "and yet," and "but" again represents his attempt to navigate the incongruity and irreconcilability of the narratives before him. These words signaling a transition in viewpoint reflect Rodrigues's struggle to come to terms with his newly realized discovery of the dialectical relationship of these narratives. To testify to the truth of the experience, Rodrigues must simultaneously affirm both sides of the dialectic; as Surin says, neither narrative can achieve ascendancy over the other, unless of course, one relinquishes the narrative of faith altogether. Rodrigues, though, does not simply jettison his faith. Instead, he desires to convey simultaneously a testimony of affirmation and a testimony of negation. On the one hand, Rodrigues is "convinced" that the peasants' death is not meaningless; on the other hand, their death exudes meaninglessness. Rodrigues's narrative of faith convinces him that the peasants now enjoy eternal happiness, but the narrative of negativity demands Rodrigues's grief and recognition of the apparent meaninglessness and God-forsakenness of the peasants' death. Rodrigues may well be a candle burning in the catacomb, but God is also silent while people are dying for the love of Him.

After the peasants' execution, Rodrigues identifies for the first time with Kichijiro's position of "weakness" and "cowardice." He too is now someone who flees the authorities out of terror and a desire to protect his own life. As Rodrigues flees by boat "trembling from head to toe," he laughs:

No matter how strong one's faith, physical fear can overwhelm one completely. . . . Now I was all alone in the black sea of the night and must take upon myself the cold and the darkness and everything else. . . . And then somehow the mouse-like face of Kichijiro, filled with terror, rose up in my imagination. Yes, that cowardly wretch . . . were I an ordinary Christian, not a priest, would I have fled in the same way? . . . How many missionaries had crossed over to this island on a tiny boat just as I had done? . . . For some reason or other I called to mind the words of Valignano at Macao: "At one time we seriously discussed the question as to whether our religious habit should be made of silk or cotton." As these words suddenly came into my mind, I looked out into the darkness and clasping my knees I *laughed* softly. . . . It seems so ludicrous that this fellow, sitting in an insect-infested little ship, dressed in the peasant clothing of Mokichi from Tomogi—that this fellow should be a priest just like them. (62–63, italics mine)

Why does Rodrigues laugh at such a time of horror? We know from incongruity theory that the greater the incongruity, the greater the paradox; the greater the paradox, the greater the laughter. Rodrigues, then, laughs because of the existential paradox he endures, and because of the insurmountable incongruity he perceives between narratives. In brief, a threefold collision of incongruous narratives evokes Rodrigues's laughter.

First, Rodrigues laughs because martyrdom in reality is a harsh and dreadful thing compared to the martyrdom in his priestly dreams of grandeur. As seen above, he suddenly apprehends the incongruity between his conception of martyrdom, and the concrete reality of martyrdom. The narrative of radical negativity—the peasants' seemingly meaningless and gross suffering accompanied by God's silence—collides with Rodrigues's Catholic narrative of faith, which perceives martyrdom as glorious in light of what many theologians would term a *theologia gloriae*, or theological focus on the glory of Christ's resurrection and triumph over death. Mokichi, the martyred peasant, represents this type of theology in the text; significantly, at the moment of his own execution he triumphantly sings this verse from a Christian hymn: "We're on the way to the temple of Paradise" (59). Within such a theology of glory, martyrdom is the natural apotheosis of faith. And yet (to borrow Rodrigues's own phrase) real-life martyrdom smacks of absurdity, ugliness, and meaninglessness rather than glory. The incongruity of these narratives, along with the paradoxical fact that they ostensibly negate one another, causes Rodrigues to laugh.

Second and similarly, Rodrigues suddenly perceives an incongruity between his traditional understanding of the role of missionary priest, and the reality of his life as missionary priest. This incongruity occasions Rodrigues's second collision of narratives. Traditional faith's narrative of the life of a missionary priest—one who serves the people, wears a habit, effects conversion—clashes with reality's narrative, in which Rodrigues cannot perform the sacraments, wears a dead peasant's clothing, and elicits condemnation and persecution. The priest, fleeing for his life in an insect-infested ship while the very peasants whose faith he had hoped to sustain die by torture, unsurprisingly laughs aloud. Rodrigues indeed laughs a second time as he reflects upon this incongruity, "These men [past Japanese missionaries] had been loved so deeply by the people. . . . They had no need to fly to the mountains for hiding like haunted men. When I reflected on my own condition a strange desire to laugh rose up within my heart" (66). The inbreaking of evil creates an astonishing gap between expectation and reality, a gap so large as to resist thought. Immanuel Kant, as we recall, states that "laughter is an affectation arising from the sudden transformation of a strained expectation into nothing."[9] Rodrigues, in accordance with Kantian theory, can only laugh to express this dissonance between expectation and reality. His laughter seems careless and odd to the casual observer, much like Kichijiro's laugh seems initially irresponsible to Rodrigues, but in actuality his laughter belies a complex theological truth language cannot capture.

A third collision of narratives occurs in this moment on the little ship: an external collision of Kichijiro and Rodrigues's respective stories. Rodrigues laughs because previously in his mind, Kichijiro's narrative of negativity had nothing whatsoever to do with his own priestly narrative of faithfulness. The two narratives are diametrically opposed in the early Rodrigues's mindset. However, as Rodrigues huddles fearfully in the roach-infested ship, he has a foretaste of his own potential for weakness and apostasy stemming from fear of physical pain. In other words, he glimpses for the first time an astonishing possible point of collision between even these two narratives—and that point is apostasy under duress. A gray area exists: apostasy and belief may not be merely antinomies, given the circumstances. Belief or at least expressions of belief prove to be radically contingent. Formerly, Rodrigues claimed, "It was impossible. Faith could not turn a man into such a coward" (24). Now, when Rodrigues fears for his own life, he realizes for the first time that those who apostatize may still possess belief, in spite of their feelings of doubt and abandonment. Rodrigues's inner dialogue poses the question: does it make one a coward to want to cling to the very life God granted? Would he himself apostatize even if he were still a believer? For the priest, the equation (belief = death) is absurd and contrary to scriptural promise; the equation (life = apostasy) even more so. The Japanese authorities have intentionally created this situation of absurdity for the oppressed Christians. This paradox continues to occasion Rodrigues's laughter throughout the text.

Laughter as Disruption of Either/Or

In Rodrigues's first letter, we discern that he is unequivocally opposed (like the Catholic Church itself) to apostasy. Apostasy itself is utterly incomprehensible to Rodrigues at this stage. Rodrigues embarks on this journey to Japan because it is "impossible to believe that their much admired teacher Ferreira, faced with the possibility of a glorious martyrdom, had groveled like a dog before the infidel" (7, 8). To be sure, apostasy reviles Rodrigues and is tantamount in his theology to cowardice. In Rodrigues's view, a person of faith embodies courage and could never therefore be an apostate or a coward. When Rodrigues meets Kichijiro on board the ship to Japan, he contemptuously assumes Kichijiro could not be a Christian because of his craven attitude:

> During the storm this pitiful coward made almost no attempt to help the sailors and now, wretchedly pale, he lay between the baggage. Splashed all around him was white vomit. . . . With the sailors we looked at the fellow with contempt. . . . This fellow . . . was just like a pig that buried its face in its own vomit. . . . Was it possible that he was of our faith? . . . No. It was impossible. Faith could not turn a man into such a coward. (24)

Here, Rodrigues indulges in traditional either/or dichotomies: either one possesses faith, or one is a coward. Either one is among the faithful martyrs, or one is a disbelieving apostate/infidel. Either one is weak, or one is strong. Nowhere is Rodrigues's either/or, black-and-white thinking better displayed than in his telling comment:

Men are born into two categories: the strong and the weak, the saints and the commonplace, the heroes and those who respect them. In times of persecution the strong are burnt in the flames and drowned in the sea; but the weak, like Kichijiro, lead a vagabond life in the mountains. As for you (I now spoke to myself) which category do you belong to? (77)

Rodrigues displays identical dichotomous thinking when he depicts the exchange between Kichijiro and the Chinese sailors, at which time Kichijiro,

pleaded for pardon in the most ugly way you could imagine. Such conduct is far from anything you could call Christian patience but this weakling's cowardice is just like that. . . . It is true, of course, that there are Japanese who endured torture for five days on end without wavering in their fidelity; but there are also cowardly weaklings like Kichijiro. (20)

Patricia Hill Collins, herself writing with an experiential knowledge of oppression as a woman of color, explains the dangers of dichotomous thinking. Either/or thought masks inequity; such thinking prevails because one side of the dichotomy is actually ideologically favored by the dominant consciousness. Writes Collins, "This emphasis on quantification and categorization occurs in conjunction with the belief that either/or categories must be ranked. The search for certainty of this sort requires that one side of a dichotomy is privileged while its other is denigrated."[10] Collins suggests that people in situations of privilege tend to dichotomize in order to maintain power; the oppressed need to shatter these false dichotomies that serve to justify and belie inequity. Liberation theologian Gustavo Guttierez once wrote that there are no innocent theologies; Collins suggests that there are no innocent dichotomies, either. To put it simply, Christians need to recognize that either/or dichotomous thought can be sin.

Rodrigues, firmly within his powerful position, affirms this either/or of strong/weak, faith/coward, believer/infidel. To do so follows the dominant consciousness of his own culture—that is, the church. But the narrative raises the question, did Christ really affirm the either/or, or was his own thinking more of the revolutionary both-and? While the Christian church arguably struggles to transcend either/or thinking through Christ's inversionary claims that the weak are indeed the strong and the poor are indeed the rich, I consider the church's transcendence of denigrating categorizations as more goal than historical actuality. Liberation theology laments that the church in praxis often has privileged one side of the dichotomy. In this the church is complicit with, rather than critical of, much of culture's systemic evils. Rodrigues is heir to this struggle. Rodrigues aligns himself with either/or thought, because to do so is to engage in thinly veiled self-affirmation, since Rodrigues includes himself in the former, infinitely preferable side of the dichotomy. When Rodrigues asks himself the question regarding his own categorization, the question is rhetorical—Rodrigues's own discussion already implies that because he is a priest, he would never consider apostasy.

When Rodrigues laughs for the first time in the novel, he laughs at the perceived incongruity between his priestly courageous self and "weak cowards" like Kichijiro. Arthur Schopenhauer, we recall, argues that all laughter is occasioned by paradox and the sudden apprehension of incongruity.[11] Rodrigues, in contrast to Kichijiro, self-righteously perceives his own faith and strength as unwavering, and laughs at the incongruity of having to trust someone on the inferior side of the dichotomy, "Don't think that because I write this way we have lost our energy and enthusiasm. On the contrary, when I reflect that I have entrusted my future to a fellow like Kichijiro, I cannot help laughing" (21).

Laughter, however, disrupts either/or thinking. For laughter can simultaneously affirm two contradictory thoughts or narratives (both-and) in a way that discursive language cannot. Rationality and cognitive discourse eschew paradox, but laughter attests to the paradox without attempting to resolve it. As we learned in Wiesel's work, those who laugh in the face of radical negation often do so in order to sustain the inexpressibility of the experience. As a move beyond language, laughter expresses the inexpressible. Similarly in *Silence*, Rodrigues's first laugh indicates the initial blurring of dichotomous distinctions and the beginning of a consciousness of ambiguity and paradox. Rodrigues laughs above because ostensibly Kichijiro is a Christian, and therefore he should be strong, not weak. But Kichijiro is a weak Christian, something that is inconceivable to Rodrigues. Kichijiro, therefore, is tantamount to an embodied oxymoron. As such, he consistently challenges Rodrigues's consciousness and disrupts his dichotomous thought. Kichijiro is a coward, but he is a coward who claims to be on Rodrigues's side; moreover, Kichijiro is a weak person on whom paradoxically the strong Rodrigues must rely. Kichijiro, this unimaginable yet undeniable and enfleshed paradox, interrupts Rodrigues's either/or consciousness—an interruption made manifest by his laughter.

But what is the secret story behind Kichijiro's laughter? Several years prior to meeting Rodrigues, the Japanese government subjected Kichijiro and his family to torture because of their Christian faith. However, Kichijiro was the only member of his family to apostatize, which meant that he had to witness his family's execution by burning at the stake. Suffering this ignominy, Kichijiro was not able to return to his native town. Kichijiro is the first Japanese that Garrpe and Rodrigues encounter, and thus they intensely question him about the situation of Christians in Japan. When Rodrigues asks Kichijiro about execution by water torture, Rodrigues reports, "His face became distorted, then suddenly he lapsed into silence. He shook his hand as though some terrible memory rose up from the past to haunt him" (17).

Kichijiro's silence in response to this question testifies to the linguistic rupture he has experienced in his encounter with a narrative-negating event, the kind of rupture to which the characters in *Beloved* and *Gates of the Forest* also bear witness. Rodrigues correctly ascertains that Kichijiro's strange attitude is a result of some "terrible memory," but he cannot comprehend that the event which Kichijiro remembers—witnessing his family's execution—so disrupts cognitive thought that he cannot speak about it: "We could not understand why Garrpe's question should make him so unhappy" (17). Kichijiro's own experience of negativity resists thought. Rodrigues seems in the narrative's beginning to have had no existential experience with an evil or a negativity that resists thought or ruptures language.

During this same interrogation, Garrpe asks Kichijiro if he is a Christian, and again Kichijiro responds only with silence, "The fellow suddenly shut up like a clam" (17). Once again, Rodrigues (mis)interprets Kichijiro's silence as stemming from cowardice rather than from the painful inexpediency of language, "Such conduct is pretty far from anything you could call Christian patience, but this weakling's cowardice is just like that. . . . Now we get some idea of why he suddenly shut up like a clam when we first mentioned the Japanese Christians. Perhaps whenever he speaks he has a dreadful fear of his own words" (20). Again with an ironic twist, Rodrigues says more than he intends. Kichijiro does fear his own inadequate words, but this fear attests more to linguistic rupture than to his own craven character.

Later, when Garrpe asks again, Kichijiro states that he is not a Christian. On another occasion, Kichijiro resorts to just shaking his head furiously. Again, such denials of faith from a person who is a practitioner of the Christian faith baffle Rodrigues. In actuality, Kichijiro exhibits a strong ambivalence toward the label "Christian," hence he alternately assumes and denies such an identity, as made manifest when he proclaims himself a Christian to prison guards in front of whom he has recently apostatized. When backed into a corner, particularly by the priests, Kichijiro deems a rejection of the name "Christian" as apposite, but he also perceives that such a denial is grossly ineffective at circumscribing his paradoxical situation. Kichijiro is a Christian who has been coerced, out of fear of death and torture, into publicly denying his Christianity—an existential paradox that plagues him and often reduces him to laughter. Kichijiro's own internal collision of narratives that ruptures language, then, is the "secret" behind his laughter, the secret Rodrigues eventually learns when he too becomes an apostate.

As we might expect, Kichijiro's laugh troubles Rodrigues, "He [Kichijiro] has the most fawning, obsequious laugh you could possibly imagine. It leaves a bad taste in our mouths. . . . The fellow intrigues me. I feel sure that bit by bit I will come to learn his secret" (25). Rodrigues's words are laden with irony; he comes to "learn" Kichijiro's "secret" just as surely as he comes to share fully in his laughter, and doing so will be the most painful lesson of Rodrigues's life. For the moment, however, Rodrigues does not understand how someone who has both seen and committed such horror can laugh, and we are reminded of Clara's admonition in *Gates of the Forest*, "You don't know yet that a man can laugh while he suffers."[12] Rodrigues misinterprets Kichijiro's laughter as obsequious, when in fact it symbolizes a far more complex existential mode-of-being-in-the-world.

In our interpretation, Kichijiro's laughter suggests that he discerns his own being to be paradoxical. He is, in short, a believing apostate. As such, he is rejected by both the Catholic Church and his own community—both communities that consider one can only be **either** an apostate **or** a believer, either a coward or a martyr. Kichijiro occupies a liminal state of nonbeing. Like all other victims of oppression, Kichijiro lives life at its limits and on its edges. He knows himself to be a "weak" Christian, a believing apostate, even though the church and Rodrigues do not acknowledge the existence of such a category. Kichijiro confesses this incessantly, "God asks me to imitate the strong, although he made me weak. Isn't this unreasonable?" (114). Throughout the narrative Kichijiro follows a strangely cyclical pattern of alternately apostatizing, then courageously turning himself in to the authorities and confessing he is a Christian, "And you officials! I am a Christian. Put me in prison" (114). The existential complexity of Kichijiro's own situation invokes this laughter. Rodrigues's preliminary moment of narrative laughter therefore foreshadows the ultimate interruption of either/or and affirmation of both-and that Rodrigues's later, more nuanced laughter will eventually make manifest. Each time Rodrigues laughs, then, he grows closer to occupying the same paradoxically existential state held by Kichijiro; until at narrative's end, Rodrigues too is a believing apostate.

Laughter as Expression of Paradoxes of the Christian Faith

Simul Justus et Peccator

Luther described all human beings as *simul justus et peccator*, that is, simultaneously justified and sinner. It is my personal view that Christian theology has not fully grasped the unique strength of such a claim, but would benefit by doing so. All Christians, Luther claimed, who truly "get" the gospel understand themselves strangely—as persons who are simultaneously righteous and sinful. Christians are justified sinners, righteous sinners, saints and sinners both at the same time. While this looks like an oxymoron, much like believing apostate, Luther argues that it is simply true according to the gospel: all Christians are embodied oxymorons. Endo suggests the same thing: on some level, are we not all believing apostates like Kichijiro and Rodrigues? Aren't we all people who often believe but often doubt, especially in times of suffering? Aren't we all sinful, yet somehow in God's eyes, not any longer? Christians understand themselves as both already redeemed and not yet redeemed—an assertion that many would surely find nonsensical. Christian theology uses the term proleptic, a word with Greek origins that means both assumed and anticipated, to describe both the kingdom of God and the redemption of the Christian.

Christian laughter can incarnate this theological and existential paradox. The both-and doctrine of *simul justus et peccator* appears illogical and absurd to an outside observer, yet nonetheless, Rodrigues's experience and Lutheran theological anthropology coincide in their understanding of the complex divine-human relationship and the Christian faith. Rodrigues's and Kichijiro's laughter reveals that either/or thinking can prove horribly inadequate in the face of radical suffering, which both characters endure. Put simply, their laughter signals a breakdown of discursive thought. Both characters understand themselves to be weak, but also Christians; believers, who are also public "apostates." Their laughter embodies the difficult existential state of both-and, and does not submit to silence in the face of linguistic rupture. Reminiscent of the whiskey priest in *The Power and the Glory*, Rodrigues ends up in the same liminal "both-and" state as Kichijiro and therefore utters the contradictory statement, "I'm no longer 'father'. . . . Even now I am the last priest in this land" (189–91).

Laughter as Interruption of Dualism of Faith and Doubt

From the very start of the narrative, Kichijiro is a person of faith who also possesses radical doubts. Kichijiro is one of the first three peasants of Tomogi taken into custody by the samurai who has learned of the existence of Christians in the village. As Kichijiro is being captured, he "snivels" and pleads, "Why has Deus Sama given us this trial? We have done no wrong" (54). Kichijiro is asking here, why does a loving God let us experience evil? What believer has not at some point asked such a question to the God that she or he loves?

In the early pages of *Silence*, however, only Kichijiro remarks on the challenge the problem of evil poses to any believer and his theology. Rodrigues ignores the problems of evil and tragic suffering as he, a person of relative power and stature, has never personally encountered them. The early Rodrigues cannot comprehend Kichijiro, who on the one hand sings triumphant Christian hymns about having "nothing to fear," but on the other is the quintessence of fear, a "whipped dog" who is as pitiful as he is weak (48). Rodrigues at this point understands only "strong faith" to be the antidote of doubt and theological skepticism as embodied by Kichijiro:

> But the funniest thing of all is Kichijiro. . . . I urged him to go to confession, and with great humility he confessed all the sins of his past life. I ordered him always to keep in mind the words of Our Lord: "He who denies my name before men him also will I deny before my Father who is in heaven." . . . This fellow is by nature utterly cowardly and seems quite unable to have the slightest courage. He has good will, however, and I told him in no uncertain terms that if he wanted to overcome this weakness of will and this cowardice . . . the remedy was not in the sake he kept drinking but in a strong faith. (42–43)

In these lines Rodrigues struggles to interpret the personhood of Kichijiro. Because Kichijiro alternates between acts of faith and acts of apostasy, acts of courage and acts of ostensible weakness, Rodrigues cannot easily fit him into his dualistic thought: "Is it that he is a good fellow at heart? Or is it that he is agreeable? Anyhow, I just can't hate him" (48). (Not without interest, Rodrigues characterizes this protean aspect of Kichijiro as "funny," perhaps a better translation would be "laughable.") Kichijiro's theological position as well as his character is slippery, too "both-and" to be easily labeled, and so Rodrigues's interpretation of him fluctuates between condemnation and gratitude.

As evidence of this, we note how frequently Rodrigues exploits transitional phrases like "anyhow," "and yet," "but," and "however," all words that indicate an oppositional statement is to follow. In the quoted passage above, however, Rodrigues cannot abide with the tension, but attempts hastily to resolve it. He ends on a decided note of condemnation, in accord with the either/or dominant consciousness of the church and its theology. He asserts that Kichijiro's doubt and cowardice could be overcome by one remedy alone: "strong faith." Faith is opposed to doubt for Rodrigues at this point, and doubt in his understanding is not, contrary to Paul Tillich, an element within faith that testifies to faith's courageous seriousness. Rodrigues's faith as it stands cannot contain Kichijiro's challenge regarding the problem of evil; for this very reason Kichijiro's (and the other peasants') suffering radically disrupts Rodrigues's dogmatic positivism. Rodrigues desires to have all the answers, yet the silence of God appears an unanswerable question on the theological horizon. Every laugh of Rodrigues's signifies a gradual chipping-away at this dichotomous thinking, each laugh is an audible testimony to the intrusion into Rodrigues's consciousness of the paradox of both-and.

Rodrigues, as he faces increasing tragedy, increasingly comes to share in Kichijiro's doubts—doubts that reach their apotheosis in Rodrigues's own forced public apostasy, which he commits because the oppressors tell him the lie that to do so will spare the lives of the peasant Christians. Rodrigues, because of Kichijiro's increasingly vocal questions of theodicy, doubts because God's silence in the face of evil and suffering begins to plague him, as the following passage vividly portrays:

> I do not believe that God has given us this trial to no purpose. I know that the day will come when we will clearly understand why this persecution with all its sufferings has been bestowed upon us—for everything that Our Lord does is for our good. And yet, even as I write these words I feel the oppressive weight in my heart of those last stammering words of Kichijiro on the morning of his departure: "Why has Deus Sama imposed this suffering upon us?" And then the resentment in those eyes that he turned

upon me. "Father," he had said, "what evil have we done?" I suppose I should simply cast from my mind these meaningless words of the coward; yet why does his plaintive voice pierce my breast with all the pain of a sharp needle? Why has our Lord imposed this torture? . . . No, Kichijiro was trying to express something different, something even more sickening. The silence of God. . . . In the face of this terrible and merciless sacrifice offered up to Him, God has remained silent. This was the problem that lay behind the plaintive question of Kichijiro. (54–55)

Rodrigues begins the above musings on an entirely different note than he ends them, and the transition is signaled by the phrase "and yet." Throughout the novel, Rodrigues repeats this highly significant phrase "and yet." This phrase's repetition signals the repeated inbreaking of paradox and ambiguity into Rodrigues's dualistic either/or consciousness. The ellipses that follow signal the rupture of language engendered by this paradox—Rodrigues is temporarily speechless. The phrase "and yet" signals Rodrigues's growing acceptance of reality as "both-and." Because faith is trust and not knowledge, Rodrigues comes to realize that it is possible to both doubt and believe. Uncertainty's intrusions into Rodrigues's consciousness are often accompanied by salvos of laughter, which interrupt the dualism of faith and doubt and testify to linguistic rupture.

Fleeing from the authorities, Rodrigues for the first time experiences oppression. He feels overwhelmed by negativity and by the ostensible lack of divine justice and divine compassion for the suffering of His own people. In other words, Rodrigues has an increasing awareness of what Paul Ricoeur terms "the scandalous theology implicit in tragedy."[13] Because ostensibly a good and omnipotent God allows such needless radical suffering and death all in the name of faith, Rodrigues comes to doubt God's very existence, while at the same time paradoxically yearning for God's existence most desperately:

If God does not exist, how can man endure the monotony of the sea and its cruel lack of emotion? (But supposing . . . of course, supposing, I mean.) From the deepest core of my being yet another voice made itself heard in a whisper. Supposing God does not exist. . . . This was a frightening fancy. If he does not exist, how absurd the whole thing becomes. What an absurd drama the lives of Mokichi and Ichizo, bound to the stake and washed by the waves. . . . Myself, too, wandering here over the desolate moun-

tains—what an absurd situation! Plucking the grass as I went
along I chewed it with my teeth, suppressing these thoughts that
rose nauseatingly in my throat. I knew well, of course, that the
greatest sin against God was despair; but the silence of God was
something I could not fathom. (68–69)

Divine silence is the paramount theological problem posed in the
text, as evidenced by its determination of the novel's title. At stake here
is God's imperviousness to suffering and evil, a concept initially unfath-
omable to Rodrigues. While he struggles to suppress such thoughts as
he wanders through the deserted hillside, he comes across a puddle. The
sight of his own face makes him laugh:

There reflected in the water was a tired, hollow face. I don't know
why, but at that moment I thought of the face of yet another man.
This was the face of a crucified man. . . . They portrayed his face—
the most pure, the most beautiful that has claimed the prayers of
man. . . . No doubt his real face was more beautiful than anything
they have envisaged. Yet the face reflected in the pool of rainwater
was heavy with mud and with stubble; it was thin and dirty, it was
the face of a haunted man filled with uneasiness and exhaustion.
Do you realize that in such circumstances a man may suddenly be
seized with a fit of laughing? I thrust my face down to the water,
twisted my lips like a madman, rolled my eyes and kept grimac-
ing and making ludicrous faces in the water. Why did I do such a
crazy thing? Why? Why? (67–68)

Why does Rodrigues laugh? Rodrigues's laughter at horror strikes
even himself as unusual and inappropriate. He laughs because doubt
intrudes upon his faith, and his faith must incorporate it. Throughout
his early letters, Rodrigues compares his own story to that of Christ's
and seeks to find a similarity between their respective stories. Rodrigues
feels later, however, that their narratives have parted ways irrevocably.
As a priest and missionary, Rodrigues understands his vocation to be
following in Christ's servantlike footsteps, bringing unbelievers to conversion and hence into the fold of divine love. As Rodrigues's musings
reveal, negativity has called the existence of the divine love into question—Rodrigues, unlike Christ, does not even know if he believes in such
a thing. Rodrigues's own vocation and mission are called into question
by the persecutions. Martyrdom is supposed to have been a beautiful

affirmation of faith, instead it has proven to be an ugly negation of life. Similarly here, Jesus' face is always portrayed as beautiful, but the face in the puddle is "haunted," "thin," and "dirty." Emulation of the life of Christ has led not to glory but to humiliation and haunting. Once again, the incongruity between following Christ in Rodrigues's dreams, and following Christ in reality reveals itself to be insurmountable. Yet already, the reader begins to wonder if Rodrigues and Christ's life-narratives are not more similar than Rodrigues is willing to grant.

Rodrigues's laughter is a mode of theological resistance. He cannot accept that reality negates his faith anymore than he can accept that the narrative of faith negates the persistence of tragedy. His repetition of the question why with regard to himself is merely an echo of the more important question he posed to God earlier regarding the presence of evil, "The only thing that kept repeating itself quietly in my mind was: Why this? Why?" (64). Rodrigues importantly does not choose unbelief or despair; he resists both modes-of-being-in-the-world, though either might be more logical than sustaining two contradictory positions at once. Rodrigues wants to protest the absurdity of the human situation; through risibility Rodrigues hopes to call divine attention to the human tragedy of suffering and absurdity.

Disgusted by God's silence, Rodrigues chooses not to echo it and instead resists the evil and suffering around him through laughter. Although Rodrigues makes a passing comparison of himself to Job, Rodrigues struggles to recognize that doubt has always had a legitimate place in the biblical tradition (especially the Hebrew Bible) in the form of lamentation. Rodrigues like many good Catholics understands despair to be the greatest sin against God. Rodrigues seems to conflate doubt and despair, as if the two were identical. Rodrigues finds his doubt disgraceful, and interprets it simply as a negation of his faith: "What is happening to you? He asked himself. 'Are you beginning to lose your faith?' said the voice from the depths of his being. Yet this voice filled him with disgust" (95).

Because of shame, Rodrigues in two instances masks his doubt from his suffering followers. He fails to realize that perhaps expressing own doubt would have comforted them by sharing in theirs. First, as the peasants pray the Lord's Prayer and ask God to deliver them from evil, Rodrigues notes in their voices a "plaintive tone." Rodrigues moves his lips along with them, but ends with an unspoken chastisement of God, "'Why have you abandoned us so completely? . . . Yet you never break the silence,' he said. 'You should not be silent forever'" (96, 104). In striking contrast, immediately thereafter, however, Rodrigues veils his own anger and assures the peasants in a voice "filled with earnest fervor," "The Lord will not abandon you for ever.... The Lord will not be silent forever" (105). Similarly and secondly, when one of the peasants tells Rodrigues she thinks she will not fear death because heaven is a place of everlasting peace and happiness, Rodrigues wants to reply, "'Heaven is not the sort of place you think it is!' But he restrained himself.... Who was he to put a cruel end to their happy dream? 'Yes,' he said blinking his eyes, 'there nothing can be stolen from us; we can be deprived of nothing'" (82).

By the novel's end, however, Rodrigues himself has become an apostate. He now stands outside the theological tradition per se, which has the unexpected side benefit of granting him theological freedom. In the end, he rejects the traditional theological understanding of doubt as mere antinomy to faith. In the words of Paul Tillich, "[Doubt] is always present as an element in the structure of faith.... There is no faith without an intrinsic 'in-spite of.'... If doubt appears, it should not be considered as the negation of faith, but as an element which was always and will always be present in the act of faith. Existential doubt and faith are poles of the same reality."[14] Perhaps the Protestant Tillich's understanding is what Endo (and his critics) have in mind when they state that Rodrigues's character is more Protestant than Catholic. For Rodrigues surely comes to embody a dialectical understanding of faith and doubt. In juxtaposition to the church's understanding of irresistible grace, in the face of radical contingency and divine silence, Rodrigues conceives of doubt as irresistible:

> And yet ... and yet ... if that man [Christ] was love itself, why had he rejected Judas in the end? ... Had he been cast aside to sink down into eternal darkness? Even as a seminarian and a priest, such doubts had arisen in his mind like dirty bubbles that rise to the surface of water in a swamp. And in such moments he tried to think of these bubbles as things that soiled the purity of his faith. But now they came upon him with a persistence that was irresistible. Shaking his head, he heaved a sigh. The Last Judgment would come. It was not given to man to understand all the mysteries of the Scriptures. Yet he wanted to know; he wanted to find out.... The priest sat down on the floor soaked with urine, and like an idiot he laughed. (164–65)

Rodrigues laughs, finally, because the dualism of faith and doubt has been irreparably ruptured. In spite of Rodrigues's best efforts to suppress the dirty bubbles of doubt, radical negation has created fissures in the early Rodrigues's positivistic faith. Rodrigues's laughter in this scene helps us to better interpret Rodrigues's doubt, which is often hidden from his followers. Above, when Rodrigues states his doubt and then ostensibly negates it with promises to the peasants, Rodrigues appears to contradict himself. However, given our understanding of laughter as a creative means of sustaining the validity of two contradictory narratives, Rodrigues is not actually fluctuating between belief and unbelief as it might seem.

On the contrary, Rodrigues simultaneously believes in the truth of both his doubt—the experience of divine abandonment and silence—and his faith—the narrative of promise expressed in his assertion "The lord will not abandon you forever." We sense Rodrigues's difficult both-and position in the lines, "There was in his heart a complexity of emotions, such as reign in the hearts of two confronting men" (177). Reminiscent of Gavriel and those oppressed by Nazi Germany, Rodrigues suffers under the weight of a dual consciousness. On the one hand, he despises his oppressor Ferriera for his doubt and apostasy, but on the other hand he recognizes Ferreira and himself as "two inseparable twins" (177). Similarly, Rodrigues appears both to believe and not to believe in the concept of heaven; in other words, he still believes in the possibility of redemption, but he can no longer conceive of redemption as mere negation of the negation. In spite of Rodrigues's obvious doubts, however, he still does not renounce his beliefs. When the samurai urges Rodrigues to apostatize, Rodrigues laughs: "'And supposing I refuse?' The priest replied quietly, laughing all the time. 'Then you'll kill me, I suppose'" (85). In all likelihood, Rodrigues cannot resist laughing at this point because part of him would truly like to apostatize—the narrative of doubt is all too real. Yet doubt is not the same as unbelief. Nor is apostasy under tragic circumstance tantamount to unbelief, as Rodrigues discovers when he apostatizes in an attempt to save innocent lives.

Rodrigues's laughter reveals that faith and doubt constitute a dialectic, not a dualism. Like Gavriel in *Gates of the Forest*, Rodrigues wants to affirm the dialectic of both God's promise and presence and God's indifference and absence, a rationally impossible task, yet the very task of tragic theology and the nuanced form of hope it engenders. Endo captures Rodrigues struggle beautifully in the following description of him, "He felt like a man who, on a rainy day, thinks of a sunlit mountain far away" (83). Rodrigues denies neither the existence of the rain, or the sunlit mountain. Neither the rain nor the sunlit mountain is prioritized, nor is it understood that the sunlit mountain will simply negate the rain. Instead, the two simply coexist. In the face of radical negation, Rodrigues faith has become a genuine hope in things unseen.

Also like Gavriel, Rodrigues expresses that he cannot pray as he once did, "Just as the water dribbles from the mouth of the man whose lips are locked by sickness, the prayer remained empty and hollow on his lips" (86). A few scenes later, symbolically, Rodrigues tries to drink some water but "it simply dribbled down from his mouth on to his hollow chest" (98). This inability to pray once again testifies to the rupture of language occasioned by radical negation, because prayer relies on words. The apostate priest Ferreira exploits the seeming inefficacy of prayer and Rodrigues's own doubt by asserting, "I prayed with all my strength; but God did nothing. . . . Prayer does nothing to alleviate suffering" (168–69). Rodrigues's prayers adopt the form of a lament rather than praise.

Rodrigues's prayers become, like Gavriel's, qualitatively different, fragmented and supplemented with laughter. In short, his prayers become protest, "his trembling lips moved a while in prayer, but the words faded from his lips. Lord, do not abandon me any more! . . . Is this prayer? For a long time I have believed that prayer is uttered to praise and glorify you; but when I speak to you it seems as though I can only blaspheme" (119). Here it is helpful to recall Wiesel's commentary on prayer, "Maybe our prayers will be against God. . . . [They are still] existentially and dialectically affirmative. For the fact that I pray means there is someone there to listen, that what I am saying is not uttered to a great void. But what I do say, I say with anger."[15] Likewise, when Rodrigues laughs and prays with anger, he does so because he chooses to sustain rather than reject his narrative of faith, thereby sustaining his relationality, albeit tenuous and troubled, with the divine. As such, both his laughter and his fragmented prayers resist despair and the temptation to allow the narrative of faith to be swallowed by the narrative of doubt and nihilism.

Interestingly and perhaps unsurprisingly, many contemporary Japanese theological critics of Endo interpret Rodrigues's apostasy as merely a blasphemous renunciation of his faith. *Silence* translator William Johnston remarks that the text is extremely controversial in Japan. The renowned Professor Tadao Yanaibara of Protestant Doshisha University, for example, writes in the *Asahi Journal*, "The martyrs heard the voice of Christ . . . but for Ferreira and Rodrigues God was silent. Does this not mean that from the beginning those priests had no faith? And for this reason Rodrigues's struggle with God is not depicted."[16] Adds Endo scholar Mark Williams:

Rodrigues' ultimate decision . . . to renounce his God and all that his life to date had stood for has been widely condemned in the Japanese Christian community as an act of heresy. Indeed several pastors were to go on public record in the months following the publication of the novel expressly forbidding their congregations from purchasing a copy of the work. . . . Endo is here guilty of giving vent to doubts concerning his faith that verge on the blasphemous.[17]

But both Yanaibara's and Williams's interpretations exhibit a profound misreading of the text because they ignore the complexity of Rodrigues's theological position. In opposition to Yanaibara's interpretation, I believe that the text dramatically depicts Rodrigues's struggle with God, yet this struggle cannot be grasped without an analysis of his laughter. Rodrigues's laughter, and not so much his words, reveals his *ongoing* struggle with the dialectic of faith and doubt and the collision of evil's story with his faith story.

Yanaibara states that God is silent for Rodrigues, but on this point Yanaibara overlooks the obvious fact that God speaks to Rodrigues through Christ on the *fumie*. Certainly, it is what Christ says that shocks Yanaibara, and not his putative silence. For Rodrigues claims that Christ himself commanded his apostasy, "The Christ in bronze speaks to the priest: 'Trample! Trample! I more than anyone know of the pain in your foot. Trample! It was to be trampled on by men that I came into this world. It was to share men's pain that I carried my cross'" (171). Yanaibara's true bone of contention is that Christ's command—that is, apostatize—diverges with the popular perception of the church's teachings on martyrdom and with Yanaibara's own theological expectations. Rodrigues's Christ speaks not of triumph or majesty, but of his share and stake in human suffering. Theologians such as Yanaibara perpetuate the church's either/or thinking problematized in the novel and emulate Rodrigues's own hasty judgment of Kichijiro as weak and unfaithful apostate, a judgment that the narrative reveals as misguided and lacking in nuance.

Laughter as Communication of Tragic Theology and Theodicy's Limits

When Rodrigues speaks above of the silence and torture of God, he struggles with the classical question of theodicy: how can we articulate that **both** God is loving and omnipotent, **and** evil abounds? Theodicy itself is faced from the get-go with the limitations of either/or thinking. How are Rodrigues and the Christian theology he represents to portray this both-and reality? Can such a both-and assertion adequately be conveyed via language? Over and over, Rodrigues, taking his spiritual cue from Kichijiro the peasant, laughs to express this paradox, which renders laughter a form of theodicy in its own right, albeit one that underscores theodicy's own limits.

Although Rodrigues persists in characterizing Kichijiro as a coward, ironically Kichijiro is the first character in the novel who is unafraid to ask the terrifying theodicean question of God's complicity in evil and radical suffering. He thus foregrounds the urgent question of theodicy in Rodrigues's consciousness. With his question of "why" a loving God would let torture befall the peasants, Kichijiro challenges the traditional doctrines of divine goodness and omnipotence. Here, in spite of entirely differing circumstances, we find an unexpected point of common ground between the "resentful" Kichijiro, and Wiesel's angry Gavriel: both protest God's perceived imperviousness and question why God allows the suffering of His people.

We must read through and beyond Rodrigues's characterization of Kichijiro as a coward to reconsider Kichijiro as a victim of the caliber of Job. Kichijiro possesses a certain Job-like courage vis-à-vis the divine in that he questions his own victimization and resists divine permission of injustice. To be sure, Endo portrays Kichijiro as *simul* hero and Judas, a fact that reminds us of Wiesel's portrayal of Judas as hero in *Gates of the Forest*. For both authors, the courage to call the divine into encounter with radical negativity verges on the blasphemous, but it is also a heroic courage. Given this consideration, it is perhaps not so surprising that both authors have been accused of blasphemy. We must read between the lines therefore and pay attention to the fact that Kichijiro cries, laughs, and protests, whereas Rodrigues remarks regarding the other peasants that in their village, "was only silence. The village itself as well as its inhabitants seemed to be accepting its suffering without protest. Long inured to suffering, the people could no longer even weep and cry in their pain" (72). In the very same scene Rodrigues describes Kichijiro as anything but silent; instead, Kichijiro displays his "servile laugh" and protests the situation, stating unequivocally as he looks down at the silent village, "It's terrible" (72).

In contrast to the silent, unweeping villagers, Kichijiro cries so often that Rodrigues interprets his weeping as further proof of his weakness. At one point, while shedding tears, Kichijiro even protests God's creation of himself as "weak" and sinful, and accuses God of unreasonableness with regard to the necessity of original sin: "But I have my cause to plead! One who has trod on the sacred image has his say too! Do you think

I trod on it willingly? My feet ached with the pain. God asks me to imitate the strong, even though he made me weak. Isn't this unreasonable?" (113–14).

Kichijiro goes on to critique radical contingency, "I am an apostate; but if I had died ten years ago I might have gone to paradise as a good Christian, not despised as an apostate. Merely because I live in a time of persecution. . . . I am sorry" (115). In the words of Stanley Cavell, radical contingency haunts every story of tragedy.[18] Kichijiro, in his acknowledgment of his situation as tragic and radically contingent, actually occupies a quite sophisticated and mature theological position. Martha Nussbaum explains that what makes a tragic situation or choice genuinely tragic is the fact that society has created a situation in which no unambiguously "right" answer is possible, no choice exists that does not involve severe negativity and/or wrongdoing.[19] Much like the protagonist Sethe in *Beloved*, Kichijiro as tragic victim must choose between incommensurate evils—in his case, apostasy or death.

In the above quote, Kichijiro breaks off in mid-sentence, again an acknowledgment of linguistic rupture in the face of tragedy, although this rupture does not result in Kichijiro relinquishing his protest. What he protests, and simultaneously attests to, is tragedy itself. Kichijiro possesses a tragic theology, a theology that acknowledges evil as irreducible and a problem for thought, yet resists evil.[20] Tragic theology, is, for our purposes, a theology that helps sustain a thinking that addresses the problem of negativity without domesticating it or explaining it away. A tragic theology grasps incongruity, without dissolving the incongruity. A tragic theology articulates and negotiates the paradoxical collision of the narrative of faith and the narrative of suffering. Tragic theology, in other words, often through the laughter of the oppressed and suffering believer, says the impossible along with Kichijiro and Gavriel: both life can be horror, and God is good. Life is *simul* tragedy and hope, and humanity is *simul justus et peccator*. Theodicy and rationality cannot express these paradoxes, as tragedy itself ruptures the language on which both rely. In place of traditional theodicy, laughter functions to express a tragic theology.

When I read Rodrigues's quick dismissal of Kichijiro as weakling, I cannot help but remember Wiesel's admonishment regarding times of extreme oppression, "Don't make facile distinctions. Don't divide them into resistance fighters and weaklings. Even the heroes perished as victims; even victims were heroes. For it came to pass in those days and in those places that a prayer on the lips was equal to a weapon in the hand."[21] Kichijiro notably still prays in times of trouble, as overheard by Rodrigues, "Quite by accident jumbled in with his sentences I caught the words 'gratia' and 'Santa Maria'" (24). It seems more rational for Kichijiro, who feels abandoned by God, to choose to reject God and believe his own apostasy. To allow himself to be overwhelmed by despair and nihilism would certainly lead to less cognitive and existential dissonance. Kichijiro's clinging to his faith in spite of the doubt to which the circumstances logically give rise is heroic despite all Rodrigues's insistence to the contrary, if heroism means, as Wiesel would assert, choosing the path of most resistance. Kichijiro seems unwilling to relinquish either faith or doubt, a courageous and difficult position to uphold. He is unwilling to let go of either the narrative of Christian faith or the narrative of tragedy and instead, as believing apostate, believes them both, paradox and all.

In the end, the stories of both Rodrigues and Kichijiro reveal that evil resists thought, true enough, but laughter likewise helps resist evil. Laughter, unlike discursive thought, acknowledges the perennial gap in rational explanations of evil. In so doing, it testifies to the limits of traditional theodicy. Try as theodicy might, an ugly gap always remains between concrete radical suffering and abstract theological explanations. In this sense there is always an ugly cockroach crawling on theology's white wall. Like Rodrigues, traditional theology often tries to ignore its repulsive ubiquity. So Christian theology faces the question: do we ignore the dirtiness of life in order to make crystal-clear theological statements? Do we act as if we have all the answers when really, suffering leaves us speechless?

Obviously, theology should not resort simply to silence. But Endo's novel teaches us that whatever theology has to say by way of response to the problem of evil should listen to those resisting believers who have undergone suffering so radical that they eventually deemed laughter as one of the most apposite responses to it—the laughter of those such as Gavriel, Rodrigues, and Sixo, whom we encounter in *Beloved*. These characters' stories reveal that laughter itself can be a creative theological and ethical response to the problem of evil. Their laughter simultaneously exposes the omnipresent problem of evil as an unanswerable question and silence as an unacceptable response to unanswerability. With respect to the problem of evil, laughter incarnates not an answer or complicity, but a response of protest and resistance. Laughter protests evil and the very problem of evil by revealing its overwhelming presence as absurd and a paradox in light of the narrative of faith.

And so, the laughter of the oppressed disrupts the banality of evil. Many contemporary thinkers such as Hannah Arendt, Lance Morrow, and David Blumenthal point out that evil has become banal in our time. Nowadays, evil masquerades as goodness, silence, injured innocence, patriotism, or "just following orders." Andrew Delbanco argues that Satan is dead, and along with him the concept of "evil." Hardly anyone believes in evil anymore. Evil is commonplace. Thus, evil is invisible. Evil has gone underground. If evil is banal, how can it be seen, let alone avoided and resisted? The laughter of the oppressed in *Silence* disallows evil's continued invisibility. The laughter of the oppressed rises above the complacent murmurings of the people to shout, hey, look at this! Really look at how absurd this situation is! Laughter highlights the absurd, rather than allowing it to pass as normal or acceptable. Laughter jars the listener out of deafness and complacency, which are forms of complicity with evil. Laughter protests things as they are by suggesting that things as they are are absurd and incongruous. More than ever, we need to be reminded that evil is real. Endo (and Wiesel and Morrison) begs that Christian theology not forget this. Surely it is the task of Christian theology to shout to the world that evil is real, in order summon our steadfast resistance.

A brief look at the infrequent laughter of the oppressors in the novel confirms the problem of evil's banality. The oppressor's laughter is qualitatively different from the laughter of the oppressed. It can best be described as mocking, derisive, triumphant, and in short, Hobbesian—"a sudden glory arising from some sudden conception of some eminency in ourselves, by comparison with the infirmity of other."[22] The interpreter, for example, exhibits this sudden glory, " 'Then the Christian God created evil men. Is that what you are saying?' . . . The interpreter laughed softly as he spoke, enjoying his victory" (88). The interpreter's laughter emits from a face "filled with hatred and resentment" (87). As for Inoue, Rodrigues remarks that his laughter too is the mocking, superior laughter characteristic of the oppressor. Inoue's laughter therefore strikes Rodrigues, whose own laughter comes from an entirely different ethical and theological position, as inauthentic, "His [Inoue's] eyes were not laughing," though "he is all the time laughing" (122). Rodrigues characterizes the prison guards' laughter as sinful and "indifferent to the fate of others. . . . Sin is for one man to walk brutally over the life of another and to be quite oblivious of the wounds he has left behind" (86). I can only think here of Arendt's apt understanding of evil as sheer thoughtlessness, hence its invisibility to most people who expect evildoers to issue transparent statements of cruel intentions. We expect devils with horns and red cloaks, but of course what we really get is ordinary people who are "just doing their job"; no wonder systemic evil is so frightening . . . and so pervasive.

Interestingly, to inflict despair on Rodrigues and get him to apostatize, all three of Rodrigues's oppressors—the interpreter, Ferriera, and Inoue—exploit the rhetoric of theodicy's failure in an effort to seduce Rodrigues into genuine unbelief and despair. They purport no evil intentions, simply rationality. Once taken into captivity, Rodrigues's first direct confrontation with the oppressors suggests that they are interested in more than merely pro forma apostasy, although they constantly insist to the contrary, "If you just go through with the formality, it won't hurt your beliefs" (118). In response to Rodrigues's comment that God is the creator of all things, the interpreter asks the age-old question of theodicy, " 'Then the Christian God created evil men. Is that what you are saying? Is evil also the work of your Deus? . . . If it is true that God is really loving and merciful, how do you explain the fact that he gives so many trials and sufferings of all kinds to man on his way to Heaven?' " (89–90). Rodrigues falls back on the traditional interpretation of suffering as punishment in his reply, "Sufferings of every kind? . . . If only man faithfully observes the commandments of our Deus he should be able to live in peace" (90).

But immediately upon leaving the interpreter's presence, Rodrigues personally experiences the failure of theodicy—the unbridgeable incongruity between his narrative of faith and the narrative of suffering of all Japanese Christians. His argument sounds weak and canned even to his own ears. Rodrigues's inner dialogue makes clear that his own theological doubts are not as different from the unbelieving interpreter's as he has made it seem. The difference between Rodrigues and the interpreter, however, is that Rodrigues's doubt does not cause him to jettison his narrative of faith; instead he struggles to incorporate his doubt into his faith by expressing to God his anger. Understanding theodicy's limits do not of necessity entail a rejection of belief:

> The prayer could not tranquilize his agonized heart, "Lord, why are you silent? Why are you always silent . . . ?" . . . His prayer was not one of thanksgiving to God; it was a prayer of petition for help; it was even an excuse for voicing his complaint and resentment. It was disgraceful for a priest to feel like this. Well he knew that his life was supposed to be devoted to the praise of God not to the expression of resentment. Yet in this day of trial, when he

felt himself like Job in his leprosy, how difficult it was to raise his voice in praise to God. (92)

Rodrigues's other two interlocutors also make a rational appeal to evil as evidence of Christianity's illogic and therefore untruth. Unprepared for such theological sophistication from his oppressors, Rodrigues is shocked by his actual encounter with the dreaded magistrate Inoue, who unexpectedly is the quintessence of rationality, "How could he have recognized one who so utterly betrayed all his expectations?" (110). As for Ferreira, he echoes Rodrigues's own logical, metaphysical concerns about suffering and divine apathy. What position could be more logical?

We want to understand Rodrigues's oppressors, then, as apostates who have authentically jettisoned their narrative of faith in the face of the failure of theodicy. Inoue, the interpreter, and Ferreira have all been baptized as Christians. All three attempt to bring Rodrigues over to their side of despair and radical doubt, which, to use Surin's terms, allows the narrative of negation to achieve sustained ascendancy over the narrative of faith. Ferreira never laughs, a sign that he has relinquished the narrative of faith and no longer labors under an incongruity of narratives. The difference between Ferreira and Rodrigues is really the cause of Rodrigues's risibility—Rodrigues understands himself to be an embodied oxymoron: a believing apostate. Ferreira, on the other hand, as far as we can tell sees himself simply as apostate; because he experiences no incongruity, he does not laugh. Ferreira feels his former self has been negated by his apostasy, and he comments, "I am not Ferreira" (150). In contrast, the laughing Rodrigues still thinks of himself as priest in spite of the paradoxical apostate label, a label he both does and does not merit. Rodrigues therefore performs the priestly sacrament of confession for Kichijiro: "No doubt his fellow priests would condemn his act as sacrilege; but even if he was betraying them, he was not betraying his Lord" (191). Rodrigues decides that neither theodicy nor unbelief are viable options; with his laughter he resists the either-or. He incarnates the both-and of the believing apostate.

To exploit Kathryn Tanner's useful distinction between everyday and academic theology, we learn from *Silence* that laughter can be understood as an everyday form of theological expression. Tragic theology, it seems, is more likely to be found in the real world, where people of faith endure the problem of evil and experience evil's "always already" externality and internality. Kichijiro, a peasant, teaches Rodrigues, a priest, not only the meaning of laughter but how to laugh. Just as Rodrigues eventually mimics Kichijiro's urgent line of theological questioning and doubt, academic and institutional theology must learn from those who endure radical suffering.

Laughter as Constructive Theology

Though many critics understand Rodrigues's theology as blasphemous, I want to argue that his emergent theology is anything but blasphemy, and in fact makes invaluable contributions to contemporary constructive theology. Rodrigues laughs for two reasons, both of which manifest a well-grounded theological position that is a far cry from heresy. First, Rodrigues's laughter is kenotic, that is self-emptying, as he comes through the experience of coerced apostasy to both understand and emulate Christ in his kenoticism. And second, Rodrigues's theology, as manifested in his laughter, is thematically Protestant and Lutheran in that it coalesces with a *theologia crucis*—a theology of the cross. Rodrigues's theology is not blasphemous, it is simply not especially Catholic, if one wants to divide Catholicism and Protestantism along traditional lines—itself a disputable distinction. Our discussion reveals that Rodrigues's paradoxical new understanding of Christ as divine yet compassionate, omnipresent companion in human suffering mirrors the theology of the cross as presented by Jürgen Moltmann, Kazoh Kitamori, and Dietrich Bonhoeffer. I understand Rodrigues's laughter at his own apostasy as a result of such a reinterpretation of Christ and not, as Endo's critics such as Yanaibara argue, as the result of a loss or negation of faith.

Laughter as Kenosis

First, Rodrigues comes to understand Christ's kenoticism at the moment of his own apostasy. Rodrigues spends the entire narrative comparing himself to Christ, and initially feels that when he is taken into captivity and unable to perform his priestly duties, he no longer follows in Christ's footsteps. However, the text's shocking climax comes when Rodrigues realizes that in the moment of radical doubt, abandonment, captivity, and impotence, he most resembles Christ. This is a possibility Rodrigues had not before considered. Endo suggests here that Rodrigues (and even us readers) underestimate the radicality of Christ's self-giving and self-offering.

The doctrine of kenosis claims that redemption is achieved through divine self-emptying. Explains one contemporary Christian theologian, "We face in Christ a Godhead self-reduced but real whose infinite power took effect in self-humiliation, whose strength was perfected in weakness . . . who emptied himself in virtue of divine fullness."[23] Endo alludes to this kenotic aspect of Christ in both his nonfiction and *Silence*. In Endo's midrashic retelling of Christ's life in the text *A Life of Jesus*, he writes:

> Concealed in the very fact of Jesus being ineffectual and weak lies the mystery of genuine Christian teaching. The meaning of the resurrection . . . is unthinkable if separated from the fact of his being ineffectual and weak. A person begins to be a follower of Jesus only by accepting the risk of becoming himself one of the powerless people in the visible world.[24]

Tellingly, in *A Life of Jesus*, Endo takes much interpretive license and interprets Christ himself as having laughed, even though scripture makes no mention of such a thing. Endo wants to rediscover the "ineffective Christ," that is, the Christ of the cross.

Endo also represents Rodrigues in *Silence* as coming to understand the radical profundity of Christ's kenotic love for humanity, "For love Christ would have apostatized. Even if it meant giving up everything he had" (170). Rodrigues's captors present him with a horrifying ethical dilemma: he must apostatize in order to save not his own life, but the lives of the peasants who will otherwise be tortured. Rodrigues gives up everything he has—that is, his vocation as a priest—in order to save the lives of others. Rodrigues tells Ferriera that he apostatized because the Christ of the *fumie* instructed him to do so: "I thought if I apostatized those miserable peasants would be saved" (175). The interpreter's Buddhist statement, "The path of mercy means that you abandon self," turns out to be true and also ironic, for Rodrigues discovers that self-abandonment is also Christianity's essence (146).

Endo suggests here that the Japanese can embrace the concept of self-abandonment because this is a familiar cultural notion owing to Buddhist influence. Throughout the novel *Silence* a polemic lurks in the subtext— can Christianity exist in the cultural context of Japan? Endo wants to answer yes, but many would disagree. Endo underscores this argument in the novel through the character of the interpreter, who argues that Japan is a swamp in which Christianity gets stuck and cannot survive. Many even today assert that being Christian and being Japanese are mutually contradictory. In other words, many believe it is not possible to live a double life as both a Christian and a Japanese. In Endo's writings, he confesses the doubleness, but defends himself against this contemporary argument that to be a Christian is somehow to betray his culture. In this way, Endo like Wiesel testifies to the doubleness aspect of being part of a minority tradition that is often not accepted by the greater culture. Endo believes the both-and is possible, though many insist on the either/or. Endo suggests in *Silence* that Japanese Catholicism adapts to Japanese (Buddhist) culture by underscoring Christ's self-emptying character. That is the important point of connection for Endo between both traditions to which he feels he belongs.

In the act of apostasy, then, Rodrigues himself becomes kenotic, self-emptying, like Christ. Here Rodrigues encounters yet another incarnate paradox: the possibility of salvific, even kenotic, apostasy. Rodrigues voluntarily gives up personal rights and ambitions and accepts suffering as a follower of Christ. In the insightful words of one Endo critic, "Imitating Christ always means willingness to relinquish self-possession. Sebastian [Rodrigues], who all his life had been possessed by the image of Christ, finds that this image demands giving up his vocation—in all its normal guises. Sebastian finds a way to conform himself to a paradigm of *kenosis* in which his vocation—not his life—is emptied into the world."[25] Rodrigues until this point has considered apostasy to be a contemptible response of weaklings, "For a long time he had felt almost no hatred for Ferreira, nothing but the pity that a superior person feels for the wretched" (130). In the end, however, Rodrigues has become Ferreira's strange twin, in that he too believes Christ would apostatize out of love. He believes apostasy can be agape, as both can be forms of kenosis. Rodrigues, apostate, paradoxically still agrees with Ferreira's writing on the prison cell wall, "*Laudate eum* [Praise Him]" (160).

Rodrigues is thus, like Kichijiro, an embodied paradox; he is a believing apostate. This incongruity and paradoxical existence makes Rodrigues laugh. Rodrigues, when Kichijiro calls him "father," laughs at the juxtaposition of this address with his other appellation "Apostate Paul": "The priest laughed. . . . He knew that they called Ferreira the Apostate Peter and himself the Apostate Paul" (190). Endo uses the trope of laughter to signal to the reader Rodrigues's emergent understanding of Christ as kenotic. The laughter also signifies the inbreaking of Rodrigues's own kenoticism, as well as his growing solidarity with the oppressed and unloved in the world.

Endo chooses laughter as an appropriate trope to convey kenoticism because laughter itself is kenotic. That is, laughter, like tears, involves a release both physical and psychological/spiritual.[26] Rodrigues releases breath with his laughter, but also and more importantly, in accordance with Freud, he experiences an invaluable catharsis of repressed confusion, bewilderment, criticism, and anger vis-à-vis the divine and existential reality. Through laughter, Rodrigues empties himself of all that needs to be said but that he cannot fully say in the midst of negativity's rupture of language. As in Genesis Yahweh fashions humanity out of breath, in *Silence* Rodrigues recreates his mode-of-being-in-the-world through laughter, an expenditure of breath.

In addition to laughter, Endo uses the imagery of face to convey to the reader that Christ and Rodrigues's narrative have at last converged in their kenoticism. When Rodrigues confesses the longing for his face to become one with Christ's, he admits likewise that he is willing to follow Christ down the path of self-emptying into suffering and if necessary, death. Says Rodrigues, "Suddenly his breast was filled with joy in the wild thought that he was united with . . . that man nailed to the cross. And that man's face pursued him like a living, vivid image. The suffering Christ! The patient Christ! From the depths of his heart he prayed that his worn face might draw near that face" (159).

Rodrigues does not see Christ's face fully and in all its reality, however, until the moment of his apostasy. "Eyes dimmed and confused the priest silently looks down at the face which he now meets for the first time since coming to this country" (170). Here, Endo suggests not only that Rodrigues sees the *fumie* for the first time, but also that Rodrigues sees Christ, the true Christ, for the first time only as he is about to trample on that face. Prior to this moment, Rodrigues did not fully understand who Christ was or what it meant to genuinely follow Christ. In the moment of his trampling, however, he realizes that Christ acts in the world redemptively through *kenosis*.

Endo depicts Rodrigues's reconception of Christ in collision not only with Rodrigues's former understanding, but also with the mainline institutionalized understanding of Christ. By juxtaposing the Roman Catholic Church's point of view in the prologue with Rodrigues's letters, Endo implicitly critiques the church, implying that it unwittingly plays down Christ's kenotic humiliation and risks glorifying martyrdom. Moreover, Endo also implicitly criticizes individual believers who are armchair martyrs—those who profess that given any circumstance, they themselves would never have apostatized. Like all good writers of tragedy, Endo wants to show that even belief, or at least professions of it, are themselves radically contingent to some degree. The prologue unequivocally states: "It was unthinkable that such a man would betray the faith, however terrible the circumstances" (3). In direct contrast to Rodrigues's later rejection of martyrdom, the writer of the prologue extols the virtues of martyrdom, "Everyone of them [the Christians], strengthened by God's grace, showed remarkable courage and even asked to be tortured, firmly declaring that they would never abandon their holy faith. . . . The heroes of Christ bore this terrible torment without flinching" (5–6).

Additionally, in the prologue the church in Rome interprets Ferreira's apostasy as "not simply the failure of one individual but a humiliating defeat for the faith itself and the whole of Europe" (7). With the use of the words "humiliating," Endo seems to underscore the fact that there are those in the church who have forgotten Christ's own humiliation, which was in fact real and necessary for our redemption. It is almost as if Endo in *Silence* offers a strange reflection on Albert Camus's warning to Christians who glorify suffering and martyrdom: "Too many people now climb on crosses merely to be seen from a greater distance, even if they have to trample somewhat on the one who has been there so long."[27] True suffering is humiliating, ugly, and self-negating, unlike the glorified, self-aggrandizing suffering of our dreams. Endo posits here this ironic possibility: for a priest in seventeenth-century Japan, choosing apostasy over martyrdom and thereby letting go of his vocation might well have been a means of shedding the last vestiges of self-glorification and pride that separated him from genuinely doing Christ's work and becoming Christ-like. For Rodrigues to discover his true vocation as Christian, he had to lose his ostensible vocation as priest.

Endo depicts this theological transformation by portraying Christ's face on the *fumie* as contrary to Rodrigues's expectations and preconceptions. Rodrigues had always envisioned the face of Christ as peaceful and beautiful, "His face bears the expression of encouragement. . . . It is a face filled with vigor and strength. . . . He felt the face of Christ looking intently at him. The clear blue eyes were gentle with compassion; the features were tranquil; it was a face filled with trust" (22, 106). When Rodrigues tramples, however, he sees the following:

> On it [the *fumie*] was a copper plate on which a Japanese craftsman had engraved that man's face. Yet the face was different from that one which the priest had gazed so often in Portugal, in Rome, in Goa, and in Macao. It was not a Christ whose face was filled with majesty and glory; neither was it a face made beautiful by endurance of pain; nor was it a face filled with the strength of a will that has repelled temptation. The face of the man who then lay at his feet was sunken and utterly exhausted. (175–76)

Suggestively, Rodrigues goes on to describe Christ's face on the *fumie* as "worn down and hollow with the constant trampling. . . . The face itself was concave" (171, 176). Endo's repeated use of the descriptive terms "hollow" and "concave" to describe Christ's true visage again serve to emphasize Christ's kenotic, voluntarily emptied character.

In a much earlier scene, when Rodrigues catches sight of his own face in a puddle, it too is "a tired, hollow face . . . thin and dirty . . . filled with uneasiness and exhaustion. Do you realize that in such circumstances a man may suddenly be seized with a fit of laughing?" (67). Christ's and Rodrigues's narratives have at last come together, as surely as their faces have become one, "Yes, his fate and that of Christ's were quite alike" (125). Endo seems to suggest here that Rodrigues has fulfilled his kenotic vocation by following Christ into suffering out of love for fellow human beings. Because Rodrigues's new understanding of both his and Christ's vocation differs so greatly from his former conception, the incongruity makes him laugh.

Rodrigues knew that as a priest his duty was to serve humanity, but he never considered the counterintuitive possibility that to serve might entail his own humiliation, and even the abandonment of his priestly vocation. Early in the narrative Rodrigues says, "I was a priest born to devote my life to the service of man. What a disgrace it would be to betray my vocation from cowardly fear" (39). When Rodrigues apostatizes, however, he reports that he feels a strange joy, "His five toes had pressed upon the face of the one he loved. He could not understand the tremendous onrush of joy that came over him at that moment" (190). Rodrigues's appropriation of a *kenosis* similar to Christ's own causes this joy. Apostasy fulfills his true priestly vocation, rather than betraying it. In the end, Rodrigues's and Christ's suffering, shame, and desire to share human pain regardless of personal cost inextricably tie the two men one to another. Rodrigues ironically discovers the true Christ not in the dogmatism of the church, but in the experience of apostasy.

Laughter as Construction of a Theology of the Cross

Through writing *Silence*, Endo arguably discovers part of what must be true of a particularly Japanese form of Christianity—Jesus must be reinterpreted as kenotic *dohansha*, the constant cosufferer and self-emptying companion of humankind.[28] Endo states that all of his writing participates in the quest for a Christianity that "fits" with the Japanese ethos, for a specifically Japanese Catholicism: "Catholicism is not a solo, but a symphony. . . .

Unless there is in that symphony a part that corresponds to Japan's mud swamp, it cannot be a true religion. What exactly this part is—that is what I want to find out."[29] For Endo this means the divine needs to be reunderstood as suffering companion, and thus a maternal figure, because the mother in Japanese culture symbolizes the self-emptying cosufferer, the incarnation of love. Writes Endo:

> In writing *Silence* I felt as though I had buried the distance I had formerly sensed between Christianity and myself. In short, that represents a change from Christianity as a paternal religion to Christianity as a maternal religion. The male image of Christ that the hero started out with is transformed into a female image. . . . The image of Christ carved on the *fumie* in silence is a maternal image, a woman seeking to suffer with her child and share her child's pain. It is not the paternal image to be found in so much western art.[30]

Rodrigues's new consciousness of Christ as cosufferer manifests a theological position that most closely approximates a Lutheran theology of the cross. In this regard, Endo seems to have written a very Protestant novel that purports to be a Catholic one. Endo himself supports this view, acknowledging that Rodrigues's faith is "close to Protestantism" and will "obviously induce criticism in theological circles."[31] It would be unfair, however, to make the totalizing claim that Catholicism does not recognize Christ's kenotic character; a so-called theologian of glory could just as easily occur with Protestantism. It is perhaps more accurate to say, therefore, that what Endo has done is produced a Catholic novel that is specifically representative of Japanese rather than Western Catholicism. Endo's Japanese form of Catholicism shares with Protestantism an emphasis on a theology of the cross, and shares with liberation theology an emphasis on listening to the voices of those who suffer. Endo uses Rodrigues's laughter to communicate this complex theological position.

A theology of the cross, a term coined by Martin Luther, reconsiders the importance of the crucified, suffering Christ for our understanding of God, and acknowledges in the words of Jürgen Moltmann that "the crucified Christ is himself a challenge to Christian theology."[32] Luther felt that the Catholicism of his day allowed the triumphalism of the resurrection to eclipse the inscrutable shame and scandal of the cross. Luther names the theology that dwells in the resurrection victory while forgetting Christ's deep suffering and humiliation a "theology of glory." By emphasizing the importance of the cross for Christian theology, Luther did not desire to eliminate Easter joy, but hoped to correct what he considered an imbalanced, inordinate doctrinal emphasis on the glory of the resurrection. A theology of the cross is a both-and theological expression of a holy paradox.

The cross involved Christ's tragic humiliation and rejection, and Luther argues that Christian theology should not forget this, though it often does in the context of a world that cherishes power and despises weakness. So Luther states, "The theologian of glory calls the bad good and the good bad; the theologian of the cross calls the thing what it actually is."[33] Though Christ's suffering has a blessed and "good" result, the crucifixion is still "bad," in the same way that all human suffering is tragic and never an unambiguous good. A theology of the cross rearticulates the importance of Christ's kenoticism as revealed on the cross. Luther wanted to rearticulate an understanding of the crucifixion and resurrection as inextricably intertwined and, to use our terms, as constituting a dialectic. Epistemologically for Luther, the divine is to be understood in *both* the scandal of the cross *and* the glory of the resurrection. The resurrection does not negate the cross' scandal, nor does the cross negate the resurrection's beauty.

Kazoh Kitamori, a Japanese Lutheran theologian and contemporary of Endo's, takes up Luther's admonition in his seminal contribution to non-Western Christian theology, entitled *Theology and the Pain of God*. In this work, Kitamori develops a Japanese theology of the cross by drawing on numerous sources both Christian and cultural, including a key passage in Buddhist scriptures that states, "Sickness is saved by sickness."[34] Kitamori writes, "God in pain is the God who resolves our human pain by his own.... Luther calls the death of Christ 'death against death' (*mors contra mortem*), I call the pain of God 'pain against pain' (*dolor contra dolorem*).... In the gospel message, God suffers pain because he embraces."[35] In all likelihood, Kitamori's work influenced Endo's own thought, given the two thinkers' cultural proximity and similar theological positions.

Expanding upon Kitamori's thought, Jürgen Moltmann, a German theologian in the West, argues that Jesus' cry of dereliction from the cross marks the beginning of a genuine Christian theology: "At the center of the Christian faith stands an unsuccessful tormented Christ, dying in forsakenness.... Jesus died crying out to God, 'My god, why has thou forsaken me?' All Christian theology and all Christian life is basically an answer to the question which Jesus asked as he died."[36] As we have seen,

Endo's Rodrigues ultimately takes this very cry of abandonment as the beginning of his own reflective theology.

Similar to Endo who yearns for a maternal image of God, Moltmann argues that a God of sheer omnipotence cannot be loved:

> What kind of poor being is a God who cannot suffer and cannot even die. . . . The one who cannot suffer cannot love either. . . . A God who is only omnipotent is in himself an incomplete being, for he cannot experience helplessness and powerlessness. Omnipotence can indeed be longed for and worshipped by helpless men, but omnipotence is never loved; it is only feared.[37]

Endo's implicit theology reflects a theology of the cross when he writes:

> Jesus displayed on the cross nothing but utter helplessness and weakness. Nowhere does the passion narrative depict Jesus except in this utterly powerless image. The reason is that love, in terms of this world's values, is forever vulnerable and helpless. . . . Jesus, powerless on the cross, is the symbol of love—nay the very incarnation of Love. . . . Jesus could not, or he did not, perform a single miracle; nor, in turn, did God extend any visible assistance or relief. If I may be allowed to say it, the narrative shows Jesus to be an utterly helpless, powerless human being. [Yet] what emerges clearly . . . is the image of Jesus as companion.[38]

Moltmann strikingly reaches this same conclusion as both Endo and his character Rodrigues regarding Jesus as cosuffering companion: "The Christ of the poor has always been the crucified Christ. . . . They find in him a Christ who does not torture them, as their masters do, but becomes their brother and companion."[39]

Endo's emphasis on the powerlessness of Christ also reminds us of the Lutheran Dietrich Bonhoeffer, who exacts from Christian thought theological honesty about God's powerlessness. Suffering at the hands of the Nazis, Bonhoeffer wrote on the wall of his own prison cell, "Only the suffering God can help." Bonhoeffer, in a well-known passage remarkably similar to Endo's above, writes:

> God would have us know that we must live as men who manage our lives without him. The God who is with us is the God who

forsakes us. . . . Before God and with God we live without God. God lets himself be pushed out of the world on the cross. He is weak and powerless in the world, and that is precisely the way, the only way, in which he is with us and helps us.[40]

Bonhoeffer's words remind us of the dialogue between Christ and Rodrigues when Rodrigues tramples on the *fumie*: "'That pain alone is enough. I understand your pain and suffering. It is for that reason that I am here.' 'Lord, I resented your silence.' 'I was not silent. I suffered beside you'" (190). In Kitamori, Moltmann, Bonhoeffer, and Rodrigues's theology of the cross, Christ remains our companion in suffering and pain, and this is his strength through weakness.[41] Those critics who maintain that Endo portrays a blasphemous theological position and a priest who "from the beginning had no faith," ignore the glaring similarity between Rodrigues's position and Lutheran orthodoxy.

In the beginning of *Silence*, Rodrigues arguably espouses a theology of glory, as reflected in his vision of Christ's face as beautiful, peaceful, and pure. Rodrigues's vision of Christ's face as in reality thin, ugly, exhausted, and suffering signals Rodrigues's transitional acceptance to a theology of the cross. It is important to note that at key moments when this new consciousness of Christ as powerless, suffering companion emerges into Rodrigues's consciousness, Rodrigues laughs:

> A different sensation filled his breast when the face of that one rose behind his closed eyelids. Now in the darkness, that face seemed close beside him. At first it was silent . . . then it seemed to speak to him: "When you suffer, I suffer with you. To the end I am close to you." . . . Unconsciously the priest laughed to himself. (161)

Most tellingly, at the end when Rodrigues himself has become a kenotic apostate, he laughs and says to Christ, "I bear no grudge against you! I am only laughing at man's fate. My faith in you is different from what it was; but I love you still" (188–89). In these lines, Rodrigues unequivocally states that his own suffering and humiliation have changed his understanding of God—his faith is "different from what it was." In other words, Rodrigues's theology has changed from a theology of glory to a genuine theology of the cross, which encompasses a both-and combination of the two. This new theology underscores the scandal of Christ's kenoticism, humiliation, and powerlessness. Rodrigues reiterates this change within his understanding in the very last lines he speaks in the text, "He was not betraying his Lord. He loved him now in a different way than before. Everything that had taken place until now had been necessary to bring him to this love. . . . Our Lord was not silent. Even if he had been silent, my life unto this day would have spoken of him" (191).

Why would espousing a theology of the cross evoke Rodrigues's laughter? Our answer to this question is three-fold. First, precisely because, as our analysis of Moltmann, Kitamori, and Bonhoeffer makes clear, a theology of the cross is paradoxical in nature. Christian theology tends not to confess its paradoxical roots, as if paradox and holy mystery are somehow more embarrassments than strengths. The laughter of the oppressed and the suffering, however, acknowledges paradox as spiritual reality. Such laughter claims the confession of paradox as theological virtue that remains true to the gospel and the paradox of the cross. Such laughter, much like apophatic mysticism, communicates the fact that sometimes the most that we can say about God is that we do not fully understand God. Paradox occasions laughter, because a paradox by definition makes two contradictory assertions simultaneously, something language cannot do. Laughter, therefore, supplements discursive thought in order to express certain difficult existential and theological truths. It highlights the limits and aporias of traditional theology. A theology of the cross embodies a both-and paradoxical style of thought, and Rodrigues laughs to express his adoption of this theology.

Like the Jewish midrash, a theology of the cross negotiates the difficult, in-one-breath affirmation of both God and world. Despite evidence to the contrary, it avows a seemingly impossible fusion between the two. For Christianity, the cross symbolizes the both-and realities that Christ is both powerful and powerless, perfectly strong and utterly weak, painfully absent yet intimately present. This should not embarrass Christian theology. Instead, it should signal to theologians that God's logic is not human logic, a revelation that invokes much needed humility and acceptance of those deemed "other" or "weak" by human standards. Rodrigues's laughter incarnates this both-and character of Christ that is a rational problem for Christianity: Christ on the cross is both divine and human, both omnipotent and impotent, both forsaken and unforsaken. Rodrigues, similar to Gavriel, is both haunted by the absence of the Messiah and blinded by His presence. Writes Moltmann, "The cross of Christ remains an offense, and Auschwitz remains Auschwitz—until the dead rise and all begin to dance because everything has become new. Until then there well be laughter underneath tears and tears within laughter."[42]

Rodrigues's laughter also expresses the both-and paradox of human existence revealed by a theology of the cross: human beings are *simul justus et peccator*. In *Silence*'s beginning, Rodrigues divides the world into neat either/or categories of weak and strong, the courageous and the cowardly, the believer and the apostate, "Men are born into two categories: the strong and the weak, the saints and the commonplace, the heroes and those who respect them" (77). By the text's end, however, Rodrigues has accepted a theology of the cross that negates either/or thinking and embraces a both-and position. This theology leads him to supersede his earlier judgments with the radically new observation, "There are neither the strong nor the weak" (190).

Endo's text sustains not only the scandal of the cross, but the related scandal of portraying an apostate as the text's hero. Kichijiro, the novel's Judas-like character, is also portrayed heroically, as is Judas himself. Rodrigues comments, "Christ wanted to save even Judas. . . . If it is not blasphemy to say so, I have the feeling that Judas was no more than an unfortunate puppet for the glory of the drama which was the life and death of Christ" (75). At the end, Kichijiro is the only person alive who recognizes that Rodrigues is still a priest and person of faith. The church on the other hand betrays Rodrigues by excommunicating him and ignoring the possibility that an apostate could still be a believer, albeit a believer whose faith has substantially changed.

By condemning Rodrigues as an apostate, the church unwittingly adopts the Japanese oppressor's consciousness that equates verbal apostasy with actual unbelief. Rodrigues's laughter interrupts this consciousness and resists it. Rodrigues, like Kichijiro, knows himself to incarnate the paradox of the believing apostate. Given this paradoxical existential condition, Rodrigues's laughter comes as no surprise. Endo's text comes perilously close to implying that Jesus himself was an "apostate" because of his cry of dereliction; perhaps for this reason Endo imagines Jesus as laughing. In *Gates of the Forest*, Wiesel too in midrashic fashion envisions the impact of a laughing Christ, "Did you know that Christ was a Jew? . . . Do you know why he was crucified? I'll tell you: because he never learned to laugh. . . . If from the cross he hadn't appealed to the Father that had forsaken him, if he'd simply laughed, then he would have triumphed over the others and himself as well" (58).

For Rodrigues, laughter manifests theological irony, irony being the condition of two opposite things coexisting at once.[43] Asks Rodrigues, "Why is human life so full of grotesque irony?" (162). In the end, Rodrigues is both a priest and not a priest, both a man of doubt and a man of faith, both sinner and justified, both hero and apostate. To say with Bonhoeffer that the God who is with us is the God who forsakes us surely defies rationality. The look of pure bewilderment on my students' faces whenever I teach Bonhoeffer helps me to remember the baffling nature of this claim. To say with Endo and the theologians of the cross that only a powerless God can help humanity sounds to human ears like linguistic nonsense, if not sheer absurdity. A theology of the cross insists that the cross remain scandalous and inscrutable, much as Rodrigues's laughter insists that negativity and human suffering remain scandalous and inexplicable. Both a theology of the cross and laughter, therefore, attempt to express the inexpressible. As the ultimate moment of radical negativity, the cross results in a linguistic rupture that a theology of the cross attempts to sustain.

The second reason Rodrigues's laughter accompanies a theology of the cross is the rupture of language. Where language fears to tread, laughter steps forth boldly. Rodrigues's character echoes a theology of the cross' claim to linguistic inexpediency, "Christianity is not what you take it to be . . . ! The priest wanted to shout this out; but the words stuck in his throat with the realization that no matter what he said no one would ever understand his present feelings—no one" (187–88). Rodrigues, like a good theologian of the cross, tries to sustain the linguistic rupture that he experiences through his encounters with radical negativity.

Rodrigues experiences linguistic rupture on three levels; indeed, the text presents him as a person who, like Christ, appears silenced. First, Rodrigues is denied his own voice through marginalization, imprisonment, and oppression. His persecutors forbid him to confess his Christianity and force him to write a book condemning his own faith. Second, the Church expels Rodrigues from his mission without hearing his side of the story, leaving those who come after him entirely ignorant of his perspective. And third, the text of *Silence* quite literally ends with Rodrigues's own silence and death, as Endo concludes the narrative with a report from a Dutch clerk instead of an entry from Rodrigues's diary. Rodrigues's life, however, Endo seems to suggest, continues to speak of Christ because he emulates Christ in his kenotic weakness, "Even now I am the last priest in this land" (191).

The third reason laughter accompanies a theology of the cross is the fact that a theology of the cross incorporates a collision of narratives— the narrative of the resurrection with the crucifixion, the narrative of divine omnipotence with the narrative of divine *kenosis*, the narrative of suffering with the narrative of redemption. A collision of the narrative of faith with the narrative of radical negativity often evokes laughter as a form of resistance to despair and disbelief. Rodrigues becomes preoccupied with persisting in his belief that Christ's *kenosis* cannot be separated from his omnipotence and redemptive power. Yet Rodrigues's view of the ugly, hollow, concave Christ as also the redemptive Christ eludes language, and Rodrigues laughs to express the absurd and paradoxical truth of his understanding. Rodrigues, in other words, wants to articulate the paradox of God's own God-forsakenness, "*Eloi, Eloi, lama sabacthani*! . . . These words were . . . issued from terror at the silence of God" (138). A theology of the cross strives to articulate this very same mystery of God's own God-forsakenness. Rodrigues, feeling personally abandoned by God himself in his persecuted state of apostasy, comes to realize that God Himself is present as cosufferer in God-forsakenness. Surely, such a statement defies all logic. But for Rodrigues, as well as for Endo and many Christians, the crucifixion makes exactly that statement.

For Rodrigues, then, laughter proves indispensable in his struggle to occupy a complex position of *theologia crucis*. On the one hand for Rodrigues, the cross is the quintessence of God's inexplicable silence and absence. On the other hand, the cross simultaneously and paradoxically functions as a symbol of God's presence and intimacy. Endo suggests the same is true for all believers. The cross functions as the nexus between Rodrigues and Christ, because Rodrigues, like Christ, suffers from God's silence and inaccessibility, and thus discovers in Christ a suffering companion. Rodrigues's own narrative of apostasy thus collides with Christ's narrative of rejection and humiliation at the intersection of the cross.

J. Louis Martyn explains that for a theology of the cross, "Until the parousia, the cross is and remains the epistemological crisis. . . . The cross is the epistemological crisis for the simple reason that while it is in the one sense followed by the resurrection it is not replaced by the resurrection."[44] Endo expresses this same dialectical concern, "The meaning of the resurrection . . . is unthinkable if separated from the fact of his being ineffectual and weak."[45] Throughout, laughter interrupts dualistic thought by instead sustaining dialectical thought, and refusing to domesticate negativity. Laughter also refuses to domesticate God by denying the possibility of God's promises. Rodrigues laughs because he has come to comprehend that both redemption and suffering, Christ and evil, kenosis and power are inscrutable yet coexistent realities. His laughter exemplifies his adoption of a theology of the cross that accepts both the narrative of faith and the narrative of tragedy as equally valid, and always in tension.

In conclusion, laughter functions as an apposite extra-linguistic resource for expression of a theology of the cross because a theology of the cross is inherently paradoxical, resistant to linguistic expressibility, and resultant from a collision of narratives. Martin Luther himself, the first theologian of the cross, saw faith and reason as incommensurable narratives whose collision evoked laughter. Reflecting upon Christ's words of faith, Luther once wrote, *"Deinde ridens dixit: Ratio dicit: Das is ein grosse lugen* (Reason laughs at my faith and says: This is a huge lie)."[46] I appreciate how in this sentence, Luther shifts from Latin, the authoritative language of the church and its theology, to German, the language of the people and everyday theologians, as if to underscore the failure of lofty discourse to express the real difficulties of the life of faith. Rodrigues would surely echo Luther's observation here that from the point of view of reason, the truth of faith is often ridiculous in its contradiction to historical experience. In *Silence*, as in Gates of the Forest, however, in the face of this paradox, laughter functions as a creative means of sustaining the validity and integrity of both of these contradictory narratives of faith and of suffering. Like a genuine theology of the cross, Rodrigues's laughter finds its strength through acknowledgment of its vulnerability, and, in the words of Moltmann, "represents a hope which is indissolubly coupled with the most intensive sense of reality."[47]

Notes

1. In my view, a book still remains to be written on the subject of the striking similarities between Jewish thought, particularly Bratzlavian Hasidism, and Lutheran thought, particularly the theology of the cross. This chapter highlights several of these similarities.

2. See Mark Williams, *Endo Shusaku: A Literature of Reconciliation* (New York: Routledge, 1999), 105.

3. Ibid., 106.

4. Ibid.

5. Ibid., 30.

6. Ibid., 106.

7. Surin, "Taking Suffering Seriously," 344.

8. Fyodor Dostoevksy, *The Brothers Karamazov*, trans. Richard Pevear and Larissa Volokhonsky (New York: Vintage, 1990), 58.

9. Quoted in Morreal, *Philosophy of Laughter and Humor*, 47.

10. Patricia Hill Collins, *Black Feminist Thought: Knowledge, Consciousness and the Politics of Empowerment* (New York: Routledge, 1991), 225.

11. Quoted in Morreal, *Philosophy of Laughter and Humor*, 52–54, 55.

12. Wiesel, *Gates of the Forest*, 174.

13. Paul Ricoeur, *The Symbolism of Evil*, trans. Emerson Buchanan (Boston: Beacon Press, 1967), 213.

14. Paul Tillich, *Dynamics of Faith* (New York: Harper and Row, 1957), 21–22.

15. Patterson, *In Dialogue and Dilemma*, 83.

16. Quoted in Endo, *Silence*, xvii.

17. Williams, *Endo Shusaku*, 107–8. As Williams's text is not a theological work and is primarily psychological, he does not explicitly offer his own opinion on the relationship of faith and doubt, or the putative blasphemy of Endo's position.

18. Quoted in Carole Ann Taylor, *The Tragedy and Comedy of Resistance: Reading Modernity through Black Women's Fiction* (Philadelphia: Pennsylvania Press, 2000), 9.

19. From a public lecture delivered by Nussbaum at the University of Virginia, Charlottesville, entitled "Tragedy and Cost-Benefit Analysis," September 13, 2000.

20. Here I am borrowing from Larry D. Bouchard's definition of a tragic theology. See Bouchard, *Tragic Method and Tragic Theology*, 8–9.

21. Wiesel and Friedlander, *Six Days of Destruction*, 52.

22. Morreal, *Philosophy of Laughter and Humor*, 20.

23. Quoted in David Ford, ed., *The Modern Theologians*, vol. 2 (Oxford: Basil Blackwell, 1989), 10.

24. Shusaku Endo, *The Life of Jesus*, trans. Richard A. Schuchert (New York: Paulist Press, 1978), 145.

25. Larry D. Bouchard, "In Front of the Mask: The Priest in Contemporary Dramas of Integrity," *Word and World* 9, no. 4 (1989): 379.

26. For an excellent discussion of the psychological functions of humor as "saving psychic resources" and a form of "soul maintenance," see Donald Capps, *A Time to Laugh: The Religion of Humor* (New York: Continuum, 2005).

27. Albert Camus, *The Fall*, trans. Justin O'Brien (New York: Modern Library, 1956), 114.

28. See Williams for an interesting discussion of the concept of *dohansha* in Endo's novels.

29. Williams, *Endo Shusaku*, 32.

30. Quoted in ibid., 123–24.

31. Quoted in ibid., 251.

32. Moltmann, *Crucified God*, 3.

33. Timothy F. Lull, ed., *Martin Luther's Basic Theological Writings* (Minneapolis: Fortress Press, 1989), 31.

34. Kazoh Kitamori, *Theology and the Pain of God* (London: SCM Press, 1965), 26.

35. Ibid., 20–21, 27.

36. Moltmann, *Crucified God*, ix, x, 4.

37. Ibid., 222–23.

38. Endo, *Life of Jesus*, 147, 150, 174.

39. Moltmann, *Crucified God*, 49.

40. Dietrich Bonhoeffer, *Letters and Papers from Prison*, ed. Eberhard Bethge (New York: Collier, 1972), 360.

41. Given our discussion of Wiesel and his emphasis on doubt and an honest acknowledgment of God's silence, it bears noting that at least two of these theologians (Moltmann and Bonhoeffer) are influenced by the event of the Holocaust and Jewish thought. Moltmann in particular publicly acknowledges his indebtedness to Wiesel, and attempts to construct a Christian theology that addresses Auschwitz.

42. Jürgen Moltmann, *Theology of Play* (New York: Harper and Row, 1972), 112.

43. I borrow this definition of irony from Frederick Buechner as depicted in his novel, *The Book of Bebb* (San Francisco: Harper and Row, 1971).

44. Charles B. Cousar, *A Theology of the Cross* (Minneapolis: Fortress, 1990), 42.

45. Endo, *Life of Jesus*, 145.

46. Quoted in Zwart, *Ethical Consensus,* 166.

47. Moltmann, *Crucified God,* 312.

5

Flowers in the Dark: African American Consciousness, Laughter, and Resistance in Toni Morrison's *Beloved*

Anything that's paradoxical has to have some humor in it or it'll crack you up. You know that? You put hot water in a cold glass, it'll crack. Because it's a contrast, a paradox. And America is such a paradoxical society, hypocritically paradoxical, that if you don't have some humor, you'll crack up.... You have to laugh at it.
—Malcolm X, *The Death and Life of Malcolm X*[1]

Other people call it humor. It's not really that. It's not sort of laughing away one's troubles.... Laughter itself for Black people has nothing to do with what's funny at all.
—Toni Morrison, interview

Dancing around the room with Sethe's apron, Beloved wants to know if there are flowers in the dark. Denver adds to the stovefire and assures her that there are.
—Toni Morrison, *Beloved*

Toni Morrison's *Beloved*, a novel set during the American slave era, presents the story of Sethe, an African American slave woman who murders her own daughter in order to save her from a life of slavery. Conjoining "laughter" and "slavery," like combining "laughter" and the "Holocaust," makes us react viscerally with discomfort and ethical apprehension. Our culture seems to have some type of "slavery etiquette" comparable to Terrence Des Pres's "Holocaust etiquette" that makes us uncomfortable to speak of laughter in conjunction with events so shameful and horrible. Nonetheless, Morrison's work unveils a profound relationship between laughter and African American consciousness. Just as Wiesel's *Gates of the Forest* occasions a reinterpretation of Jewish laughter amidst the Holocaust, Morrison's *Beloved* occasions a much-needed reinterpretation of black laughter as an ethical and theological resource. As was the case for Wiesel and Endo, nearly all critics simply ignore the laughter in *Beloved*'s pages. When the novel was made into a film, the filmmakers omitted all of the strange but crucial narrative moments of laughter. Why is this? Perhaps the novel's intensely tragic and disturbing subject matter causes us to shy away from the messy and seemingly "unserious" question of the laughter in the story. Yet still we must ask, what does the laughter of the oppressed mean?

Beloved, though fiction, has a profound historical epicenter even beyond being based on the historical era of African American slavery. The real life of Margaret Garner inspired Morrison to write *Beloved*. As the editor of *The Black Book* in the 1970s, Morrison came across an obscure article from 1856 in the *American Baptist* entitled "A Visit to the Slave Mother Who Killed Her Child." In this article, Morrison discovered the following story that gave birth to her fictional character Sethe:

> She [Margaret Garner] said that when the officers and slaveholders came to the house in which they were concealed, she caught a shovel and struck two of her children on the head, and she took a knife and cut the throat of the third, and tried to kill the other—that if they had given her time, she would have killed them all—that with regard to herself, she cared but little; but she was unwilling to have her children suffer as she had done.
>
> I inquired if she was not excited almost to madness when she committed the act. No, she replied, I was as cool as I now am; and would much rather kill them at once, and thus end their sufferings, than have them taken back to slavery, and be murdered by piecemeal.[2]

Commenting on the article and its readers, Morrison states, "I wondered if they knew the complicated psychic power one had to exercise to resist devastation."[3] The article does not provide the complex context and background to Garner's real-life tale, so Morrison, much like the midrash, reconstructs it through the fictional Sethe's psychic struggle to cope with her murder of her own child Beloved, along with the other characters' simultaneous struggles to resist slavery and its devastating psychological, spiritual, and emotional aftermath. In the narrative, Beloved emerges as a composite character who represents not only Sethe's dead child but all of the deceased children of slavery who died midpassage. Morrison, then, similar to Wiesel and Endo, writes to tell the untold stories of the marginalized that history books and the media fail to tell.

Of particular interest is the laughter of three of *Beloved*'s characters: Baby Suggs, Sixo, and Paul D, all of whom struggle to endure the radically negating experience of slavery and its consequences. Laughter functions in the text as a creative, counterhegemonic mode of ethical and theological resistance for the oppressed African American community. By engaging *Beloved* with the works of James Cone, Dwight Hopkins, Patricia Hill Collins, Audre Lorde, Mikhail Bahktin, Lawrence Levine, and others, I aim to show that laughter can function as an empowering and invaluable interruption of both the system and the state of oppression. To appropriate Beloved's own metaphor quoted in this chapter's epigraph, laughter blooms within the story as an incongruous flower of resistance in the dark world of dehumanization.

Baby Suggs

We turn first to the character of Baby Suggs, an especially interesting case for our discussion of laughter. Although Baby Suggs, as spiritual leader of her community, preaches laughter as resistance for most of her life, she ultimately abandons laughter. If a collision of narratives engenders laughter, does this mean the narrative of tragedy has overwhelmed Baby Suggs? Has she let go of her narrative of faith?

Baby Suggs, Sethe's mother-in-law, was a slave at Sweet Home until her son, Halle, bought her freedom from the slave master by working overtime for five years of Sundays. Although Baby Suggs gained her freedom, she must leave her son behind, and her life remains scarred by the irreparable wounds inflicted by slavery: "In all of Baby's life, as well as Sethe's own, men and women were moved around like checkers. Anybody Baby Suggs knew, let alone loved, who hadn't run off or been hanged, got rented out, loaned out, bought up, brought back, stored up, mortgaged, won, stolen or seized" (5).

In spite of this tragic existence, Baby Suggs emerges for a time as the model of resistance and spiritual leadership for her community. Those around her refer to her as Baby Suggs, holy. Rather than succumb to despair, Baby Suggs decides that:

Because slave life had "busted her legs, back, head, eyes, hands, kidneys, womb and tongue," she had nothing left to make a living with but her heart—which she put to work at once. Accepting no title of honor before her name, but allowing a small caress after it, she became an unchurched preacher, one who visited pulpits and opened her great heart to those who could use it. In winter and fall she carried it to AME's and Baptists, Holinesses and Sanctified, the Church of the Redeemer and the Redeemed. Uncalled, unrobed, unanointed, she let her great heart beat in their presence. (87)

Baby Suggs therefore is rooted in the tradition of African American spirituality and takes the pulpit when called by the Spirit.

Laughter as Deconstruction of the Oppressive Consciousness

Baby's laughter-as-resistance manifests predominantly an ethical, humanistic concern, although with subtle theological undertones. In other words, Morrison appears less concerned than Endo and Wiesel with God's silence and more preoccupied with the secular question: in light of slavery, what can be said about humanity and how we should live? Baby's laughter has the same critical purpose as African American spirituality: to deconstruct both white theology and the white hegemonic consciousness.

Baby Suggs's rootedness in African American slave religion can be discerned in two main ways: (1) her use of a worship space in the woods and (2) the fact that, as a woman, she preaches at all. First, her outdoor preaching in the Clearing has obvious roots in a slave worship tradition known as the bush arbor, a space in the woods created by slaves to be used for clandestine meetings of worship. We read, "When warm weather came, Baby Suggs, holy, followed by every black man, woman and child who could make it through, took her great heart to the Clearing—a wide-open place cut deep in the woods nobody knew for what at the end of a path known only to deer" (87). In a seminal text entitled *Slave Religion: The "Invisible Institution" in the Antebellum South*, Albert Raboteau explains that although Christianity had pervaded the slave community, slaves had an extensive religious life of their own outside the institutional church, "In the secrecy of the quarters or the seclusion of the bush arbors ('hush harbors') the slaves made Christianity truly their own."[4] Dissatisfied with worship in the white churches that ad nauseam preached subservience to slave masters, many slaves held their own worship services outdoors in the words or in their living space. In the words of one ex-slave, these special clandestine worship services took place "cause we wanted to serve God in our own way."[5]

Despite its pervasiveness, slave religion earned the later name the "invisible institution," both because of the slaves' surreptitiousness and scholarship's longstanding failure to study their practices. These secret outdoor gatherings, of which Baby Suggs's meetings are a likely offspring, were entirely distinctive and responded to the needs of the African American community by negating white theology and revaluing black identity and being. Dwight Hopkins argues that by seizing the sacred domain of the bush arbor or prayer ground, African Americans helped sustain and constitute a distinctive identity.[6]

Upon first arriving in the North, Baby Suggs refers to her involvement with the invisible institution. Responding to Ms. Bodwin's inquiry about her churchgoing habits, Baby's cryptic answer suggests that although she has not set foot in a church for the ten years of her enslavement at Sweet Home, she has consistently worshiped with other African Americans in "some kind of way." She responds ambiguously, "I ain't set foot in one [a church] in ten years. . . . Wasn't none. I dislike the place I was before this last one, but I did get to church every Sunday some kind of way" (146). Baby Suggs's comment contains the implicit critique that white churches are not authentic churches at all; when asked why she does not go to church, she replies, "Wasn't none." Undoubtedly churches in the South were available, but Baby Suggs's response implies that, as white institutions tainted with racism, they did not meet her worship needs. Baby Suggs's comment that she nonetheless worshipped "every Sunday some kind of way" most likely refers to the stolen prayer meetings of slave religion.

Given Baby Suggs's (and obviously Morrison's) knowledge and acquaintance with slave religion, she symbolizes and embodies the mode-of-being-as-resistance that accompanied the tradition. Historically, slave prayer meetings often functioned as an occasion to plan physical liberation as well as spiritual liberation. The unique African American theology developed by the slaves was so liberating that it frequently crystallized into courageous acts of physical resistance. Nat Turner and a vast number of other African American revolutionaries, for example, led slave revolts with explicit religious validation for their uprising. Understanding full well the connection between theological liberty and acts of resistance seeking physical liberty, slave owners passed reactionary laws, punishable by death, forbidding slaves to practice Christianity on their own.

As Dwight Hopkins and George Cummings conclude in their study of slave narratives, slave religion must be considered in and of itself a form of resistance:

> Assembled deep in the woods . . . African Americans found worship space in which to thrive by maintaining morale in situations that seemed hopeless; preserving mental sanity in the face of the irrational white world . . . synthesizing memories of African religious structures and practices with reinterpreted Christian belief to build a unique African American theology under slavery, organizing and plotting slave political and cultural resistance.[7]

Summarizes Hopkins, "Bush arbors epitomized black hands and hearts creating space for the poor to encounter the holy . . . and not only fashion their secret and novel approach to the divinity, but also resist and reinvent themselves over against oppressive structures."[8] In the sacred domain of the Clearing, the recently liberated Baby Suggs provides just such a place where the poor and black can come to collectively restore their strength to face a world of prejudice and socioeconomic oppression that persists even in the North.

Besides embodying resistance by creating a distinct religious consciousness and worship space for slaves, Baby Suggs's rootedness in slave religion can be seen in a second way. In the Invisible Institution, many years before most white mainline churches had ordained a single woman, a preacher was anyone, male or female, who was, as Raboteau describes, "licensed only by the Spirit." Morrison describes Baby as uncalled, unrobed, and unchurched. Delores Williams helps us understand that in stark contrast to the white institutional church in the antebellum period, black communities granted older women the authoritative voice for educating other slaves and children in African American Christianity, as the women were the ones who stayed behind while men worked in the fields.[9] In the *Black Book* article on which Morrison based *Beloved*, Margaret Garner's real-life mother-in-law is a preacher, the inspiration for the character of Baby Suggs.

Laughter as Grace

During Baby Suggs's meetings, then, she creates a space wherein the people can resist and reinvent themselves under her spiritual guidance. Not only does Baby incorporate into her unconventional "service" traditionally African American forms of worship such as the ring shout dance and call and response preaching, but also she extends to her people the unusual invitation to laugh, dance, and sing in the midst of tragic suffering:

> After situating herself on a huge flat-sided rock, Baby Suggs bowed her head and prayed silently. . . . Then she shouted, "Let the children come!" and they ran from the trees toward her.
>
> "Let your mothers hear you laugh," she told them, and the woods rang. The adults looked on and could not help smiling.
>
> Then "Let the grown men come," she shouted. They stepped out one by one from among the ringing trees.
>
> "Let your wives and your children see you dance," she told them and groundlife shuddered under their feet.
>
> Finally she called the women to her. "Cry," she told them. "For the living and the dead. Just cry." And without covering their eyes, the women let loose.
>
> It started that way: laughing children, dancing men, crying women and then it got mixed up. . . . In the silence that followed Baby Suggs, holy, offered up to them her great big heart.
>
> She did not tell them to clean up their lives or to go and sin no more. She did not tell them they were the blessed of the earth, its inheriting meek or its glorybound pure.
>
> She told them that the only grace they could have was the grace they could imagine. That if they could not see it, they would not have it. (87–88)

Baby Suggs, therefore, much like the rebbe and Gavriel in *Gates of the Forest*, urges the people to laugh, as well as sing and dance—all alternative modes of expression the dominant Christian theology and practice does not embrace. Yet there is a noteworthy shift of emphasis from Wiesel's Gavriel and Endo's Rodrigues to Morrison's Baby Suggs: Baby's preoccupation is not as much with the problem of evil and its relationship to God, as it is with the problem of evil and its relationship to humanity. Baby Suggs in her sermon avoids God-language, probably because of its corruption by white Christians. In Baby's sermon, grace is apparently not divine gift, because the human imagination creates grace. Baby's personal experience transforms her religious tradition in this regard: in her understanding, liberation is ultimately a human possibility, rather than a divine one. Or better: liberation comes *both* from humanity *and* from God because either/or interpretations fail to describe the complexity of the divine-human interaction within the Christian faith.

Baby does, after all, inaugurate her sermon above with a prayer, yet the remainder of the address is solely to the community. Here, we are reminded of Gavriel who both hopes and cannot hope, and who comments, "Everything is true and everything is a lie; men love and kill one another; God bids them pray and yet their prayers change nothing" (9). Although the later Baby Suggs abandons even this position, the early Baby adopts an ethical position that reveals a humanistic religious dimension. In fact, at this point in the narrative, Baby might well agree with the Hasidic aphorism that a person must pray as if all depended on God and act as if all depended on humanity.

Laughter as Alternative Black Consciousness and Identity Creation

Baby Suggs therefore embodies a paradox and incarnates a fractured faith, much like her fictional counterparts Gavriel and Rodrigues. Also like Gavriel and Rodrigues, the laughter Baby Suggs preaches is born from a collision of narratives. Like Rodrigues who experienced multiple simultaneous collisions of narratives, Baby Suggs's collision of narratives occurs on three different levels of experience, all of which rupture language and therefore engender laughter.

First, Baby experiences the collision of an emerging black consciousness with white consciousness and ideology. In Baby Suggs's preaching, she rejects the white consciousness, which aims to inculcate in the slaves feelings of subservience and inferiority and respect for a divinely sanctioned white dominance. White churches preached ad nauseam to the slaves passages such as Ephesians 6:5, Colossians 3:22, and 1 Peter 2:18. All of these Bible verses instruct slaves to obey their masters in all things and not to sin against them; they served therefore as the theological undergirding for white dominance. Baby Suggs, however, straightforwardly rejects the theology of these passages and their otherworldly promise of heavenly reward for subservience: "She did not tell them to clean up their lives or to go and sin no more. She did not tell them they were the blessed of the earth, its inheriting meek or its glorybound pure" (87–88). Baby Suggs realizes that to say such things would be tantamount to subscribing to a white consciousness that would foster quietism and passivity among the people, who are still struggling for physical, legal, psychological, emotional, and socioeconomic liberation from slavery's oppression.

In *The Failure of White Theology*, Patrick Bascio points out that black religion is a religion of protest that functions as a critical corrective to white theology and consciousness, "Black religion began the process of decolonizing theology when it insisted that God was the freeing one who was at work in history setting the victims free."[10] Baby Suggs with her laughter, dance, and speech wants to decolonize white consciousness and theology and replace it with an African American consciousness of liberation, self-valuation, and resistance. Black feminist critic Deborah McDowell notes that African American laughter often can be "law-breaking" and "truth-breaking," and an expression of what Henri Bergson terms "topsy-turvydom."[11] In lieu of quietism, Baby hopes to incite protest. Her message unveils a theology of protest. To quote Hopkins and Cummings, "The slaves constantly had to struggle with unraveling the false theological consciousness existentially imposed by white definition."[12] Baby Suggs's preaching is a conscious and deliberate attempt at this unraveling. Her laughter is a conduit of protest essential to this end.

Baby Suggs's "preaching" and laughter, then, manifest a decolonized version of white theological anthropology, a new vision of who African Americans are and their created purpose. Baby Suggs attempts to convince her people that African Americans are not worthless, unintelligent, and subhuman as those within the corridors of power have tried desperately to make them believe. States Cone, "Black consciousness is an attempt to recover a past deliberately destroyed by slave masters. . . . There is only one course of action for the black community, and that is to destroy the oppressor's definition of blackness."[13] Schoolteacher, for example, tells his nephews to list Sethe's "animal characteristics" on a sheet of paper, and proceeds to allow his boys to rape her. The whites in the narrative conceive of blacks as "a people who needed every care and guidance in the world to keep them from the cannibal life they preferred" (151). Morrison adds, "White people believed that whatever the manners, under every dark skin was a jungle" (198).

In direct opposition to this white consciousness and anthropology, Baby Suggs provides the people with a new black consciousness. Through laughter and dance, she encourages the people to rediscover themselves as lovable, beautiful, and chosen. They are, she assures them, and here no doubt the novel's title refers to the African American people as a whole—the beloved, of one another and of God. Writes Cone, "The essence of antebellum black religion was the emphasis on the *sombodiness* of black slaves . . . even though they were treated as things. . . . To be enslaved is to be declared nobody."[14] In contrast to white preaching, Baby Suggs's sermons and worship in the woods affirm the somebodiness of African Americans. Her message incarnates the biblical verse Morrison chose as the novel's epigraph, Romans 9:25: "I will call them my people, which were not my people; and her beloved, which was not beloved."

In the most important sermon in the novel, Baby Suggs once again urges the people to laugh as she imparts to the community a new sense of identity and self-worth, and fittingly repeats the phrase from Romans "O my people." This sermon makes explicit Baby Suggs's effort to unravel the false theological consciousness and false anthropology of white ideology, as well as to replace it with a black understanding of the self as lovable, valuable, and self-determined:

> "Here," she said, "in this here place, we flesh; flesh that weeps, laughs; flesh that dances on bare feet in grass. Love it. Love it hard. Yonder they do not love your flesh. They despise it. They don't love your eyes; they'd just as soon pick 'em out. No more do they love the skin on your back. Yonder they flay it. And O my people they do not love your hands. Those they only use, tie, bind, chop off and leave empty. Love your hands! Love them. Raise them up and kiss them. Touch others with them, pat them together, stroke them on your face 'cause they don't love that either. *You* got to love it, you! And no, they ain't in love with your mouth. Yonder, out there, they will see it broken and break it again. . . . And O my people, out yonder, hear me, they do not love your neck unnoosed and straight. So love your neck; put a hand on it, grace it, stroke it and hold it up. . . . More than your life-holding womb and your life-giving private parts, hear me now, love your heart. For this is the prize." Saying no more, she stood up then and danced with her twisted hip the rest of what her heart had to say while the others opened their mouths and gave her the music. (88–89)

Here, as in Wiesel and Endo, Morrison's novel suggests that African Americans too experience a linguistic rupture, for all they have suffered cannot ever be fully said. No white person can ever fully understand the pain of the experience of slavery. Thus, Baby Suggs laughs and dances "with her twisted hip the rest of what her heart had to say." Racism and oppression so distort language that they rupture it and render it incapable of expressing the African American condition of suffering and protest. In the face of this crisis of representation, laughter helps deconstruct white racist thinking, in Patricia Hill Collins's sense of deconstruction: exposing a concept as ideological or culturally constructed rather than as a natural or simple reflection of reality.

Baby Suggs's laughter juxtaposes the white hegemonic narrative with the black-consciousness narrative, and forces the former to encounter the latter. This juxtaposition has the effect of rupturing a simple hegemony. In so doing, Baby Suggs exposes white hegemony and white theology as empty ideology fueled by insecurity and hatred. With this incitation to laughter and love, Baby Suggs imparts to her people a radically new self-consciousness and form of resistance. Womanist theologian Kelly Brown Douglas reminds us that slavery was part of a greater ideological structure, which presupposed both hierarchical relationships between human beings and the inferiority of people of color.[15] The dominant culture taught African Americans self-hate, low self-esteem, subservience, and submissive acceptance of an unchangeable inferiority.

Moreover, white society hoped that African Americans would internalize this valuation of themselves and thereby accept subservience as manifest destiny. Cone argues that white people did everything in their power to define black reality as servanthood and black existence as "nonbeing."[16] The prevailing definition of black as nonbeing and worthy of death is the thrust behind Baby Suggs assertion, "They do not love your neck unnoosed." However, Baby Suggs shatters precisely this false ethical consciousness of the white oppressive system. She effectively deconstructs such an understanding of blackness by exposing it as externally imposed, entirely ungenuine, and therefore absurdly laughable.

In its humanistic assertion of a radically autonomous will that can kill the beast of tradition and supposedly authoritative voices, Baby's laughter in this "sermon" evokes comparison to that of Friedrich Nietzsche's Zarathustra. Zarathustra states, "Not by wrath does one kill but by laughter."[17] Although Baby would reject Zarathustra's nihilism, and radical relativism and individualism, we can certainly imagine her saying along with him, "Verily, you who are good and just, there is much about you that is laughable, and especially your fear of that which has hitherto been called devil."[18]

White consciousness demonizes the black person, and Nietzsche's use of laughter lends support for our interpretation that Baby's laughter unmasks this consciousness of the putative "good and just" as mere ideology. Moreover, Nietzsche helps us understand Baby Suggs's laughter as annihilative. Her laughter counters the deleterious effects of tradition and civil and religious authority. For Nietzsche as for Morrison, laughter gives the unvoiced a voice of power, will, and self-valuation. For Morrison, however, the will-to-power embodied in laughter contains an eminent danger, as the will-to-power can lead one to become an oppressor like Schoolteacher, or to become an oppressed person like Sethe, who chooses to murder her own child. Nietzsche's own writing, for example, was used to support the Nazi will-to-power. Morrison on the other hand suggests that if the will-to-power leads one to think one can possess others, it destroys itself. Even Sethe, who sought her whole life to escape being possessed by others, frighteningly repeats to Beloved, "You are mine/You are mine/You are mine" (216).

Baby Suggs, like Zarathustra, rejects the dominant consciousness as false and misleading, fostering the slumber of the masses. All too often, Baby has heard Christianity exploited to foster inferiority and quietism—"she did not tell them they were the glorybound pure and to go and sin no more"—and so she tries to interrupt this theological anthropology. Baby Suggs encourages the people to self-love and self-affirmation, in spite of the fact that the dominant culture encourages only their self-hatred and self-negation.

Cone agrees that an authentic black consciousness insists on self-understanding and self-creation of the kind advocated by Baby Suggs: "There is only one possible authentic existence in this society, and that is to force a revolutionary confrontation with the structures of white power by saying yes to the essence of their blackness . . . affirming that which the oppressor regards as degrading."[19] By asking the people to laugh even though their oppressors want them to weep, Baby Suggs invites them to share in this independent consciousness. Gavriel makes this very same point, "To weep is to play their game. I won't" (7). Baby Suggs, then, like Gavriel, with her laughter jettisons the despair, tears, and self-loathing her oppressors strive relentlessly to inflict. Her laughter interrupts not only white hegemonic theology, but also both the system of oppression and the state of despair and paralysis that accompanies it.

By laughing, Baby Suggs expresses that the two opposing narratives of white and black consciousness are in conflict, creating a paradoxical both-and existence for African Americans. Where racism has become banal and accepted, no paradox or opposing narratives remains in the mind of the oppressed. With a laugh, Baby Suggs signals her nonacceptance of racism and calls attention to its absurdity. The laughter of the black oppressed interrupts the banality of the systemic evil of racism. Baby Suggs's laughter manifests an independent African American consciousness that exists in tension with the hegemonic consciousness. As Collins points out, oppressive structures try to eliminate an independent consciousness precisely because it empowers the oppressed to counter hegemony: "Suppressing the knowledge produced by an oppressed group makes it easier for dominant groups to rule because [of] the seeming absence of an independent consciousness in the oppressed. . . . One key reason that standpoints of oppressed groups are suppressed is that self-defined standpoints can stimulate resistance."[20]

Baby Suggs's laughter thus must be considered a highly creative ethical and theological response, a transformative mode-of-being-in-the-world. By laughing, Baby creatively brings to consciousness a potential narrative of celebration, self-affirmation, love, hope, protest—a narrative of hope deliberately made inaccessible to African Americans by whites. Baby confronts the white voice with the heretofore silenced black voice and black laughter. Baby embodies what Kelly Brown Douglas terms a spirituality of resistance, a resistance with theological roots but imperative ethical, historical, and activist components:

> A spirituality of resistance implies . . . that if an oppressed people
> have pride in their own culture and historical heritage, as well as
> a knowledge that they are children of God, then they will not be
> as vulnerable to the oppressive structures, systems, and ideologies
> that attempt to convince them that they are nobody and that their
> lives are not worth living.[21]

Baby urges her people to self-definition because she understands, in the words of African American poet Audre Lorde, "It is axiomatic that if we do not define ourselves for ourselves, we will be defined by others—for their use and to our detriment."[22]

Baby's laughter is creative because it entirely contradicts history; African Americans have been denied the very narrative Baby Suggs's laughter suggests can be actualized. Baby's laughter anticipates the future and is a manifestation of what Cone terms the "apocalyptic imagination":

> It was a hope *against* the hopes of this world. . . . This transcendent
> element of hope . . . elevated black people above the limitations of
> the slave experience, and enabled them to view black humanity
> independently of their oppressors. . . . The strongest counterweight
> to the obstacles in the way of historical liberation is that vision of
> the future defined by the oppressed black slaves.[23]

Baby Suggs has faith that her people can achieve this level of self-definition and self-love, but not through mere language, which cannot express the paradox of the African American dual consciousness. Instead,

Baby uses laughter and song to capture the contradictions and both-and character of her experience of oppression. Cone says that black music (and we can add black laughter) "unites the joy and the sorrow, the love and the hate, the hope and despair of the black people. It is necessary to grasp the contradictions inherent in black experience. Who could possibly understand these paradoxical affirmations but the people who live them?"[24] In the midst of tragedy, Baby's laughter functions to resist passivity, despair, subservience, and hopelessness by its insistence on the impossible possibility of regeneration—the grace the people can imagine.

Laughter as Protesting Hope in the Face of Evil

The second collision experienced by Baby Suggs involves the collision of the narrative of faith with the narrative of negativity, as was the case for Gavriel and Rodrigues. For Baby, her narrative of human potential for love and grace collides with the narrative of white cruelty and oppression. In the background of this collision lies the familiar problem of evil and theodicy, which, as we have seen in Wiesel and Endo, ruptures language and engenders laughter. Baby herself states clearly that the horror of reality (slavery) has ruptured language for her and other African Americans, "Every mention of her past life hurt. Everything in it was painful or lost. She [Sethe] and Baby Suggs had agreed without saying so that it was unspeakable" (58). Also, at the end of Baby's life, "Except for an occasional request for color she said practically nothing" (105). Here we see another manifestation of the crisis of representation engendered by an encounter with oppression and suffering.

Baby Suggs laughs because words cannot adequately circumscribe the "in-spite-of," "not-yet" aspect of her faith and her hope, a faith in humanity that persists in the face of tragedy. Ricoeur explains, "The existential-historical condition of evil constitutes the challenge to which religion brings the reply of an 'in spite of . . . ,' an 'even though. . . .' This tie between challenge and reply is the tie of hope. . . . The confession of the inscrutability of evil closes the way of explanation only so as to hold open that of regeneration."[25] Baby Suggs's laughter manifests a hope that acknowledges its coexistence with radical evil. It responds to and challenges an evil that is inscrutable, unspeakable, and otherwise crippling. Morrison says, "Black people never annihilate evil. . . . They accept it. It's almost like a fourth dimension in their lives."[26]

As is the case for Gavriel and Rodrigues, Baby's collision of her narrative of faith and negativity involves at least in part God's ostensible absence and lack of justice and benevolence, as revealed in the following dialogue she has with Stamp Paid:

"You saying God give up? Nothing left for us but pour out our own blood?"

"I'm saying they came in my yard."

"You punishing Him ain't you."

"Not like He punish me." (179)

On another occasion, Stamp Paid tells us, "Her [Baby Suggs's] authority in the pulpit, her dance in the Clearing, her powerful Call . . . all that had been mocked and rebuked by the bloodspill in her backyard. God puzzled her and she was too ashamed of him to say so" (177). Just as Hasidic thought cannot ever fully reconcile a just God to the *Shoah*, African American theology struggles to reconcile God's justice with the experience of slavery. While we should never conflate the two distinct experiences of oppression, the similarities provide an interesting point of departure for dialogue across communities. The black theologian William Jones for example daringly raises the question of divine racism, asking, "Is God a white racist?"[27] Similarly, in *Beloved*, characters besides Baby Suggs often raise the questions of theodicy or a tragic theology: When Amy Denver asks, "Wonder what God had in mind"; Sethe, nearly dead from attempting to escape slavery, echoes, "Good question. . . . What did He have in mind?" (80). Even more poignantly, Paul D at one point asks, "How much is a nigger supposed to take? Tell me. . . . Why? Why? Why? Why? Why?" (235). Morrison's narrative leaves these questions open-ended and unanswered.

Sethe's drastic murder shatters religious thought for many of the characters in the novel. Baby eventually abandons the question of a tragic theology and adopts a tragic anthropology instead, "[On] the afternoon of the last day of her life . . . she got out of bed . . . and announced to Sethe and Denver the lesson she had learned from her sixty years a slave and ten years free: that there was no bad luck in the world but whitepeople" (104).

At the very end, Baby feels betrayed by God, but most betrayed by humanity. When Stamp Paid tells Baby Suggs that she has given up because she blames God, she shifts the focus of the problematic by three times repeating the phrase, "I'm saying they [white folks] came in my yard" (179). The goodness and grace she believed humanity could possess and create have been irrevocably violated, and she feels that humanity is powerless to alter historical circumstance. Prior to Beloved's death, Baby's laughter manifested a time when she, like Gavriel and Rodrigues, was able to sustain the dialectical tension between hope and radical evil. For a time, with her work in the Clearing, Baby succeeded in sustaining this impossible fusion of the memory of hope and the memory of horror. When Baby is no longer able to sustain the tension, her laughter ends, and Baby Suggs chooses to retire to her bed to contemplate color.

The third and final collision of narratives Baby undergoes is the collision between her own narrative of resistance and the narrative of Beloved's death. Up until the point of Sethe's murder of Beloved, Baby has fought back against the tragic forces in her life, and refused to be silenced. Baby Suggs becomes an example of a character who can no longer sustain the dialectic between the narrative of hope and the narrative of tragedy any longer. In short, she stops laughing, "Except for an occasional request for color she said practically nothing" (104). In the murder of Beloved, Baby realizes that slavery's effects were worse than she ever imagined possible. This narrative of tragedy is so great it appears it may eclipse her narrative of hope.

We recall that Surin claims that in the situation of radical negativity, the narrative of faith collides with the narrative of its negation, but neither achieves an ascendancy over the other.[28] Thanks to Surin's analysis, we can see that Baby Suggs, understandably, is an example of someone who can no longer sustain the paradoxical balancing act of simultaneously affirming both contradictory narratives. In this regard, Baby appears similar to Endo's characters Inoue and Ferreria, who have also abandoned their faith. In short, the narrative of negativity has gained ascendancy over Baby's narrative of faith in humanity, grace, and goodness. With her relinquishment of the narrative of faith in humanity, she no longer possesses risibility. For Baby Suggs, the narrative of the Beloved's murder eclipses the possibility of a counternarrative of hope. Baby goes to bed to contemplate color and gives up speech, as if the struggle to affirm the possibility of hope had become too difficult. Baby's refusal to laugh signals that she no longer experiences paradox and incongruity. She does not laugh because she no longer feels the both-and character of existence and the in-spite-of character of the life of faith. The narrative very sympathetically portrays Baby as someone who can no longer continue the struggle of laughter.

Although Baby Suggs has learned to expect little from white people, she nonetheless comments prior to Beloved's death that even though she was a slave at Sweet Home, "Nobody, but nobody, knocked her down. Not once . . . Even when she slipped in cow dung and broke every egg in her apron, nobody said you-black-bitch-what's-the-matter-with-you and nobody knocked her down" (139). Baby thinks that given her experience of radical suffering as a slave, she has experienced the quintessence of rejection and pain; thus she asks, "What was left to hurt her now?" (139).

Morrison seems to suggest that what is left to hurt Baby is the impossible possibility of rejection and cruelty from her own community. It undoubtedly devastates her to acknowledge that not a single member of her community warned her of the impending approach of the slave owners on the day Sethe murdered Beloved, "Nobody warned them, and he'd [Stamp Paid] always believed it wasn't the exhaustion from a long day's gorging that dulled them, but some other thing—like, well, like meanness—that let them stand aside" (157). Moreover, the knowledge that her own daughter-in-law would kill her own African American child, one of their own beloved, devastates her completely. The white folks have won at last, Baby seems to suggest; they have created a system so oppressive that blacks will kill and reject one another. Baby had learned to live with and against white killing, but Sethe's murder ruptures her narrative of faith so radically that the dialectic cannot be sustained.

Two final comments must be made regarding Baby Suggs's ostensible abandonment of the struggle for hope and protesting laughter. First, going to bed to contemplate color is an activity enshrouded in ambiguity. Does Baby Suggs contemplate color in an attempt to avoid the societal, dichotomous either/or of black and white? Is she attempting to recover what she has lost, or has she merely lost the narrative of hope? These questions are not really answerable from textual clues, and offer us hope that maybe she did not abandon protest.

Second, in spite of this unanswerability, whatever Baby Suggs's final stance, the early Baby Suggs's embodiment of resistance outlives her. Her laughter bequeaths a legacy of resistance to all who knew her. She serves as the model of resistance for each of the other character for the rest of their lives. When Sethe, for example, considers letting love in the form of Paul D into her life it is Baby Suggs's voice she hears, urging her to visit the Clearing, and overcome her fear by "laying down sword and shield" (86). Says Sethe, "Nine years without the fingers or the voice of Baby Suggs was too much" (87). At the very same moment, to honor and remember

Baby Suggs, "the mountain to his sky," Stamp Paid chooses to reconcile with Sethe, "While Stamp Paid was making up his mind to visit 124, for Baby Suggs's sake, Sethe was trying to take her advice: to lay it all down, sword and shield" (173). And finally, when Denver makes the transformative choice to leave home and get help for Sethe and Beloved, she does so only because she hears in her spiritual memory the sound of Baby Suggs laughter, "And then Baby Suggs laughed, clear as anything . . . 'There ain't no defense . . . Know it, and go on out the yard. Go on'" (244).

Sixo

Sixo is the second character in *Beloved* whose laughter during the horrors of slavery functions as a creative, counterhegemonic mode of ethical and theological resistance for the disenfranchised African American community. Sixo, a slave, lives on Mr. Garner's plantation Sweet Home at the same time as Halle, Sethe, and Paul D. Sixo's own particular style of resistance is more difficult to discern and interpret than Baby Suggs's is, in part because he, unlike Baby Suggs, lives his entire life enslaved and has far more limited access to means of resistance. Morrison does not give readers as much access to his psychological and emotional interiority. Whereas Baby Suggs is a preacher who consistently exteriorizes her spirituality of resistance, Sixo, on the other hand, we are told, "Stopped speaking English because there was no future in it" (25).

Laughter as Speech-act of Resistance to Racially Constructed Language

Initially, Sixo's partial adoption of silence seems a sign of resignation to despair and acquiescence to the futility of resistance. In analyzing Sixo's life and death as embodiments of resistance, however, we must keep in mind Cone's precautionary statement, "Not all slaves chose to risk their lives in an insurrection; and that did not mean that they accepted the values of their masters. The vast majority of slaves chose other forms of resistance. . . . If we are to interpret rightly the minds of black slaves, we must feel our way into their world, becoming sensitive to the many ways they resisted white slaveholders."[29] For four reasons, therefore, Sixo's cessation of speech cannot be interpreted as acquiescence to the state of oppression and its accompanying despair.

First and perhaps most importantly, whereas Baby proceeds existentially from laughter to silence, Sixo proceeds from silence to laughter, a sign that he continues to attempt to express the inexpressible, unlike Baby who unfortunately no longer has the strength to sustain the paradox.

Indeed, as we shall see in the end, Sixo's silence is better construed as a precursor to his laughter, as a testimony to the linguistic rupture experienced by the slaves that creates the space for laughter as extra-linguistic mode of resistance.

Second and relatedly, as Cone reminds us, ordinary linguistic resistance was denied slaves, "Slaves knew that any *open* assertion of their being would be regarded as a threat by slave masters, who were virtually outside the law and could make decisions of life and death even on whim."[30] It is constitutive of the very nature of marginalization that the marginalized are denied a voice; oppression sustains its systemic grip by aspiring to virtual invisibility through the silencing of dissenting voices. Hegemonic thinking absolutizes itself, excluding a priori the potential worth of modes of thought other than the ideology endemic to the dominant culture. For Sixo, then, who unlike Baby is still a slave, remaining silent is his way of expressing the question, why speak when no one who actually needs to hear what you have to say will listen?

Dwight Hopkins identifies four areas/disciplines of society that symbolize the means used by the dominant culture to uphold the status quo—namely, political economy, everyday ordinary living, racial and cultural identity, and language.[31] The hegemonic culture proclaims these disciplines as objective, scientific, and value-neutral, yet, argues Hopkins, in reality the dominant white culture exploits all four sociocultural spheres to sustain the slave's oppression and marginalized existence. The slave therefore, is restricted from accessing these disciplines' "legitimate" interpretive power. Sixo, therefore, is denied legitimate access to language as a sociopolitical resource, because those in power refuse to acknowledge his voice. However, slaves often transform these four spheres of hegemony into what Hopkins terms disciplines of creativity: "Hence they [these four areas] exhibit potential transformative spaces of maneuver and counter-hegemonic acts of liberation. . . . In the four disciplines of creativity, we discover sites of struggle and contestation."[32] Sixo transforms the sphere of language into a space of struggle, and we anticipate that laughter plays a crucial counterhegemonic role in this sphere, as a subversive speech-act and mode of resistance in the face of language's inaccessibility.

Third, we can interpret Sixo's rejection of "English" (note the cultural specificity of the term) as an implicit aggressive critique of the language of the white slave owners. Sixo's oppressors, along with the white imperialists who began the slave trade, undeniably use the English language to perpetuate dominance and their own egregious ideology. Sixo's refusal to participate in such language games (and his eventual laughter) bespeak his understanding of the ideological undergirdings and hence inexpediency of his own tongue. Sixo's refusal to speak is an articulation of the question, why speak when what you are saying will be misconstrued, distorted, and used against you?

Morrison explains that language is inherently problematic for African Americans because it is always, and has been since the inception of slavery, racially constructed. States Morrison, "Language . . . can powerfully evoke and enforce hidden signs of racial superiority, cultural hegemony, and dismissive 'othering' of people and language. . . . [I try to] free up the language from its almost always predictable employment of racially informed and determined chains."[33] Sixo's silence is a first step toward decolonizing language by calling attention to its desperate need for transformation.

And fourth, Paul Ricoeur reminds us that tragedy and radical negativity inherently resist thought and rupture language. Morrison's *Beloved* shows clearly that this was indeed the case with the horrors of enslavement and racism. In the novel, African Americans "neither described nor asked about the sorrow that drove them from one place to another. The whites didn't bear speaking on. Everybody knew" (53). During Baby Suggs's own enslaved days at Sweet Home, "Baby Suggs talked as little as she could get away with because what was there to say that the roots of her tongue could manage" (141). Sixo's silence therefore is a tacit acknowledgment of the inexpediency of language in these times of radical negativity—the roots of his tongue can in no way adequately articulate all that he endures. Fittingly, Dwight Hopkins entitled his book on slavery, *Cut Loose Your Stammering Tongue.*

For all these reasons, Sixo's silence cannot be dismissed out of hand as acquiescence to despair and defeatism. But perhaps even more importantly, Sixo's other behaviors reveal without a doubt that Sixo moves beyond mere silence to active resistance to the system and state of oppression. When Sixo begins plotting his escape, he begins to speak English again. Moreover, bearing striking resemblance to the early Baby Suggs, Sixo practices all of the subversive, extra-linguistic forms of resistance originally advocated by Baby Suggs: dance, song, and finally, laughter.

Sixo, however, unlike Baby Suggs, is forced to rely more heavily on the former supra-linguistic forms of expression, as he is still enslaved and therefore denied access to language as a resource for resistance. For example, when Sixo is caught attempting to escape Sweet Home, he begins immediately to sing. Schoolteacher finds such singing so incongruous and verging on madness that he decides to burn Sixo alive, declaring, "This one will never be suitable" (226). Adds Morrison, "The song must have convinced him" (226). Sixo also, we discover, dances alone at night in the woods to cope with his grief at his separation from his love, the Thirty-Mile Woman Patsy. "Sixo went among trees at night. For dancing, he said, to keep his bloodlines open, he said. Privately, alone, he did it. None of the rest of them had seen him at it, but they could imagine it, and the picture they pictured made them eager to laugh at him—in daylight, that is, when it was safe" (25).

Sixo tells his friends about his dancing immediately after he regales them with his tale of a successful rendezvous with the Thirty-Mile Woman—a young girl so named because Sixo walks two thirty-four-mile trips within the span of three months in order to court her. At last, he convinces her to walk one-third of the way, and they are able to spend a few precious hours together in the woods making love. This rendezvous with the Thirty-Mile Woman must be seen as an incredible act of resistance in and of itself, for neither Sixo or Patsy "could go anywhere on business of their own" (24). The surreptitious meeting requires slipping away on Sixo's one afternoon off a week, walking thirty miles on foot in one day, Sixo's puncturing the girl's calf to simulate snakebite as an excuse for being late to work, and the solidarity of all Sixo's friends to cover for his fatigue upon his return to Sweet Home. The entire meeting is undoubtedly punishable by death or a severe beating, should either party be caught: "Since the Thirty-Mile Woman was already fourteen and scheduled for somebody's arms, the danger was real" (24).

Laughter as Identity and Community Creation

One of the most basic human dignities denied the slaves is the right to love and be with the person of their choosing. Though only a teenager, Patsy is "scheduled" for someone else's arms—with this choice of transactional terms Morrison underscores the businesslike objectification of slaves and their treatment as nonpersons. Families like Baby Suggs's are ruthlessly split apart on the auction block, and female slaves are forced to "breed" often with other slaves, or worse, with the slave owners themselves. In the world of slavery and domination, blacks are consistently objectified, and are not acting subjects. African American feminist ethicist bell hooks explains that the oppressed must defy such objectification:

> As subjects, people have the right to define their own reality, establish their own identities, name their history. As objects, one's reality is defined by others, one's identity created by others, one's history

named only in ways that define one's relationship to those who are subject. . . . Oppressed people resist by identifying themselves as subjects, by defining their reality, shaping their new identity, naming their history, telling their story.[34]

Sixo certainly tells his own story here, "He told the story to Paul F, Halle and Paul D in the peculiar way that made them cry-laugh," but furthermore, he resists objectification within a system of servitude by reclaiming himself as an acting subject. His solitary dance in the woods, moving to a rhythm uniquely of his own creation, symbolizes this reclamation and self-empowerment. In loving Patsy, a choice that is entirely independent of the dominant ideology, Sixo effectively challenges the ubiquitous external assaults on his being. Against all odds, Sixo chooses to love a woman whom the dominant culture would deem not "his" to love. While all the other Sweet Home men desire Sethe, as she is the only black woman Mr. Garner has placed in their immediate midst as available to them, Sixo makes choices beyond Mr. Garner's pseudo-choices, thereby defining his own reality, "Because of the Thirty-Mile Woman Sixo was the only one not paralyzed by yearning for Sethe" (25). Sixo asserts himself as a self-valuing person worthy of love and of making his own decisions.

In so doing, Sixo exhibits the independent consciousness preached by Baby Suggs. For him, this consciousness is an indispensable weapon of resistance, capable of exposing the dominant consciousness as oppressive ideology and thereby empowering him for greater acts of revolution. African American folk literature is replete with resistance stories of the Way-Maker who collaborates with black humanity to "make a way out of no way." In our narrative, when Sethe longs for the presence of Baby Suggs she affirms her existence as a way-maker, saying, "Just let me feel your fingers again on the back of my neck and I will lay it all down, make a way out of this no way" (95). Similarly, Sixo's love, rendezvous, and sexual encounter with the Thirty-Mile Woman all exemplify the way in which he miraculously makes a way out of no way.

Unsurprisingly, a closer look at the text reveals that Sixo therefore comes to embody in the eyes of the other slaves a heroic paradigm of liberation. His laughter engenders solidarity. Indeed, much like Baby Suggs, we can argue that he creates around himself a culture of resistance, in which he inspires others to actively participate. Womanist minister and professor of African American studies Cheryl Townsend Gilkes offers the following elucidating definition of a culture of resistance:

Oppressed people often try to develop and instill values that differ drastically from those communicated by the dominant culture. . . . In the African-American experience, such innovation and resistance has been a response to the constant pressure to devise "a way out of no way." . . . Culture is composed of people's collective and cumulative efforts at prescriptions for human behavior. Cultures of resistance are no different, except that they are constructed in opposition to a more powerful dominant culture. In order to construct oppositional ways of thinking and acting, people must be able to idealize their oppositional alternatives. They must be able to point to people who embody those roles in order to be socialized or to socialize others. . . . The actors in these new or refashioned roles are charged with maintaining an alternative, critical worldview within a community under pressure to conform to dominant ways.[35]

Although Townsend Gilkes is not discussing the slave era, the phrase culture of resistance still applies to both Baby Suggs and Sixo, both of whom construct a way of thinking and acting that is oppositional to the dominant culture. Both characters, each within their respective settings, embody an alternative, critical worldview that instills in those around them a yearning for liberation and self-empowerment. Such an interpretation accords with Hopkins, who asserts that even the seemingly disempowered slaves had their own particular culture of resistance and ethic of survival even in the grips of white supremacy.

Interestingly, Hopkins and Cummings identify as central to this ethic of survival the slaves' "taking-not-stealing practice":

Instead of obeying their earthly owners, African American chattel . . . differentiated between stealing and taking. They defined "stealing" as the illegal removal of a fellow bondservant's private property and taking as the removal of that which they believed the master had wrongfully stolen from the slaves. . . . The necessity of sheer survival mandated that they had to preserve their lives, that is, their humanity, by removing the basic provisions from the master's till. . . . A perspective from below, a perspective of black human survival, identified and affirmed right and wrong in contrast to those white folks who held privilege and power in society.[36]

In *Beloved*, Sixo embodies the taking-not-stealing ethic of survival; indeed, it is he who introduces it to the others at Sweet Home as a mode of resistance. Sethe, as she "takes" from her employer even as a freedwoman years after Sixo's death, still recollects Sixo's example as an embodiment of an alternative, critical worldview:

> "Did you steal that shoat? You stole that shoat." Schoolteacher was quiet but firm, like he was just going through the motions—not expecting an answer that mattered. Sixo sat there, not even getting up to plead or deny. He just sat there, the streak-of-lean in his hand, the gristle clustered in the tin plate like gemstones—rough, unpolished, but loot nevertheless.
>
> "You stole that shoat, didn't you?"
>
> "No, Sir." Said Sixo, but he had the decency to keep his eyes on the meat.
>
> "You telling me you didn't steal it, and I'm looking right at you?"
>
> "No, sir, I didn't steal it."
>
> Schoolteacher smiled. "Did you kill it?"
>
> "Yes, sir. I killed it. . . ."
>
> "Well, then. Did you eat it?"
>
> "Yes, sir. I sure did."
>
> "And you telling me that's not stealing?"
>
> "No, sir. It ain't."
>
> "What is it then?"
>
> "Improving your property, sir."
>
> "What?"

"Sixo plant rye to give the high piece a better chance. Sixo take and feed the soil, give you more crop. Sixo take and feed Sixo give you more work." (190)

Here, Sixo differentiates between stealing and taking, as he insists to Schoolteacher that he has not *stolen* the shoat but "Sixo *take* and feed Sixo." Again, Sixo's independent consciousness results in rebellious action. Sixo has self-defined the situation and his proper place in it. His actions contain an aggressive social critique and oppositional worldview that even Schoolteacher recognizes as precociously beyond the pale of the hegemonic worldview, "Clever, but schoolteacher beat him anyway to show him that definitions belonged to the definers—not the defined" (191).

For the most part, Sixo's existence is defined by the slave owners. Even his "name"—six, zero—is the very quintessence of dehumanization, as it is merely a number that presumably comes straight from his bill of sale, assigned to him by the definers. The act of naming was so important to slaves, because it was a right that they were for the most part denied, once again revealing the slave's limited access to language. Baby Suggs's refusal to relinquish her real name, for example, signifies her active commitment to self-definition. Baby's bill-of-sale name is Jenny Whitlow, yet she refuses to accept this name. She tells Mr. Garner as she begins her life of freedom, "Suggs is my name, sir. From my husband. He didn't call me Jenny"; and Mr. Garner answers, " 'If I was you I'd stick to Jenny Whitlow. Mrs. Baby Suggs ain't no name for a freed Negro.' Maybe not, she thought, but Baby Suggs was all she had left of the 'husband' she claimed" (142). When asked about the significance of names, Morrison herself replied in an interview,

I never knew the real names of my father's friends. . . . They used other names. A part of that had to do with cultural orphanage, part of it with the rejection of the name given to them under circumstances not of their choosing. If you come from Africa, your name is gone. . . . That's a huge psychological scar. The best thing you can do is take another name which is yours because it reflects something about you or your own choice.[37]

Although Sixo does seem to go by the name given him by the oppressors, with his final breath he subverts the name by himself designating a name for his creation—that is, his unborn child, "Seven-O."

Additionally, Sixo becomes a definer by his actions, actions proceeding from an alternative consciousness that at every turn challenges the dominant consciousness. In particular, Sixo possesses and practices his own moral code, rather than merely adopting that of the white slave owners, who dictate that stealing from their superfluity is an absolute moral wrong. Cone comments on the practice of slave "stealing," "Black people rejected these definitions of good and bad. . . . They formulated a *new* law and a *new* morality that reflected the requirements of *black* existence. . . . To be right meant doing whatever was necessary to stay alive with dignity. To be wrong meant accepting without struggle the place masters had defined."[38]

Despite the fact that "after the conversation about the shoat, Sixo is tied up with the stock at night," the other slaves clearly consider his behavior to be right, and not wrong. Indeed, the other slaves at Sweet Home eventually adopt Sixo's moral code as their own, "They began to pilfer in earnest, and it became not only their right but their obligation" (191). Sixo's practice of taking-not-stealing as an ethics of survival is part of the culture of resistance that he creates at Sweet Home. Even though he is punished and locked up in a pen at night, Sixo does not acquiesce to despair or helplessness. Instead, he begins to plot his escape in earnest, and we are told, "Sixo keeps a nail in his mouth now, to help him undo the rope when he has to" (223). The nail in Sixo's mouth is literal, but it also functions figuratively as the protesting hope, always just below the surface of the silenced tongue, that Sixo sustains in spite of hopelessness.

Laughter as Transcendence of Fear

Sixo's position vis-à-vis the dominant white slave owners is extraordinarily dangerous. On some level Paul and the others know that to side with him in the hours of darkness is tantamount to participating in his vision of liberation, which he plans to actualize. Oddly, Paul D and the other Sweet Home men "laugh" at Sixo's dancing, but only in the daylight "when it's safe." To laugh with Sixo at night means to participate in his broader scheme for liberation, for it is during the nighttime hours that the Sweet Home slaves plan to run away from the plantation across the Ohio River to freedom. And it is none other than Sixo who instigates and orchestrates this plan of escape, the plot that indeed results in Sethe's and Patsy's freedom, and creates a way out of no way:

> Sixo, hitching up the horses, is speaking English again and tells Halle what his Thirty-Mile Woman told him. That seven Negroes

on her place were joining two others going North. . . . Sixo was going, his woman was going. . . .

Now all they have to do is wait through the spring, till the corn is as high as it ever got and the moon as fat.

And plan. Is it better to leave in the dark to get a better start, or go at daybreak to be able to see the way better? Sixo spits at the suggestion. Night gives them more time and the protection of color. He does not ask them if they are afraid. He manages some dry runs to the corn at night, burying blankets and two knives near the creek. (222)

Sixo does not ask them if they are afraid because he himself has transcended fear, the debilitating fear that is the result of the psychological abuse of oppression. Here we are reminded of Gavriel, whose laugh was the "laugh of a man who has known total fear and is no longer afraid of anyone or anything" (18).

It is not coincidental that Sixo, the character in the novel who laughs most poignantly and incongruously, is the character who dreams the most of freedom. While Baby Suggs leaves those around her to ponder her final statement that white folks have robbed her of everything, Sixo leaves his friends to ponder his incongruous laughter at the moment of his death. In contemplating escape, the ultimate act of resistance and liberation, Sixo once again thinks outside the box of his companions, thinks with an independent consciousness. While all the other slaves sleep, he alone "creeps" at night. While all the other slaves contemplate legally buying themselves out of slavery, Sixo plans real escape. Sethe explains:

We should have begun to plan. But we didn't. I don't know what we thought—but getting away was a money thing to us. Buy out. Running was nowhere on our minds. All of us? Some? Where to? How to go? It was Sixo who brought it up, finally. . . . Sixo started watching the sky. He was the only one who crept at night and Halle said that's how he learned about the train. . . . Halle was pointing over the stable. . . . "Sixo say freedom is that way. A whole train is going and if we can get there, don't need to be no buy-out." . . . Sixo watched the sky. Not the high part, the low part where it touched the trees. You could tell his mind was gone from Sweet Home. (197)

In these lines, we note that even Sethe notices how Sixo thinks beyond the status quo of white consciousness—"you could tell his mind was gone

from Sweet Home." In contemplating a future of freedom, a possibility
that Schoolteacher attempts to teach the slaves is an impossibility, Sixo
successfully thinks beyond oppression and its ideology. Patricia Hill Collins comments that even if change cannot be brought about externally
in society itself, African Americans can develop and sustain a changed
consciousness as a sphere of freedom. She adds, "People experience and
resist oppression on three levels: the level of personal biography; the
group or community level of the cultural context created by race, class,
and gender; and the systemic level of social institutions. . . . This level of
individual consciousness is a fundamental area where new knowledge
can generate change."[39] Not coincidentally, when Sixo begins planning
his freedom, he also resumes speaking English.

As a slave, Sixo is unable to resist oppression at the systemic level,
but the narrative is replete with instances of Sixo resisting oppression at
the level of personal biography. In dancing, singing, taking-not-stealing,
plotting escape, and eventually by laughing, Sixo manifests and sustains a
changed consciousness, one that is liberated from the white slave owners'
ideology. Sixo accordingly frequently offers an alternative (and correct)
interpretation of events that is opposed to that of white consciousness,
and leads the other slaves in laughter at the ridiculousness of white ignorance, "Sixo said the doctor made Mrs. Garner sick. Said he was giving
her to drink what stallions got when they broke a leg and no gunpowder
could be spared, and had it not been for schoolteacher's new rules, he
would have told her so. They laughed at him. Sixo had a knowing tale
about everything" (219). Within this changed consciousness, not only
is Sixo "free" psychologically and spiritually on the "inside," he also is
empowered enough to begin to dream of actualized freedom, and to take
active steps to bring such dreams to fruition. More importantly, Sixo's
"new knowledge" spills over to the group, generating change and resistance at the communal level, as Halle and the slaves learn of this radically
new possibility of freedom and share this knowledge with one another:
"Sixo say freedom is that way" (197).

The apotheosis of Sixo's life of resistance is his final laughter as he
laughs in the face of death. Sixo's planned escape goes horribly wrong,
and both he and Paul D are captured. When Sixo is captured, he sings, but
his singing is a subversive act of resistance in that it secretly allows Sethe
and the Thirty-Mile Woman to escape. Sixo selflessly and effectively creates a scene that distracts Schoolteacher and the men long enough for
the women to get away. While singing, Sixo grabs one of the men's rifles
and is able to strike him with it, in his only act of violent resistance.

Sixo's incongruous singing and physical retaliation leads Schoolteacher to consider Sixo mad and therefore unfit even for slavery. Schoolteacher horrifically proceeds to burn Sixo alive on the spot:

> The fire keeps failing and the whitemen are put out with them-selves for not being prepared for this emergency. They came to capture, not to kill. What they can manage is only enough for cooking hominy. Dry faggots are scarce and the grass is slick with dew. By the light of the hominy fire Sixo straightens. He is through with his song. He laughs, a rippling sound like Sethe's sons make when they tumble in hay or splash in rainwater. His feet are cook-ing; the cloth of his trousers smokes. He laughs. Something is funny. Paul D guesses what it is when Sixo interrupts his laughter to call out, "Seven-O! Seven-O!"
>
> Smoky, stubborn fire. They shoot him to shut him up. Have to. (226)

Sixo, therefore, laughs not only at the moment of his death, but also laughs at death itself. This image of a slave man being burned alive while laughing jolts the reader, shocks us with its terrifying pain and incongruity. The image is undeniably grotesque. His laughter, because it transcends fear, terrifies his oppressors, but they have to "shut him up." I am reminded of the words of Jürgen Moltmann: "The power of the pow-erless lies in such liberations from fear, in their laughter at the expense of deified rulers who are nothing after all but dolled-up dwarfs. People who are no longer afraid . . . can no longer be ruled with ease, although of course they can be shot."[40]

Laughter as Manifestation of Dual Consciousness

Susan Corey's analysis of Morrison's use of the grotesque in *Beloved*, although she does not specifically analyze the character of Sixo or his laughter, helps us to unpack the complexity of Sixo's laughter in his crucial death-scene. Drawing on Mikhail Bakhtin, Corey defines the grotesque as an "aesthetic phenomenon that encourages the creation of meaning and the discovery of new connections through its effect of shock, con-fusion, disorder, or contradiction. The grotesque breaks the boundar-ies of normalcy in some way and always points toward the mysterious and inexplicable."[41] Undoubtedly Sixo's laughter shocks the white slave owners who surround him in the same way that Sixo's song does—both are inexplicable, bafflingly contradictory, and seemingly without cause.

The white slave owners can only attribute his laughter to madness. It is not "sane"—that is, in line with hegemonic white thought.

Yet it is precisely the glaring inexplicability of Sixo's laughter that warrants our analysis. With Sixo's laughter, Morrison draws attention to its occasion: the gross injustice of the existing social system in which a man can be burned alive on a whim, without repercussion, because of a song. Morrison herself writes of her use of the grotesque, "Something really terrible . . . is always a push toward the abyss somewhere to see what is remarkable, because that's the way to find out what is heroic. That's the way I know why such people survive, who went under, who didn't, . . . because our existence here has been grotesque."[42]

Sixo laughs because the situation is absurd, as indeed slavery is absurd—a grotesque exaggeration and materialization of a will-to-power. Cone defines the absurd as that which is meaningless, "We [African Americans] are seeking meaning in a world permeated with philosophical and theological absurdities."[43] Sixo's laugh is heroic because it is a mode of survival, of resistance to the despair and quietism inflicted by existential meaninglessness.

Morrison presents us with a disturbing and grotesquely distorted image because she wants to disorient us into recognizing that the image merely reflects the reality of slave life, which indeed was a grotesque distortion of life. Explains Corey:

> The grotesque enables a writer to challenge conventional ideals, values, and structures; and to expose evil or oppressive social institutions and practices. Thus the grotesque assists a writer to present a paradoxical vision of a world "held largely by the devil," yet infused with moments of grace and hope for renewal through contact with a larger world of meanings. . . . The grotesque has the effect of . . . undermining the established order and exposing oppressive systems. . . . The grotesque allows the writer to challenge any final or closed version of the truth . . . and to explore the paradoxical, ambiguous, mixed nature of human life.[44]

Morrison uses the image of Sixo being burned alive to expose the evil and absurdity of the slave institution, along with the paradox of Sixo's existence. Yet we must explore the precise nature of the paradoxes that Sixo's death exposes in order to discover wherein lies the puzzling grace and renewal to which Corey alludes.

Mikhail Bahktin not only notes that laughter is an essential element of the grotesque, but also states that without the principle of laughter the genre of the grotesque would be impossible. Bahktin argues for a reinterpretation of the ambivalence of the grotesque. In his mind, the grotesque bespeaks the reality of debasement and horror on the one hand, and the possibility of regeneration and renewal on the other. In Bahktin's view, the latter positive purpose of the grotesque is largely ignored. Laughter is appropriate to the grotesque for Bahktin because it too shares this ambivalence and regenerating potential. Laughter is appropriate to the grotesque situation because it attests to this dual consciousness—the coexistence of horror and hope, meaninglessness and meaning, terror and faith in regeneration—in a way that language cannot. Laughter attests to the possibility of regeneration but only paradoxically and painfully, because the need for regeneration is necessitated by a grotesque situation wherein regeneration is grossly absent.

Bahktin's discussion of laughter accords with our theological interpretation of laughter as an attempt by the suffering individual to sustain the integrity of both the narrative of faith and the narrative of negativity and to hold both narratives in dialectical tension. Laughter sustains a certain ambivalence, capturing a both-and existential situation in a way that cognitive discourse cannot attain without reductionistic tendencies toward either/or. In Sixo's death scene, therefore, Morrison uses the grotesque image and Sixo's laughter to sustain the paradox of his existence and to thrust this paradox into the reader's consciousness.

Sixo's experience of the world as paradoxical and incongruous on multiple levels occasions his laughter. According to Arthur Schopenhauer:

All laughter . . . is occasioned by a paradox. . . . Accordingly the phenomenon of laughter always signifies the sudden apprehension of an incongruity between such a conception and the real object thought under it, thus between the abstract and the concrete object of perception. The greater and more unexpected, in the apprehension of the laugher, this incongruity is, the more violent will be his laughter.[45]

Sixo experiences paradox in that he is both African and American (note that there is no existential option of either/or). He is not free in a country that upholds liberty as its highest ideal. Sixo labors under the existential burden of being dually defined. He is defined by contradiction. He strives for self-definition, yet any emerging self-valuation always competes with the hegemonic definition of blacks as inferior nonbeings. I am reminded of Malxolm X, who argued that black life in America is an absurd paradox:

> Anything that's paradoxical has to have some humor in it, or it'll crack you up. . . . Because it's a contrast, a paradox. And America is such a paradoxical society, hypocritically paradoxical, that if you don't have some humor, you'll crack up. . . . You have to be able to laugh to stand up and sing, "My country 'tis of thee, sweet land of liberty." *That's* a joke. And if you don't laugh at it, it'll crack you up.[46]

W. E. B. DuBois states that racism imposes an existential dilemma on its victims that results in an identity crisis and struggle. Dubois characterizes this dilemma as the African American experience of a "double self." Writes Dubois, "One feels his two-ness—an American Negro, two souls, two thoughts, two unreconciled strivings, two warring ideals in one dark body. . . . The history of the American Negro is the history of this strife."[47] A greater incongruity than the intrinsic value of African Americans as persons and the severely subordinate value placed on them by white society can perhaps not be imagined. Thus the incisive violence of Sixo's death-laughter, a laughter arising out of "two-ness."

Cone adds that slavery imposes another existential paradox on all who are enslaved, "Under the law, slaves were property and persons. But the two definitions together were absurd, because property and persons are mutually exclusive modes of being which negate one another."[48] Once again, laughter steps in to capture the actual coexistence of two modes of being that ostensibly negate one another. Language cannot possibly express such an existential dilemma in its fullness. It defies rationality to assert that I am both person and property, both liberated and enslaved, both utterly affirmed and utterly negated. And so, Sixo for a time jettisons speech altogether, and in his final moments, chooses only to laugh. Laughter, unlike language, holds both sides of these paradoxes in dialectical tension, thereby reflecting Sixo's actual experience of the commingling of these oppositional states. Discursive thought asserts the either/or, whereas laughter can incarnate the inherently complex both-and, in-spite-of character of the existence and resistance of the marginalized. Sixo's very existence is shot through with paradox, and his laughter functions to sustain this paradox and live through it.

Fascinatingly, many African American theorists, particularly black women who labor under a double oppression, argue that either/or thought is inherently hegemonic and ideological. bell hooks claims either/or dichotomous thinking to be "the central ideological component of all systems of domination in western society."[49] hooks seems to suggest that the fundamental problem with dichotomous thought is that it is always, if only surreptitiously, hierarchical. She writes, "Either/or dichotomous thinking categorizes people, things and ideas in terms of their difference from one another."[50] Collins argues the same in her book *Black Feminist Thought:* "This emphasis on quantification and categorization occurs in conjunction with the belief that either/or categories must be ranked. The search for certainty of this sort requires that one side of a dichotomy is privileged while its other is denigrated."[51]

In the either/or schema, then, the two concepts or parties being compared are not only different, but also are implicitly unequal. Either/or implies not only a comparison but a contrast; the two concepts are opposed to one another, and one side of the either/or dichotomy is more "right" or better than the other. For example either you are black, or you are white; you cannot be both (hence the difficulty our society has had in accepting the ambiguity of interracial couples). Either God (and hence life) is good and just, or life is bad and unjust. Either you are enslaved, or you are free. Either one is American, or one is African. Either Sixo is defeated, or he is triumphant. Either Sethe is the savior of her children, or she is their murderer. As a society we hate ambiguity, and when we encounter it, we are intolerant of it, striving to reduce it to either/or.[52] This is particularly true, all too true, in the realm of ethics and theology.

But as *Beloved* and *Silence* and *Gates of the Forest* testify, sometimes ambiguity is real. Sometimes we live existentially in the both-and, and it is there that we must live, find or create meaning, believe or not believe, and make ethical decisions. Theology ignores this truth to its peril, according to Cone who states, "Theological language must be paradoxical because the necessity of affirming two dimensions of reality which appear to be contradictory."[53] Either/or discursive thought is often reductionistic, and therefore theology needs to reevaluate its use of it. Many African American thinkers point out that either/or thought is usually racist, sexist, classist—in short, ideological and resulting in the explicit marginalization of certain people's experiences. A good case in point is the glaring fact that theology has for too long ignored the experience of the oppressed, and their laughter.

Dominant, hegemonic thought has a hidden drive to sustain and reinforce either/or thinking, because this is its ideological scaffolding. Thus Schoolteacher and the whites categorize Sixo and Sethe as "mad," just as Janos and the other Nazis consider Gavriel mad; all these characters reject either/or and befuddle those at the top of the systems of domination. Morrison's text reminds us of these dangers of either/or, and the potentially rich ethical and theological resource of both-and modes of thought.

Sixo labors under the paradox of both-and in the sense that that although he is radically dehumanized, he on several levels indefatigably affirms his humanity and that of the other slaves. First, his laughter and song allow the Thirty-Mile Woman to escape. Second, Sixo's laughter asserts that he affirms himself as worthy of life even in the face of Schoolteacher's absurd death-dealing. For surely, if Sixo merely accepted Schoolteacher's view of himself, there would be no perceived incongruity, no paradox, and consequently no laughter. Sixo's laughter therefore attests to his refusal to accept the oppressor's view of his person as nonbeing. We must understand such a psychological feat of nonacquiescence as an incredible act of resistance, as whites condition slaves to internalize a negative self-image and sense of inferiority. Cone explains, "There is such a thing as living physically while being dead spiritually. As long as blacks let whites define the limits of their being, blacks are dead. 'To be or not to be' is thus a dilemma for the black community: to assert one's humanity and be killed, or to cling to life and sink into nonhumanity."[54]

Laughter as Deconstruction of Oppression

Paradoxically, then, it is genuine life Sixo chooses by choosing death, even though choosing to resist and assert his humanity results in his physical death. Cone's assertion that clinging to life can result in nonhumanity is nowhere better revealed than in this comparison of Sixo and Paul D. Reflecting on Sixo and his life and death, Paul D says admiringly, "Now *there* was a man. . . . Himself . . . didn't compare" (22). Paul D chooses not to resist and to live, but it is he who ends up feeling unhuman, wearing a three-bit animal collar and envying a rooster, Mister, for his vastly greater freedom:

> Mister, he looked so . . . free. Better than me. Stronger, tougher. . . . Mister was allowed to be and stay what he was. But I wasn't allowed to be and stay what I was. . . . Wasn't no way I'd ever be Paul D again, living or dead. Schoolteacher changed me. I was something else and that something was less than a chicken sitting in the sun on a tub. (72)

Paul D concludes: "He couldn't figure out why it took so long. He may as well have jumped in the fire with Sixo and they both could have had a good laugh" (219). Ironically, Sixo is dead but spiritually and psychologically alive; whereas Paul D is alive but emotionally and psychically dead. In the words of Ignazio Silone, "Freedom is not something you get as a present. . . . You can live in a dictatorship and be free—on one condition: that you fight the dictatorship. The man who thinks with his own mind and keeps it uncorrupted is free."[55]

Sixo's laughter witnesses to a psychological and spiritual form of freedom, even though he is physically bound and facing death. Morrison, commenting on another of her characters, says, "He is the thing I keep calling a 'free man,' not free in the legal sense, but free in his head. . . . I'm interested in characters who are lawless in that regard. They make up their lives."[56] We say the same of Sixo—he is free in his head. Cone asserts that slaves not only seek freedom-from-bondage, they also exhibit what he terms freedom-in-bondage.[57] Sixo's laughter therefore manifests his freedom-in-bondage, an emotional, spiritual, and psychological freedom.

Morrison comments on her work, "What's important . . . is the process by which we construct and deconstruct reality in order to be able to function in it. I'm trying to explore how a people . . . absorbs and rejects information on a very personal level about something [slavery] that is undigestible and unabsorbable, completely."[58] Schoolteacher decides at the moment he begins to burn Sixo alive that Sixo is not even worthy of life, commenting, "This one will never be suitable" (226). Sixo's laughter and song, however, deconstruct this negation of his being. It is the cruel nature of oppression that the oppressors can make flippant life-and-death decisions of this kind for the oppressed. However, it is also the nature of oppression that the oppressed can, to the extent they are able, deconstruct and resist this definition of themselves as subhuman and reject it, which Sixo powerfully does. Indeed, what can be more incredible than the fact that those oppressed by Christian thought such as the slaves did not simply reject the faith outright? Instead, although Christianity for centuries was used to justify oppression, millions of its victims reinterpreted it to justify their liberation. It is an astounding example of deconstruction.

Sixo's laughter, then, much like Gavriel's, ruptures the dualism of hope and tragedy. Although usually we consider tragedy to be a situation of hopelessness, this kind of laughter asserts the paradoxical notion of tragic hope. Utilizing Cornel West's terms, we can say that Sixo's laughter is a form of "aggressive waiting," or a mode of "revolutionary patience."[59] Sixo's laughter takes on a proleptic, anticipatory character. Sixo, similar to the Hasid, inculcates "a certain kind of joy that will be justified only retroactively."[60] Sixo's laughter attests to the already-but-not-yet liberation he experiences through the possession of an independent consciousness. His laughter imaginatively recreates both the present and the future by its very existence. And even though Sixo does not live to see his son born or his dreams of freedom actualized, his laughter transforms his mode-of-being by naming the present as absurd in the anticipation of freedom.

He laughs (and dances and sings) for the imagined future, in which liberation is universal and pervades all levels of existence, in a manner reminiscent of Wiesel's comment, "Even if we find no faith we must raise it up in the hope that one day we will understand why, and that one day we will be able to give a reason for believing."[61] Sixo believes and hopes for freedom in order that one day such hope might be justified. His laughter is proleptic liberation, or to borrow a term from Cone, a form of proleptic transcendence.

Laughter as Demystification of Power

Michel Foucault insightfully argues that power relationships always structurally include resistance to that very power:

> Where there is power, there is resistance. . . . [A relationship of power] depends on a multiplicity of points of resistance: these play the role of adversary, target, support or handle in power relations. These points of resistance are present everywhere in the power network. Hence there is no single locus of great Refusal, no soul of revolt, source of all rebellions, or pure law of the revolutionary. Instead there is a plurality of resistances. . . . And it is doubtless the strategic codification of these points of resistance that make a revolution possible.[62]

As Kelly Brown Douglas points out, Foucault has a bottom-up analysis of power relationships. In his theory, institutional change always begins below, at the microlevels of society, with people who alter microlevel relationships. For our purposes, Foucault's analysis is helpful because it demystifies power by democratizing both power and resistance. Power relationships are sustained at least in part by those who are in them; hence they are also changed by those in them.

Foucault's radical reunderstanding of power helps us interpret Sixo's character. Foucault's analysis is radical because it places the potentiality for revolutionary change within societal power structures into the hands of those who are seemingly disempowered. Paradoxically then, the seemingly powerless individuals like Sixo in reality are empowered through resistance. Thanks to Foucault, we discern that systemic change begins with the smallest individual act of resistance, with, for example, the slightest shift in the balance of power between a slave and his master. Every microlevel act, therefore, even a laugh of the oppressed, takes on potential revolutionary significance.

In *Beloved*, Sixo fearlessly alters his power relationship with Schoolteacher, by taking-not-stealing food he considers himself entitled to, loving the woman of his choice, attempting escape, and finally by singing and laughing in his master's face even as he is murdered. Sixo's laughter is defiant and emancipatory. Laughter is a preservation of Sixo's dignity, as Schoolteacher expects and desires Sixo to cry and despair in the moment of terror. Of course, Sixo's joyous laughter and song appear so unanticipated and strange to Schoolteacher that he attributes them to madness. Sixo's laugh so disturbs and violates Schoolteacher's sense of absolute control over his slaves that Schoolteacher finds it unbearable. Schoolteacher reseizes a semblance of control in the situation by not passively allowing the fire do his killing for him, "They shoot him [Sixo] to shut him up. Have to" (226). Schoolteacher "'has to" shoot Sixo because he cannot allow his precocious laughter, which alters and upsets the power relationship between them in a way that is evident to all present, to continue.

For certainly, the slaves around Sixo interpret his laughter as liberation from fear and indignity. Like Gavriel's and Baby Suggs's, Sixo's laughter emancipates. Laughter is repeatedly associated throughout *Beloved* with actualized moments of freedom, both psychological and physical. When, for example, Baby Suggs reaches freedom in Ohio we read, "her own heartbeat. Had it been there all along? . . . She felt like a fool and began to laugh out loud. . . . She couldn't stop laughing. . . . She covered her mouth to keep from laughing too loud" (141). Similarly, in the beautiful scene when Sethe and the girls temporarily celebrate their freedom from the past and skate carefree over the ice, the mother and daughters all laugh repeatedly as "nobody saw them falling" (175). When Sethe, at last a free woman, relaxes after her daring escape to the North, "Sethe's laugh of delight was so loud the crawling-already baby blinked. . . . She [Sethe] didn't cry. . . . Baby Suggs came in and laughed at them" (93–94). But in the end, Sixo dies. Is his laughter still emancipatory despite the fact that the oppressors "win" in his case?

As strange as it may seem, Sixo's laughter as he is put to death represents the apotheosis of his lifetime of heroic gestures of defiance and self-valuation. Paul D affirms that he watches Sixo, "whom he loved better than his brothers, roast without a tear just so the roasters would know what a man was like" (126). Paul D wishes that he could sing and laugh along with Sixo, but at that time he has not yet reached the freedom-in-bondage state of resistance that Sixo has. Comments Paul D on Sixo's final song, "He thinks he should have sung along. Loud, something loud and rolling to go with Sixo's tune, but the words put him off, he didn't understand the words. Although it shouldn't have mattered because he understood the sound: hatred so loose it was juba" (227).

Here again, one of Morrison's characters testifies to the fact that language cannot speak to the unspeakable horror they have endured. We never learn the words to Sixo's song, nor do the slaves understand or repeat the words, because the negativity is so radical language is ruptured by it. During the antebellum period, slaves were jailed for singing the spiritual, "We'll soon be free." When forbidden to sing, slaves hummed the song, and Albert Raboteau argues that the song itself nonetheless functioned as an indirect form of social criticism.[63] Sixo's wordless song also conveys an aggressive social critique of white ideology and practice: unleashed hatred that dances its way into the consciousness of the hearer. Sixo's words to his song are not important. What is most important is the fact that he can still sing, when every reason for singing has been taken away from him. Cone concurs, "It does not matter what oppressors say or do or what they try to make us out to be. We know we have a freedom not made of human hands. It is this faith that defines our person, and thus enables black people to sing when the world says they have nothing to sing about."[64]

Paul D describes Sixo's laughter as oddly joyful, "What a laugh. So rippling and full of glee it put out the fire" (229). The narrator compares it to the laughter of a child at play—"a rippling sound like Sethe's sons make when they tumble in hay or splash in rainwater." Sixo's laughter baffles the white onlookers as incomprehensible in its glee. It interrupts the state of oppression, that is, the emotional states of despair and misery and the psychological states of learned helplessness and learned inferiority. Also, Sixo's laugh interrupts the system of oppression—"puts out the fire"—because it shifts the burden of bewilderment, paradox, and hermeneutical chaos onto white shoulders.

Laughter as Tragic Hope

Schoolteacher and his men have taken away every reason for laughter and joy, yet Sixo laughs anyway, manifesting an independent consciousness that has survived against all odds. Writes Dwight Hopkins of slave laughter,

African Americans worked with the Spirit of freedom within their own souls by employing laughter to declare a statement about the unbroken self. Whites with power cannot fathom the logic of laughter gushing forth from black bodies lame with injury. Indeed, black laughter, expressed in excruciating pain, creates and exhibits its own rhetoric of survival, resistance, and self-transformation for the black oppressed.[65]

Sixo is unafraid to die, and this fearlessness makes him free, much like the ex-slave Frederick Douglas who reflects, "I had reached the point at which I was not afraid to die. This Spirit made me a freeman in fact, while I remained a slave in form."[66]

Cornel West argues for an interpretation of African American laughter as conveying a worldview of tragic hope. For West, the African American consciousness places "an enduring emphasis on the tragic facts of human existence: death, disease, disappointment, dread, and despair. . . . But the radically comic character of African American life—the pervasive sense of joy, laughter, and ingenious humor in the black community—flows primarily from the African American preoccupation with tragedy."[67] Sixo laughs not only in spite of tragedy, but because of it. Like much of African American laughter as described by West and Hopkins, Sixo's laughter commingles hope and tragedy, joy and pain, despair and love.

This admixture leads us to one final paradox of the situation of Sixo's death that we have not yet mentioned. Sixo's grotesque death is also, a moment pregnant, quite literally, with regeneration and hope. Sixo's death accords perfectly with Bakhtin's argument for an understanding of the grotesque as ambivalent, and never mere negation. Bahktin argues that death in the grotesque is better understood as "birth-giving-death":

Laughter degrades and materializes. . . . Degradation here means . . . the contact with earth as an element that swallows up and gives birth at the same time. To degrade is to bury, to sow, and to kill simultaneously, in order to bring forth something more and better. . . . Degradation digs a bodily grave for a new birth; it has not only a destructive, negative aspect, but also a regenerating one. . . . Grotesque realism knows no other lower level; it is the fruitful earth and the womb. It is always conceiving.[68]

Sixo's death is shot through with this Bakhtinian two-sidedness of the both-and; his final moment marks not only death, debasement, and hopelessness but also conception, regeneration, and hope. For in Sixo's final moments the one word he shouts in the midst of his laughter is the word: Seven-O. Sixo sings and resists Schoolteacher and his men in order to distract them from the fact that the Thirty-Mile Woman is escaping up the river. In effect, Sixo sacrifices his life in order to save the Thirty-Mile Woman. But Sixo saves more than just her; through an oblique remark made by Paul D we discover that the shout Seven-O! indicates that Sixo has just learned the Thirty-Mile Woman is pregnant with his unborn child. "Something is funny, Paul D guesses what it is when Sixo interrupts his laughter to call out, 'Seven-O! Seven-O!' . . . Seven-O! Seven-O because his Thirty-Mile Woman got away with his blossoming seed" (226, 228–29).

Because of Sixo's sacrifice, this child and its mother make their way to freedom in the North. Because of Sixo's life of resistance and love, this child was conceived against all odds. In the midst of the oppressor's death dealing, Sixo succeeds in life-giving. Although the white men want to rob Sixo of both life and dignity, Sixo's laughter suggests that their victory is penultimate, as the ultimate triumph of love and freedom is Sixo's as yet unborn child in the soon-to-be-free Thirty-Mile Woman's womb. The joke, in other words, is on them.

In a strange turn of events, then, Sixo's choice of death, which seems the quintessence of passivity, becomes an act of resistance. The choice of death, rather than a life of egregious oppression, is indeed the central theme of *Beloved*. Sethe chooses death for herself and her children rather than return to a life of enslavement; but she is apprehended prior to carrying out her suicide. James Cone asserts, "Black resistance has roots stretching back to the slave ships. . . . It began when the first black person decided that death would be preferable to slavery."[69] Dwight Hopkins concurs, "To claim control over and freedom for the black body . . . was to assert that one's humanity reflected sacred creation. . . . Suicide suggested an ultimate determination to remove an unpaid labor commodity from the slave system and, consequently, was a blow against the macropolitical economy."[70]

We must recognize also that Margaret Garner was not the only slave attempting suicide and murdering her children as a means of resistance to enslavement. Suicide by fasting was so common on slave ships that a compulsory feeding device was implemented. Historian William Cheek reports that the agony of slavery pushed some black men and women to commit acts of self-violence as a means of resistance. Slaves would routinely chop off their own fingers and toes, eat dirt in order to induce serious illness or death, and commit infanticide. Notes Delores Williams, "African American women . . . killed their children to keep them from a life of enslavement. . . . A mother on a Georgia plantation killed thirteen of her babies to save them from slavery."[71] Our analysis of Sixo's laughter and death therefore is crucial, as it provides with a key for better understanding the complexities of Sethe's murder of Beloved.

Paul D

Laughter as Mode of Survival

The third and final character in the novel whose laugh merits our analysis is Paul D. Paul D learns much from Sixo's embodiment of resistance and eventually comes to emulate him. But when Paul D first shows up at 124 Bluestone Road, he is a "walking man" just trying to leave the past behind:

> He didn't believe he could live with a woman—any woman—for over two out of three months. That was about as long as he could abide one place . . . walking off when he got ready was the only way he could convince himself that he would no longer have to sleep, pee, eat or swing a sledge hammer in chains. . . . After Alfred he had shut down a generous portion of his head, . . . for more required him to dwell on Halle's face and Sixo laughing. (40–41)

Paul D tries to forget about his tragic past and his time spent on the chain gang in Alfred because the memories are excruciating to relive. For Paul D, as for Sethe, "The future was a matter of keeping the past at bay. . . . Every mention of her past life hurt. Everything in it was painful or lost. . . . The hurt was always there—like a tender place in the corner of her mouth that the bit left" (42, 58).

For Morrison, however, a process of reclamation is essential. Paul D's refusal to not think about Sixo laughing is dangerous, because Paul D could learn so much from Sixo's means of resistance and struggle for identity. For Morrison, African Americans have no genuine future until the past has been confronted and reclaimed, "The past, until you confront it, until you live through it, keeps coming back in other forms. . . . There is a necessity for remembering the horror, but of course there's a necessity for remembering it in a manner in which it can be digested, in a manner in which the memory is not destructive."[72] Morrison says that none of the characters in *Beloved* want to remember, because they are afraid. Beloved, however, as ghost and victim of the tragedy of slavery, represents the slave-past that "haunts" the novel's characters. She is the past that will not let them go, and "comes back in other forms." Sethe and Denver's need to address this unspoken grief in their past quite literally compels them to call Beloved into the flesh, "Sethe and Denver decided to end the persecution by calling for the ghost that tried them so. 'Come on. Come on. You may as well just come on'" (4).

Beloved's incarnation in flesh and blood forces each of the characters in turn to confront this painful past. To use Morrison's own term from the novel, Beloved is a "rememory" they all cannot avoid bumping into. Paul D, however, seeks to avoid the past, locking his memories away in the "tobacco tin" of his heart, which he explains is rusted shut: "It was some time before he could put Alfred, Georgia, Sixo, Schoolteacher, Halle, his brothers, Sethe, Mister, the taste of iron, the sight of butter, the smell of hickory, notebook paper, one by one, into the tobacco tin lodged in his chest. By the time he got to 124 nothing in this world could pry it open" (113). Paul D begins to tell Sethe about his painful past but then chooses to stop, "He would not pry it [the lid of the tobacco tin buried in his chest] loose now in front of this sweet sturdy woman, for if she got a whiff of the contents it would shame him" (73). The past for Paul D is unspeakable because of its accompanying shame.

Fittingly, when Paul D first steps into 124 Bluestone Road, his first action is to exorcise the ghost of Beloved—but unsuccessfully, as she later resurrects in the flesh. Because Paul D seeks to avoid the past rather than learn from it, throughout the story he despises Beloved and seeks to avoid her. Paul D asks Sethe to make Beloved move out, and when she will not cooperate, Paul D himself moves out of the house into the storehouse. Nonetheless, Beloved still makes her way to the shed where she seduces Paul D, which opens his tobacco tin, "He didn't hear the whisper that the flakes of rust made either as they fell away from the seams of his tobacco tin" (117).

Ironically, Paul D urges Sethe to "go inside"—explore her emotional interiority and the way the past has affected her—seemingly without seeing that he needs to explore his own interior life. Paul D tells Sethe, "Go as far inside as you need to, I'll hold your ankles. Make sure you get back out. . . . We can make a life, girl. A life" (46). Up until that moment, Paul D had decided to stay on the move and love small: "The best thing, he knew, was to love just a little bit; everything, just a little bit, so when they broke its back, or shoved it in a croaker sack, well, maybe you'd have a little love left over for the next one" (45).

Yet Paul D mistakenly thinks he can make a new life without first facing the ugly stained contents of the tobacco tin in his own heart. In order for Paul D to face the future and obtain the life with Sethe that he desires, he must first confront his own past as well as Sethe's. Beloved embodies not only the tragic slave-past that both Paul D and Sethe share, but also the dead daughter Sethe murdered—a secret element of Sethe's past about which Paul D knows nothing. Paul D's sexual encounter with Beloved signifies this ambivalent and essential encounter with the past. By the novel's end Paul D himself recognizes this ambivalence: "Afterward, beached and gobbling air, in the midst of repulsion and personal shame, he was thankful too for having been escorted to some ocean-deep place he once belonged to" (264).

Beloved is thus a highly ambivalent figure in Paul D's psyche, but on the positive side his sexual encounters with her are necessary for him for several reasons. On the one hand, he must experience intimacy with her because repeatedly confronting the past is the key to his future, the key to his overcoming his fear of loving someone fully and staying put long enough in one place to have a real relationship. On the other hand, Paul D's encounter with Beloved is frightening and painful, as it symbolizes his betrayal of Sethe as a result of knowledge of her past. Once he sleeps with Beloved, the distance between him and Sethe grows, "Sethe scares me. I scare me. And that girl in her house scares me the most" (234). Not coincidentally, just after Paul D sleeps with Beloved, Stamp Paid forces Paul D to come face-to-face with Sethe's past—the knowledge of Beloved, and that Sethe murdered her as a baby. Paul D cannot accept this fact and moves out for good. The encounter with the past has swallowed his hopes for a future, just as Sethe's obsession with Beloved/the past has made her forget about a future with Paul D. Paul D permits this memory to become destructive as he wields it as a weapon of judgment and criticism of Sethe. As Paul D departs, he, like Schoolteacher, accuses Sethe of being subhuman, and leaves her with the parting words, "You got two feet, Sethe, not four" (165).

In the criticism of the novel, no moment is more overlooked than the conversation between Paul D and Stamp Paid just before Paul D's unexpected return to Sethe and Bluestone Road. Even in the film version of *Beloved*, which otherwise follows the novel to the letter, the filmmakers chose to omit this strange scene. Why? In this crucial scene, just prior to his return to Sethe, Paul D laughs. But his laughter bewilders us, because nothing is ostensibly funny. What Paul D jokes about is so horrible as to make one cringe.

Paul D has heard about Sethe's second murder attempt on the day of Beloved's exorcism by the community. Sethe, reliving the past, hallucinates that Denver's new employer Mr. Bodwin is Schoolteacher, and she proceeds to reenact the murders of that fateful day—with one exception. This time around she tries to kill the white man and not her own child. When Paul D hears this news of Sethe's second murder, he laughs at it and says to Stamp Paid:

"Yeah. Damn. That woman is crazy. Crazy."

"Yeah, well, ain't we all?"

They laughed then. A rusty chuckle at first and then more, louder and louder until Stamp took out his pocket handkerchief and wiped his eyes while Paul D pressed the heel of his hand in his own. As the scene neither one had witnessed took shape before them, its seriousness and embarrassment made them shake with laughter.

"Every time a whiteman come to the door she got to kill somebody?"

"For all she know, the man could be coming for the rent."

"Good thing they don't deliver mail out that way."

"Wouldn't nobody get no letter."

"Except the postman."

"Be a mighty hard message."

"And his last."

When their laughter was spent, they took deep breaths and shook their heads. (265)

Almost immediately after laughing at this horror, Paul D returns to Sethe, to stay with her and "put his story next to hers" (273).

Paul D's laughter shocks and disorients the reader. Nothing seems "funny" in the traditional sense, yet Paul D and Stamp Paid laugh until the tears roll down. In a 1985 interview (notably a year in which Morrison would have been writing *Beloved*), Morrison stated:

> Other people call it humor. It's not really that. It's not sort of laughing away one's troubles. And laughter itself for Black people has nothing to do with what's funny at all. And taking that which is peripheral, or violent or doomed or something that nobody else sees any value in and making value out of it or having a psychological attitude about duress is part of what made us stay alive and fairly coherent and irony is a part of that—being able to see the underside of something as well. . . . I am conscious of . . . how Black people during that time [slavery] apprehend life simply because they didn't trust anybody else's version of it.[73]

Paul D's laughter in this scene seems to fall under Morrison's characterization of having nothing to do with humor, and more with coping and survival. Paul D and Stamp Paid take that which is violent and valueless and see its ironic, valuable underside. In *Black Culture and Black Consciousness* Lawrence Levine notes, "The oblique jokes of southern blacks were able to draw humor from the most painful situation. . . . [Black laughter] . . . is from the time of slavery on . . . essential to black survival and the maintenance of group sanity and integrity."[74] Paul D's laughter, like Sixo's, captures the both-and paradoxical nature of black consciousness. As such his laughter appears mad, incongruous to those outside the slave experience. African American laughter separates the oppressed from the oppressor, by fostering group solidarity among those with the experiential knowledge necessary to "get" the joke. According to Levine, laughter fosters group identification and community by widening the gap between those inside and outside the laughter, "Black laughter provided a sense of the total black condition not only by putting whites and their racial system in perspective but also by supplying an important degree of self and group knowledge."[75] For this reason, to those on the outside, Paul D's laughter makes very little sense at first hearing. Levine explains:

> A substantial percentage of Negro humor, even had it been revealed to whites, would simply not have struck them as funny.

The experiences, the perspective, and the needs of many black Americans so often diverged from those of the majority of white Americans that their humor with its incisive commentary upon reality from the vantage point of black consciousness was not easily comprehensible to whites.... These fragile jokes ... revealed the ... agonizing difficulty of the black's situation in a way which many white contemporaries would have found difficult to fathom, or *at least difficult to fathom as humor*.[76]

Even today, the complexities of Paul D's laughter make it difficult to interpret, particularly for a white audience.

However, Sixo and Baby Suggs's laughter shed light on Paul D's. As we recall from chapter two, Schophenhauer claims that laughter stems from paradox, from the perception of incongruity.[77] To preserve sanity, Paul D must navigate the muddy waters of paradox under which both he and Sethe as ex-slaves labor. Like Sixo, Paul D laughs because he encounters paradoxical incongruity. An impossible incongruity exists between the person he knows Sethe to be—a woman who loves her children dearly—and the person slavery has caused her to become—a murderer of her children. Quite literally, Paul D cannot accept that Sethe is the murderess pictured in the newspaper clipping, as revealed in his repetition of the phrase, "That ain't her mouth" (154).

As many have said, although Beloved as the resurrection of Sethe's crime haunts the novel's pages, the infinitely more nefarious ghost that the text posits is slavery and its universally haunting legacy. For Paul D, Sethe must be one or the other—either mother or murderess. She cannot kill in order to save. Certainly, white hegemonic thought enforces this either/or distinction, because to acknowledge the situation's tragic circumstance would be tantamount to admitting society's inherent structure creates murderers out of mothers. The whites in the narrative condemn Sethe's choice and imprison her without trial. They exhibit bewilderment at her behavior and repeat the question, "What she go and do that for?" (150). Schoolteacher's nephew even compares himself to Sethe in order to conclude he would never have been capable of such an act: "The woman—something was wrong with her. . . . What she go and do that for? On account of a beating? Hell, he'd been beat a million times and he was white. . . . But no beating ever made him . . . I mean no way he could have . . . What she go and do that for?" (150). For the whites to acknowledge the situation's ambiguity would be to acknowledge their own complicity in Sethe's rough choice.

Martha Nussbaum explains that what makes a tragic situation or choice genuinely tragic is the fact that there is no right answer, no choice available that does not involve severe moral wrongdoing.[78] Lawrence Langer, writing on the Holocaust, calls these "choiceless choices."[79] Sethe has a choiceless choice: she and her children can live (and be raped, tortured, and treated like animals), or they can die (and be free but no longer alive). For Sethe, either she takes her own life and her children's lives and strikes a blow at the political economy, or she lives as a slave and is allowed no personal liberty. Nussbaum reminds us that Hegel points out the political significance of tragedy: it motivates us to imagine a society structured in such a way that choices between fundamental values and entitlements would be eliminated. Morrison's novel is political through and through. Her tragedy, like all tragedies, is a tale that must be told because it forces us as a society to ask the Hegelian question: is there a rearrangement of society's structure that could eliminate the tragic choiceless choice?

As we know, the question is not merely fictional. Historically, many slaves committed infanticide, suicide, and self-mutilation. We want to slap the facile label of insanity on such actions, because to do so allows us to overlook the systemic evil that is their breeding ground. Systemic evil is banal, whereas moral evil is striking, but only because it makes it easy to point fingers of blame away from ourselves. (We saw this again recently in the post-Katrina media obsession with "looting," rather than with the fact that 28 percent of New Orleans residents not only were starving, but lived in abject poverty even prior to the hurricane.) In my view, the slaves' actions such as suicide and infanticide, while perhaps morally objectionable, nonetheless level an aggressive, terrifying social critique. Sethe's murder of Beloved forces us to ask the tragic question: can we restructure society so that mothers would not rather kill their children than have them live in it? If the whites in the narrative really answered their own question, "what she go and do that for," they would find themselves immersed in cognitive dissonance. For the answer is: because *we* have made of her life a horror. White ideology has set up a tragic either/or decision for Sethe. Yet, whites must realize, as the slaves do, that the dichotomy is artificially inflicted and could be otherwise. Slavery could be eliminated, and human beings would not have to choose between death and death-in-life. The real choice is for a more just society, but it is eclipsed by the people's self-righteous obsession with Sethe's individual choice.

Laughter as Transformative Consciousness

Interpreting the laughter in the narrative thus helps us to interpret
Sethe's action in a more ethically and theologically sophisticated way.
The laughter of the oppressed in the story begs us to dispense with the
lens of the either/or hegemonic dichotomy, and instead to see the situation's complexity. We should interpret Sethe's choice with Paul Ricoeur's
hermeneutic of an ethics of distress, or what we might even call a tragic
ethic. The situation is not either/or, either Sethe is a good mother or she
is a terrible mother/murderer; in point of fact the situation is both-and.
Sethe is both a mother who dearly loves her children and the murderer of
those very same babies. The paradox is: she does kill her babies in order
that they may live. Rationally, this is absurd. Logically, it makes no sense.
Language cannot capture such a paradox, but laughter can because it
holds the both-and together in the one moment.

When Paul D initially leaves Sethe in horror at her actions, he
interprets her murder of Beloved in the exact same manner as white
hegemonic thought. In an exact parallel to Schoolteacher who lists
Sethe's animal characteristics, Paul D accuses Sethe of being an animal,
and behaving as if she has "four feet, not two." Yet Paul D must reclaim
his past and have his own interpretation of Sethe's actions, rather than
merely echoing the sentiment of the white dominant consciousness. Paul
D at this point fails to have the independent consciousness exhibited by
both Sixo and the early Baby Suggs. His later laughter signals his new
ownership of his black consciousness.

Morrison reveals this about Paul D through the subtle issue of his
name. The name Paul D is clearly a generic bill-of-sale name given from
the slave owners. He and the other men with him have no individual
personhood in the eyes of the whites; hence, they are all named Paul—
Paul A, Paul B, and so on. But more importantly, in spite of the fact that
Paul D has been gone from Sweet Home for several decades, when he
arrives at Bluestone Road, Denver addresses him as Mr. D. Paul D cor-
rects the girl and says, "Garner, baby. Paul D Garner." Delores Williams
explains, "Some ex-slaves kept the names they had because, in freedom,
they wanted to indicate that they had been 'raised' by quality white folk
during slavery."[80] Paul D is not to blame for this identity crisis, as Major
Jones explains:

> A part of the black man's identity problem lies in the fact that he
> has not been too sure who he was at any given moment. . . . A part
> of the dehumanizing process was to strip him of his original sense

of personhood. . . . His self-identity was to be related to that of his
master. . . . He was never sure of himself. . . . He bore no name of
his own; he had acquired the name of his master.[81]

Yet Paul D must come to realize that by keeping the name Garner, he
still allows himself to be defined, rather than strive for self-definition.

Right after Paul D laughs at Sethe's crime and just before he returns
to Sethe, Paul D runs into Denver again. In spite of having been cor-
rected the last time, Denver greets Paul D with the exact same words,
"Good morning, Mr. D." But this time Paul D does not correct her, and
merely answers, "Well, it is now" (266). Most critical literature overlooks
this small but significant moment. Paul D always believed he was a man
because Mr. Garner raised good slaves. He believed he was a valuable
person because Mr. Garner said so. But Paul D begins to realize that the
name Garner still signifies oppression: "Is that where the manhood lay?
In the naming done by a whiteman?" (125). Through the character of
Paul D, therefore, Morrison's narrative exposes the lie of benevolent slavery. Unleashing the contents of his own tobacco tin, Paul D goes through
the following thought process:

> For years Paul D believed schoolteacher broke into children what
> Garner had raised into men. And it was that that made them run
> off. Now, plagued by the contents of his tobacco tin, he wondered
> how much difference there really was between before schooteacher
> and after. Garner called and announced them men—but only on
> Sweet Home, and by his leave. Was he naming what he saw or creat-
> ing what he did not? That was the wonder of Sixo, and even Halle; it
> was always clear to Paul D that those two were men whether Garner
> said so or not. It troubled him that, concerning his own manhood,
> he could not satisfy himself on that point. . . . Suppose Garner woke
> up one morning and changed his mind? Took the word away. Would
> they have run then? . . . Why did the brothers need the one whole
> night to decide? To discuss whether they would join Sixo and Halle.
> Because they had been isolated in a wonderful lie, . . . ignorant of or
> amused by Sixo's dark stories. (220–21)

In truth, Paul D is inherently worthy of life and freedom, and not
because Mr. Garner says so. Before Paul D achieved an independent
consciousness, he allowed shame to overcome him. Whites see him as
shameful and so he feels shame. Understandably Paul D for most of his

life appropriated hegemonic thought as his own thought. Traci West notes that the shame that victims of violence experience is itself "a powerful covert weapon of domination"; as a result blacks need to struggle "against the colonizing process which teaches us forms of self-hatred."[82]

Paul D struggles throughout the narrative to rid himself of this shame and its accompanying shame that is oppression's hangover. Hopkins says that the most sinister scheme of the oppressor is to convince the oppressed that the oppressor's voice and interests are the same as the oppressed's. The results of such an internalization have tragic consequences. But fortunately, once Paul D emancipates himself from the oppressive consciousness of black blame, he comes to realize that he is not to blame for his past, nor is Sethe unambiguously to blame for hers. In the words of Audre Lorde, "The true focus of revolutionary change is never merely the oppressive situations which we seek to escape, but that piece of the oppressor which is planted deep in each of us."[83]

Paul D's release of the name Garner means he has at last triumphed over that piece of the oppressor he has internalized. Paul D reclaims and accepts both his and Sethe's painful past, which prepares him to move ahead to a future. Laughing at the oppression has helped Paul D achieve this emancipation, for Hopkins notes:

> Joking fosters a leveling of the apparent omnipotence of the monopolizers of divine creation. When the exploiter is laughed at, he or she can be better seen as just another human being and not some type of demi-god to be feared sheepishly and automatically by the least in society. The very process of laughing . . . helps to alleviate the insanity of being victimized by abuse. Thus one continues down the path of co-constituting the new self.[84]

Not coincidentally, Paul D liberates himself from the pain of the past at the same time the community exorcizes Beloved from 124 Bluestone Road. Beloved's exorcism therefore at least in part symbolizes Paul D's transformation in consciousness. Delores Williams explains that a transformation of consciousness is when oppressed people arrive at self or group identity through a newly acquired awareness of self-worth and appreciation of their own community. Paul D's laughter symbolizes that this transformation of consciousness has transpired—previously he could only wish that he could laugh along with Sixo. Confused about his identity, Paul D previously could not share in Sixo's emotional and psychological liberation and resistance. But once he is free enough in his mind to laugh at oppression and its absurd repercussions, Paul D is empowered and liberated from his former days of being a walking man with a tobacco tin heart. Paul D's laughter thus signifies that a certain *metanoia*, or conversion, has occurred in his thought and psyche. Writes Hopkins, "To be free calls for the oppressed to think they are free. . . . Part of preparing for this struggle and participating in it demands a radical *metanoia* (or conversion) of the thought processes of those at the bottom of society. One of the greatest chains with which oppression enslaves the oppressed is the chain around the *mind* of the marginalized."[85]

American philosopher Kenneth Burke explains that a purpose of humor is to attain maximum consciousness, both of self and of others.[86] Humor enables us to grow in self-awareness. With his "humor," Paul D emancipates himself from the chains of the dominant consciousness. Cone remarks, "For the slaves, their consciousness is defined by masters and rulers. . . . The victims of such attitudes have only two alternatives: 1) to accept the oppressors' value system and thus be contented with the place set for them by others or 2) to find a completely new way of looking at reality that enables them to fight against oppression."[87] For Paul D, the lens of risibility enables him to construe another reality with a self-defined consciousness.

Paul D's joking about the system that has turned the kind-hearted Sethe into a monster who would kill anyone white who entered her sphere of vision, including her own mailman, articulates a criticism against such a system. Previously, Paul D misdirected this critique and unwittingly appropriated the white consciousness by accusing Sethe of having "two feet not four," the very same dehumanizing characteristic Schoolteacher had ascribed to her. Once Paul D laughs and returns to Sethe, however, we see that he has jettisoned his internalized perception of Sethe as animallike in her murder, thereby abandoning the white consciousness. In the end, Sethe asks Paul D if he has come back to her to "count her feet"; Paul D replies, "Rub your feet" (272).

With a laugh, Paul D takes his judgment and anger toward Sethe and redirects it toward white society. This redirection exactly parallels Sethe's attempt to stab the white man rather than her own child the second time around. Henri Bergson argues that laughter is inversionary, that is, it trivializes or degrades "ideas and personages normally held to be lofty or noble, and the advancement of those normally consigned to an inferior or inconsequential position."[88] While the dominant consciousness degrades Sethe, laughter turns this thought on its head. Paul D's laughter unmasks the system as absurd, as laughable.

Freud explains, "Tendentious jokes are especially favored in order to make aggressiveness or criticism possible against persons in exalted positions who claim to exercise authority. The joke then represents a rebellion against that authority, a liberation from its pressure."[89] Paul D's laughter interrupts the system of oppression. It strikes a blow at the status quo by rebelling against its absurdity. More importantly, it liberates Paul D from his own shame that enables him to return to the woman he loves without judging her in the same way he has judged himself for so long. To quote Levine, Paul D's unexpected joke illustrates the ethical resistance in African American humor:

> Jokes about . . . forms of racial violence illustrate [that] . . . humor . . . is not resigned; it is rebellious and signifies the victory of the ego which refuses to be hurt by the arrow of adversity and instead attempts to become impervious to the wounds dealt it by the outside world. [In black humor] . . . the outer world was reduced to pygmy proportions, the situation was dwarfed, and the joke-tellers and their audiences were allowed to set aside, or at least to minimize, the pain and defeat imposed upon them by the external world.[90]

In short, Paul D's laughter frees him for a future his oppressors sought to deny him.

In the end, Paul D finds genuine liberation, the kind that Sixo and Baby Suggs experienced only proleptically. Along the way to liberation and freedom, Paul D follows the "tree flowers" in order to find his way north. Throughout the story, Morrison uses the trope of flowers to symbolically represent the flourishing of this incongruous form of protesting hope, which can lead to survival. Baby Suggs, for example, puts flowers in her hat that dark day Schoolteacher comes for Sethe: "She cut through a stalk of insistent rue. Its flowers she stuck through a split in her hat" (138). Another name for rue, interestingly, is "herb of grace," and grace for Baby was a sign of a protesting hope's flourishing. Sethe, at Sweet Home, similarly brought a fistful of flowers into Mrs. Garner's kitchen everyday, "just to be able to work in it, feel like some part of it was hers, to take the ugly out of it" (22). And finally, the dead child Beloved asks her sister Denver, "Are there flowers in the dark?" (121).

A belief that flowers can grow in the dark is irrational, impossible, absurd; much as Baby Suggs's, Sixo's, and Paul D's faith in liberation in the midst of enslavement and horror is paradoxical, irrational, and absurd. Surely, both beliefs are laughable to many. However, the text tells us Beloved's question is rightly answered in the affirmative—flowers do bloom in the dark, Denver "adds sticks to the stovefire and assures her there are." And Paul D, having followed the flowers along his twisted path to freedom, returns finally to Sethe and 124, only to be "amazed by the riot of late-summer flowers" (121). Throughout the narrative, laughter testifies to the existence of such flowers, even though they are not yet fully allowed into the light. When Paul D laughs and returns to Sethe, it is because he rediscovers the possibility of a future.

In conclusion, Paul D, much like Gavriel and Rodrigues, endures the paradox of existence by allowing the narrative of slavery's past tragedy to remain in conflict and unresolved tension with the narrative of future hope. In what we can interpret as a final act of resistance, perhaps the most poignant of the novel, Paul D asks for Sethe's permission to place his "story next to hers" (273). Laughter seems to have shown Paul D that one cannot reconcile the narratives of memory and hope, nor does one need to do so in order to survive. When Sethe thinks that Paul D wants her to choose between Denver and him—that is, choose between past and future narratives, Paul D responds, "I'm not asking you to choose. . . . It's not about choosing somebody over her—it's making space for somebody along with her" (45). Morrison, like Wiesel, seems to suggest that for some horrors, no genuine answer is possible. Also like Wiesel, however, she suggests that creating a space for the juxtaposition of narratives opens up the possibility of an in-spite-of future.

What is possible, in other words, is Paul D's proposal that Paul D and Sethe not only juxtapose their past and future narratives, but also that they juxtapose each of their respective narratives, one with another. Paul D knows that the future, however hopeful, can never negate the past. But in contrast to Baby Suggs, he also affirms that the past should equally never negate the possibility of a future, " 'Sethe,' he says, 'me and you, we got more yesterday than anybody. We need some kind of tomorrow' " (273). Paul D thus leaves us with a strange twist on Surin: love *intentionally* takes the disparate narratives of two people—narratives often in conflict and ravaged by contingency—and simultaneously affirms the identity and integrity of both, without prioritizing one over the other.

Morrison's novel reminds us that where there is rupture and pain, love can still create solidarity and beauty without negating or denying rupture. Wiesel and Endo both share Morrison's implicit conclusion that a juxtaposition of narratives shares the burden of suffering, even if this suffering remains unredeemed and inexplicable. Endo writes that Rodrigues, who has juxtaposed his narrative with both Kichijiro's and

Christ's, discovers that a "sense of suffering shared softly eased his heart and mind more than the sweetest water."[91] Similarly, Wiesel writes in *Gates*, "You say, 'I'm alone.' Some one answers, 'I'm alone too.' . . . A bridge is thrown between the two abysses. . . . We are alone, yes, but inside this solitude we are brothers."[92] In the end, all three authors redefine love as a resistant mode-of-being that juxtaposes another person's narrative, however shattered and broken, alongside one's own and refuses to let go. Christian theology and ethics, as they struggle to make *agape* and social justice real in the real world of conflicting narratives, should heed these insightful authors' injunction to listen to one another, to affirm the integrity of other people's narratives, and to place these narratives next to our own. The laughter of the oppressed cries hear us! Hear our stories! Do we hear?

Notes

1. I am grateful to Dr. James Cone, who pointed out to me this significant quote from Malcolm X in Peter Goldman, *The Death and Life of Malcolm X* (Urbana: University of Illinois Press, 1973), 24–25.

2. Quoted in Gurleen Grewal, *Circles of Sorrow, Lines of Struggle: The Novels of Toni Morrison* (Baton Rouge: Louisiana State University Press, 1998), 98.

3. Quoted in Grewal, *Circles of Sorrow*, 98.

4. Albert J. Raboteau, *Slave Religion: The "Invisible Institution" in the Antebellum South* (Oxford: Oxford University Press, 1978), 212, 213.

5. Dwight Hopkins and George Cummings, eds., *Cut Loose Your Stammering Tongue: Black Theology in Slave Narratives* (Maryknoll, NY: Orbis, 1991), 152.

6. See Dwight Hopkins, *Down, Up and Over: Slave Religion and Black Theology* (Minneapolis: Fortress Press, 2000).

7. Hopkins and Cummings, *Cut Loose*, 41.

8. Hopkins, *Down, Up and Over*, 138.

9. See Delores Williams, *Sisters of the Wilderness: The Challenge of Womanist God-Talk* (Maryknoll, NY: Orbis, 1993).

10. Patrick Bascio, *The Failure of White Theology: A Black Theological Perspective* (New York: Peter Lang, 1994), 67.

11. Henri Bergson, *Laughter: An Essay on the Meaning of the Comic* (New York: MacMillan, 1913), 94. Quoted in Cheryl Sanders, ed., *Living the Intersection: Womanism and Afrocentrism in Theology* (Minneapolis, MN: Fortress Press, 1995), 99.

12. Hopkins and Cummings, *Cut Loose*, 31.

13. James Cone, *A Black Theology of Liberation* (Maryknoll, NY: Orbis, 1986), 12–13.

14. James Cone, *The Spirituals and the Blues* (Maryknoll, NY: Orbis, 1972), 16, 33.

15. Kelly Brown Douglas, *The Black Christ* (Maryknoll, NY: Orbis, 1994), 10.

16. James Cone, *God of the Oppressed* (Minneapolis: Seabury Press, 1975), 2, 5.

17. Nietzsche, *Thus Spoke Zarathustra*, 144.

18. Ibid., 315.

19. Cone, *Black Theology of Liberation*, 15.

20. Collins, *Black Feminist Thought*, 5, 28.

21. Kelly Brown Douglas, *The Black Christ* (Maryknoll, NY: Orbis, 1994), 105.

22. Quoted in Collins, *Black Feminist Thought*, 26.

23. Cone, *Spirituals and the Blues*, 90–91.

24. Ibid., 5.

25. Paul Ricoeur, *Figuring the Sacred: Religion, Narrative, and Imagination*, ed. Mark I. Wallace, trans. David Pellauer (Minneapolis: Augsburg, 1995), 76, 82.

26. Danille Taylor-Guthrie, ed., *Conversations with Toni Morrison* (Jackson: Mississippi University Press, 1994), 8.

27. Quoted in Bascio, *Failure of White Theology*, 120.

28. Surin, "Taking Suffering Seriously," 344.

29. Cone, *Spirituals and the Blues*, 135.

30. Ibid., 68.

31. Hopkins, *Down, Up and Over*, 2.

32. Ibid., 3.

33. Toni Morrison, *Playing in the Dark: Whiteness and the Literary Imagination* (Cambridge, MA: Harvard University Press, 1992), x–xi.

34. Quoted in Collins, *Black Feminist Thought*, 69, 34.

35. Cheryl Townsend Gilkes, *If It Wasn't for the Women: Black Women's Experience and Womanist Culture in Church and Community* (Maryknoll, NY: Orbis, 2001), 144.

36. Hopkins and Cummings, *Cut Loose*, 37.

37. Taylor-Guthrie, *Conversations with Toni Morrison*, 126.

38. Cone, *Spirituals and the Blues*, 26.

39. Collins, *Black Feminist Theology*, 227.

40. Moltmann, *Theology of Play*, 14.

41. Susan Corey, "The Religious Dimensions of the Grotesque in Literature: Toni Morrison's *Beloved*," in *The Grotesque in Art and Literature*, edited by James Luther Adams and William Yates (Grand Rapids: Eerdmans, 1997), 229.

42. Taylor-Guthrie, *Conversations with Toni Morrison*, 180.

43. Cone, *Black Theology of Liberation*, 16.

44. Corey, "Religious Dimensions," 229, 230.

45. Quoted in Morreal, *Philosophy of Laughter and Humor*, 52–54, 55.

46. Quoted in Goldman, *Death and Life of Malcolm X*, 24–25.

47. Quoted in Major Jones, *Black Awareness: A Theology of Hope* (Nashville: Abingdon, 1971), 65.

48. Cone, *Spirituals and the Blues*, 21.

49. Collins, *Black Feminist Theology*, 68.

50. Ibid.

51. Ibid., 225.

52. Elie Wiesel states, "Ambiguity is the name of our sickness, of everybody's sickness. What are we looking for in life, in existence, in history, in our own being? For the One to do away with ambiguity." See Cargas, *In Conversation with Elie Wiesel*, 18.

53. Quoted in Douglas, *Black Christ*, 59.

54. Cone, *Black Theology of Liberation*, 11.

55. Quoted in ibid., 88.

56. Taylor-Guthrie, *Conversations with Toni Morrison*, 19.

57. Cone, *Spirituals and the Blues*, 28.

58. Ibid., 235.

59. Cornel West, *Prophesy Deliverance!: An Afro-American Revolutionary Christianity* (Philadelphia: Westminster, 1982), 152.

60. Elie Wiesel, *Four Hasidic Masters and Their Struggle with Melancholy* (Notre Dame, IN: University of Notre Dame Press, 1978), 123.

61. Ekkehard Schuster and Reinhold Boscher-Kimmig, *Hope Against Hope: Johann Baptist Metz and Elie Wiesel Speak Out on the Holocaust*, trans. J. Matthew Ashley (New York: Paulist Press, 1962), 95.

62. Quoted in Kelly Brown Douglas, *Sexuality and the Black Church* (Maryknoll, NY: Orbis, 1999), 20.

63. Albert J. Raboteau, *Slave Religion: The Invisible Institution in the Antebellum South* (Oxford: Oxford University Press, 1978), 248–49.

64. Cone, *God of the Oppressed*, 13.

65. Hopkins, *Down, Up and Over*, 256.

66. Quoted in ibid., 271.

67. West, *Prophesy Deliverance!*, 151.

68. Bakhtin, *Rabelais and His World*, 20–21.

69. Cone, *Spirituals and the Blues*, 24.

70. Hopkins, *Down, Up and Over*, 128.

71. Williams, *Sisters in the Wilderness*, 136.

72. Taylor-Guthrie, *Conversations with Toni Morrison*, 241, 247.

73. Ibid., 175.

74. Lawrence W. Levine, *Black Culture and Black Consciousness: Afro-American Folk Thought From Slavery to Freedom* (Oxford: Oxford University Press, 1977), 314, 338.

75. Ibid., 320. See also 359.

76. Ibid., 313, italics mine.

77. Quoted in Morreal, *The Philosophy of Laughter and Horror*, 54–55.

78. All of Nussbaum's comments in this paragraph come from a public lecture delivered by Nussbaum at the University of Virginia, Charlottesville, entitled "Tragedy and Cost-Benefit Analysis," September 13, 2000.

79. Lawrence Langer, *Versions of Survival: The Holocaust and the Human Spirit* (Albany, NY: SUNY Press, 1982), 72.

80. Williams, *Sisters in the Wilderness*, 76.

81. Jones, *Black Awareness*, 63–64.

82. Traci West, *Wounds of the Spirit: Black Women, Violence, and Resistance Ethics* (New York: NYU Press, 1999), 75.

83. Quoted in Collins, *Black Feminist Theology*, 229.

84. Hopkins, *Down, Up and Over*, 255.

85. Ibid., 246.

86. Quoted in Levine, *Black Culture*, 321.

87. Cone, *God of the Oppressed*, 33.

88. Quoted in Levine, *Black Culture*, 300.

89. Freud, *Jokes*, 125.

90. Levine, *Black Culture*, 343.

91. Endo, *Silence*, 99.

92. Wiesel, *Gates of the Forest* (New York: Schocken, 1966), 177, 193.

Conclusion:
Toward a Theology of Laughter

"Theology is born of imagination yoked to the service of life."
—Miguel De Unamuno, *Tragic Sense of Life*

Now that Christian theology has at long last opened its ears to the laughter of the oppressed, it is time to use what we have heard to construct an informed theology of laughter. Faith and laughter are inextricably intertwined, and this interrelationship summons us to reflect further on the creative potential of a theology of laughter. While we can no longer simply say with Augustine, Chrysostom, and Niebuhr that laughter is always blasphemous, derisive, and inessential to faith, we still need to summarize our answer to the question, what has Christian theology learned from the laughter of the oppressed about tragedy, theodicy, faith, and even theology itself? For laughter informs our understanding of theology's undertaking, as surely as theology informed our understanding of laughter. Five preliminary characteristics of a theology of laughter emerge.

1. *Faith and hope are paradoxical and proleptic.* First, a theology of laughter increases our consciousness of faith and hope, post-*Shoah*, post-slavery, post-Hiroshima, as inherently paradoxical. As our analysis of laughter in extremis shows, the narrative of faith perennially collides with the narrative of empirical, historical reality. This collision is so absurd in its incongruity of narratives as to evoke our laughter. To add to Tertullian, we not only believe, but laugh, because ontologically our life (and death) is often absurd. In the words of German theologian Helmut

Thielicke, "The absolute is always on the edge of ridiculousness when it collides with the contingent."[1] Spanish philosopher and poet Miguel de Unamuno states, "Athanasius had the supreme audacity of faith, that of asserting things mutually contradictory. . . . Reason . . . laughs at my faith and despises it."[2] Unamuno deems grasping this paradoxical collision between faith and reality as possession of a tragic sense of life, but a sense upon which hope not only can, but must be built. And so, faith is born of the very stuff that also engenders laughter—contradiction, incongruity, and paradox. Theology must confess the incongruity of its own endeavors. To do so helps theology maintain its necessary humility, as a set of questions rather than purely a set of answers.

A theology of laughter exposes the fact that faith is contrarational or metaempirical, to use Unamuno's and Peter Berger's terms, respectively.[3] Theology undoubtedly fears the label "irrational." However, I would argue that this fear owes in large part to theology's misunderstanding of the nature of evil. Theology should not be ashamed of its contrarational status, because evil, unless we are complicit with it, resists rational thought and comprehension. Epistemologically speaking, to live by reason alone would mean a refusal to acknowledge both evil and theology's appropriate metaempirical response to evil: hope. A theology of hope must be the counterpart of a theology of laughter.

For hope, too, can be classified as metaempirical if not paradoxical. Hope, which lies at the center of theology, is by definition at least somewhat incongruous with reality. Writes Unamuno,

> Tragedy [is] . . . is the expression of a conflict between what the world is as scientific reason shows it to be, and what we wish that it might be, as our religious faith affirms it to be. . . . In the depths of the abyss, the despair of the heart and of the will and of the skepticism of reason meet face to face and embrace like brothers. . . . It is from this embrace, this tragic . . . embrace, that the wellspring of life will flow, a life serious and terrible. . . . It is despair and despair alone that begets heroic hope, absurd hope, mad hope. *Spero quia absurdam*, it ought to have been said, rather than *credo*.[4]

For Unamuno, life is a conflict between two narratives: the narrative of reason and reality and the narrative of faith, the narrative of facts and the narrative of longing. This collision can lead to despair or hope, but when it leads to hope, that hope is heroic but appears to many eyes as madness. We hope because it is absurd.

Faith itself is paradoxical, then, because it espouses hope as one of its foundational tenets. In Christian theology, hope is based on promise, and Jürgen Moltmann explains:

> If the word is a word of promise, then that means that this word has not yet found a reality congruous with it, but that on the contrary it stands in contradiction to the reality open to experience now and heretofore. It is only for that reason that the word of promise can give rise to doubt that measures the word by the standard of reality [and] to the faith that measures the present reality by the standard of the word.[5]

Hope itself, then, as Moltmann points out, is based on a contradictory juxtaposition of the narrative of faith and the narrative of reality. In the words of contemporary liberal evangelical writer and political activist Jim Wallis, "Hope is believing in spite of the evidence, then watching the evidence change."[6]

For Christianity, however, these two narratives' point of collision is the cross of Christ. The cross reminds us that Christian theology should not shy away from contradiction but instead inquire into the fruitfulness and meaningfulness of such contradictions. Christian hope is therefore paradoxical in that it is simultaneously congruous (with the incarnation) and incongruous (with much of empirical reality and historical experience).

A theology of laughter insists that Christian hope both fractures narratives of suffering and negativity and is fractured *by* such confrontations. Hope is congruous with the reality of the incarnation, yet Christian hope acknowledges the proleptic and therefore fragmentary nature of its narrative of redemption. A theology of laughter affirms that redemption's "already" aspect is as real as redemption's "not yet." A theology of laughter underscores the fact that the not-yet, in-spite-of character of our hope is excruciating, yet hope is not to be relinquished.

Living in hope thus means living proleptically, living in the "not yet" in order to actualize and create a world congruous with it. To use Ernst Bloch's terms, hope means living in accordance with an "anticipatory consciousness."[7] A euphemistic synonym for contrarational might then be imaginative. As Karl Barth once said, a person without an imagination is like a person who lacks a leg—the same is true for theologians.[8] Theology is not irrational but imaginative, in British philosopher Mary Warnock's sense of seeing-as.[9] A theology of laughter sees the world as what it genuinely is if *everyone's* life-story, including that of the marginal-ized, is taken into account; it sees the world as a place of radical cruelty and pain as well as a place of radical beauty and redemption.

Theology's task, therefore, is to imaginatively live by and sustain the word of promise even in the face of its ostensible negation. Through the lives of the characters Sixo, Gavriel, and Rodrigues, Morrison, Wiesel, and Endo all suggest that living by logic alone in liminal situations, without any form of anticipatory consciousness, results in despair if not annihilation. These authors depict the laughter of the disempowered and suffering as promethean. If Sixo, or any member of the African American community for that matter, had waited around for someone to offer him an alternative consciousness rather than creatively constructing one, Morrison implies that he would have died moaning rather than laughing.

Likewise, theology should be unafraid to be promethean. A theology of laughter teaches us that theology should not fear the scandal of mak-ing affirmations that contradict the dominant consciousness. After all, the laughter of the oppressed does just that. Phenomenologically, much about the world and our lives defies rationality, and faith and reason, it must be confessed with Martin Luther, are often locked in combative embrace, laughing one at the other. The narratives of faith and reason are, though they often intersect, in paradoxical conflict, and no end is in sight for their wrestling. As our analysis of Wiesel reminds us, however, creative think-ing climbs on the giant shoulders of logical rationalism in order to glimpse redemption through the clouds of catastrophe.[10] Theology should exhibit just such creative thinking, and recall moreover that almost all creative thought contains elements of the contrarational, and that is its peculiar strength. Theology should strive to offer an imaginative, transformative mode-of-being-in-the-world to those who will listen.

2. *Theology needs to avoid dichotomous thought.* Second and relat-edly, a theology of laughter eschews dichotomous thought, and, with Athanasius, is unafraid of the scandal of both-and assertions. It reminds us that theology, in order to be true to laughter and faith, must embrace and express the both-and character of human experience. Theologians of laughter remind us that human beings are *simul justus et peccator*, the divine is both absent and present, redemption is both already and not-yet, and life is both horror and love. Theologians of laughter listen to the oppressed persons of faith who cry out for our recognition of what they describe as the "doubleness" of their experience as both children of God and the rejected of humanity. A theology of laughter in this way recognizes and holds in awesome wonder the deep complexity of

human experience. A theology of laughter sets the narratives of promise and rejection side-by-side and demands that both narratives be told and retold as well as heard and reheard. In short, a theology of laughter affirms the constructive value of juxtapositions. In so doing, theology does more than pay lip service to diversity; instead, it celebrates otherness with a steadfast refusal to conflate diverse experiences into a false synthesis.

A theology of laughter deconstructs either/or thinking and unmasks its potential to be either unrepresentative of experience and reality or worse, ideological. Endo's and Morrison's works, for example, show us that polarizing thought masks a hegemonic consciousness. A theology of laughter recognizes that dichotomous thought is usually sin—a grasping after power and placement of ourselves on the "righteous" side of the dichotomy. This revolutionary insight grants theology not only the freedom but also the responsibility to reject either/or thought, along with its concomitant conscious or unconscious desire to dominate others. The "us" vs. "them" mentality pervades world history and is used even today on the international political scene to legitimate violence, terrorism, and war in all corners of the globe. Even here at home, the "United" States are divided into red and blue states. A theology of laughter, following the thought of Martin Luther King Jr., rejects these "us-them" distinctions as false dichotomies, because "an element of goodness may be found even in our worst enemy. . . . There is some good in the worst of us and some evil in the best of us."[11] For theologians of laughter, Christ's death on the cross shatters the pernicious "us-them" dichotomy that lies at the heart of anti-Semitism, racism, misogyny, nationalism, hate, and genocide.

Theologians of laughter insist that theology can and should think creatively and subversively, providing an alternative consciousness to collide with the dominant consciousness when necessary. To put it simply, theology should not disinherit its scriptural legacy of prophetic critique. A theology of laughter does not back down from the claim that the existence of the faithful is indeed a curious admixture of hope and anguish, violence and blessing, exile and presence, negativity and promise. A theology of laughter, in other words, strives to master the fine art of "zusammendinken," thinking together frames of reference that are habitually opposed.[12] A theology of laughter remembers the definition of genius widely attributed to Einstein: one who sustains two contradictory thoughts at once. People of faith, therefore, are called to be geniuses. Dichotomous thought stands in need of an interruption, and a theology of laughter, unsilenced as it is by paradox and the task of *zusammendinken*, stands in a unique position to provide such an interruption.

3. *Christian theology should sustain a commitment to theological honesty.* Third, a theology of laughter insists on the virtue and necessity of theological honesty vis-à-vis the problem of evil and the provisional nature of all theological statements. In this way, a theology of laughter acknowledges the problematic of human finitude. A theology of laughter upholds a hermeneutics of suspicion with regard to answers and claims of conclusiveness with regard to the problems of evil and human suffering. A theology of laughter shows us that Christian thought cannot afford to ignore Friedrich Nietzsche's critique, "If you should wish to emerge out of this insufficiency of Christianity, then ponder the experience of two millennia: which, clothed in the modesty of the question, speaks thus, 'If Christ really intended to redeem the world, must he not be said to have failed?'"[13] Religious faith as well as reason, in short, are wounded and fractured by the litany of atrocities we call history, and particularly the twentieth century. Even what little of the twenty-first century we have experienced has been filled with war, poverty, natural disasters, genocide in the Sudan, and discussions of the Christian legitimacy of torture, to name only a few. Theology refuses to acknowledge these painful aspects of human life to its own detriment, as to do so leads thinkers like Nietzsche to abandon theology in disgust at its unwillingness to confront its own limitations.

A theology of laughter underscores the fact that theology must incorporate Nietzsche's critique into itself in order to speak to the modern and postmodern human experience. Theologians of laughter must ask themselves the grim question: how do we dare speak of redemption in a world that is obviously so unredeemed? Taking a cue from Nietzsche, we theologians must realize that if we are not honest about the grim picture of humanity painted by history, then we condemn theology to irrelevance. Yet neither can despair be theology's answer. If the popular works of Wiesel, Endo, and Morrison are any indication, the problems of evil and the unanswerability of human suffering are paramount concerns for culture and its "everyday" theologians and ethicists—that is, real people struggling to live real lives amidst cancer, terrorism, hurricanes, war, racism, sexism, oppression, suffering, death, murder, and everything else covered on the nightly news.[14]

Aspiring to the virtue of theological honesty, a theology of laughter confesses its own inadequacies, and endeavors to sustain a hermeneutics of rupture. This is necessary because a theology of laughter reveals that history has ruptured language, human relationships, and theology itself.

Modern events such as the Holocaust have rendered us strangers to God, one another, and even ourselves. Theology should not disavow the crisis of representation to which all three works discussed here attest. Theology must concede, with Hannah Arendt, that horrors happen that are soul-destroying. In response to Toni Morrison and Nietzsche, theology must confess that egregious history has ruptured our faith in humanity and our understanding of our ethical and moral capabilities, "We are . . . illogical and thus unjust beings and can recognize this: this is one of the greatest and most irresolvable discords of existence."[15] Similarly, with Wiesel, Endo, and others, post-*Shoah* Christian thought must admit that historical happenings fracture God-language and language itself. The laughter of the oppressed reveals that in spite of these ruptures, conduits of protest, resistance, and hope remain to those who creatively construct them. A theology of laughter asserts that possibilities, many of them transformative though counterintuitive, abound within contingency and tragedy. A theology of laughter reminds us that evil must always be recognized, but it also must equally be resisted and condemned.

As final part and parcel of honesty, a theology of laughter attests to the worthiness, yet provisional and fragmentary nature of all theological statements and doctrines. A theology of laughter, ruptured as it is by col-lisional narratives, can only claim to have told the "whole truth" in so far as it reveals this truth to be baffling, ambiguous, and self-contradictory. A theology of laughter therefore creates a new space within theology for reconsidering the work and importance of critical doubt as an element within faith. In doing so, theology leaves room for both historical experience and for God. A theology of laughter invites theology to consider itself open and dialogical, and therefore willing to juxtapose its own narrative and doctrines with any and all counternarratives the world's future and God have to offer.

4. *Theology should confess the problematic of a theology of suffering.* A theology of laughter suggests that if Christian theology truly hears the voices of Morrison, Endo, and Wiesel and learns from this dialectical engagement with culture, Christian theology must overcome its proclivity to legitimate human suffering. Christian theology must jettison its rose-colored glasses and look instead to the paradoxical scandal of the cross of Christ. Rationalizing pain and suffering in the name of providence or otherworldly redemption not only alienates many suffering persons from the Christian faith, but also cripples post-Holocaust Jewish-Christian dialogue and impedes active resistance to social injustice. Christian theology must speak out against those who would use its tenets inappropriately to

construe a theology of suffering in which human suffering is interpreted as always necessary and redemptive. The cross in the twenty-first century must no longer be used to justify hegemony, oppression, or quietism. A theology of laughter remembers that even thoughtlessness is a sin for which we must seek forgiveness. A theology of laughter dictates that Christian theology must become repentant as well as responsible for all that has been done and will be done in its name.

Taking its cue from the laughter of the oppressed, Christian theology should sustain an interpretation of suffering as unsolvable mystery, just as surely as it sustains an understanding of love as impossible possibility. In the words of Unamuno, whom all three authors echo, theology should remember that "the only mystery really mysterious is the mystery of suffering."[16] Theologians, in order to do theology well, need to hear the testimony of those in pain and victimized by violence in any form. A theology of laughter resists the perennial danger of domesticating negativity with a disingenuous sleight-of-hand. A theology of laughter considers the problem of evil with utmost seriousness, and always sustains the narrative of hope only in juxtaposition and tension with the memory of radical suffering. Theologians such as James Cone who successfully bridge the gap between everyday theology and academic theology repeatedly make this claim. A theology of laughter underscores Cone's words, "There is no answer that faith can give for suffering that removes its contradiction. Faith in Christ therefore does not explain evil, it empowers us to fight against evil."[17] A theology of laughter reminds us that for every testimony to the power of evil, we must in the same breath testify to the power of resistance in the face of that evil. Such a reading of history transforms history into a place of hope. A theology of laughter's attention to stories of resistance reminds me of something I always tell my students when I teach the Holocaust: the only thing as incredible as the atrocities committed by human beings against one another are the selfless, kenotic acts of resistance committed by human beings on behalf of one another. Such is the mystery of human life.

Understanding suffering in this way generates within theology an increased consciousness of the need for solidarity, compassion, and genuine listening amidst the altarity and diversity of human narratives. Comprehending the fragility of goodness, promise, and justice in the face of radical negativity need not fill us with resignation. Such an understanding can just as surely make us more, and not less, willing to strive for the fulfillment of these longings for God and God's justice. Indeed, a genuine understanding of radical contingency summons us to an even

greater consciousness of ethical and moral responsibility and account-
ability. As Moltmann has said:

> This may sound like a contradiction but is in fact an inescapable
> correlation. Only those who are capable of joy can feel pain at
> their own and other people's suffering. A man [*sic*] who can laugh
> can also weep. . . . Where freedom is near, the chains begin to
> hurt. Where the Kingdom of God is at hand, we feel the abyss of
> God-forsakenness.[18]

In short, remembering suffering as enigma helps prevent theology from
becoming platitudinous.

    5. *Theology must acknowledge the limits of theodicy.* Fifth and finally, a
theology of laughter unveils the potential failure of theodicy. In the face
of radical suffering that has ruptured traditional frameworks of thought
and belief, a theology of laughter confesses that theodicy too has become
for many an impossible possibility. Though traditional theology tends
to absolutize its knowledge, a theology of laughter is unafraid to sometimes concede ignorance on this side of the eschaton. The divine's ways,
a theology of laughter suggests, cannot always be justified, at least for the
time being and not by finite human thought. Nonetheless, as Moltmann
says, hope is possible, as long as it is indissolubly coupled with the most
intensive sense of reality. Fusing the world and God is no easy task, and
theology must realize that theodicy is not the only way to sustain this
fusion. As Wiesel has shown, arguing with God and lamenting God's ways
does not entail an abandonment of the divine-human relationship, but a
legitimate means of upholding it. Judaism grants this legacy to Christianity, but all too often Christianity has returned this gift unopened.

    A theology of laughter insists that a justification or legitimization of
the empirical state of the world is not necessary in order for life, theology,
and the divine-human relationship to continue and attain meaningfulness.
Knowledge does not always bring joy. Faith, for a theology of laughter,
always maintains an awareness of its in-spite-of character. In spite of evil,
a theology of laughter joyously affirms a bond between God and world
while admitting all the while that such a bond is paradoxical, raising more
questions than it answers. In so far as theodicy does not acknowledge its
own incapability fully to overcome the problem of evil, theodicy must be
abandoned as an affront to the real memory of suffering.

    In the end, a theology of laughter coalesces with contemporary
philosopher and Holocaust scholar John Roth's notion of a theodicy of

protest. A theology of laughter, in other words, asks us to take up with Roth a position of antitheodicy that acknowledges the incomprehensibility of suffering yet encourages us to continue the fight of resistance. With Roth, a theology of laughter urges us to transform our otherwise Nietzschean dissent and anger at the world's lack of redemption into a religious response:

> A protesting theodicy . . . supposes that human life is always under siege. All gains are precarious, periodic, and problematic. . . . Yet the human prospect is not hopeless, nor is it without reasons for joy and thanksgiving. In fact, that prospect can be enhanced to the degree that the widespread experience of despair is turned on itself to yield a spirit of dissent. . . . God's promises call for protests.[19]

Notes

1. Quoted in Peter Berger, *Redeeming Laughter: The Comic Dimension of Human Experience* (New York: Walter de Gruyter, 1997), 194.

2. Miguel de Unamuno, *Tragic Sense of Life* (New York: Dover Publications, 1954), 292.

3. Berger, *Redeeming Laughter*, 210; Unamuno, 198.

4. Ibid., 324.

5. Jürgen Moltmann, *Theology of Hope* (Minneapolis: Fortress Press, 1967), 103–4.

6. Quoted in Paul Rogat Loeb, ed., *The Impossible Will Take a Little While: A Citizen's Guide to Hope in a Time of Fear* (New York: Basic Books, 2004), 5.

7. See Ernst Bloch, *The Principle of Hope*, 3 vols. (Cambridge, MA: MIT Press, 1986).

8. Karl Barth, *Church Dogmatics*, vol. 3.1 (Edinburgh: T & T Clark, 1958), 91.

9. See Mary Warnock, *Imagination* (Berkeley: University of California Press, 1976).

10. Mordechai Rotenberg, *Dialogue with Deviance: The Hasidic Ethic and the Theory of Social Contraction* (Lanham, MD: University Press of America, 1993), 177, 173.

11. Martin Luther King Jr., *Strength to Love* (Philadelphia: Fortress Press, 1963), 51.

12. Arthur Koestler asserts *zusammendinken* is the goal of humor; we say the same for a theology of laughter. See Berger, *Redeeming Laughter*, 61.

13. Friedrich Nietzsche, *Human, All Too Human: A Book for Free Spirits* (Cambridge: Cambridge University Press, 1986), 235.

14. As a theologian of laughter, I am amazed by the immense popularity of comedian Jon Stewart's mock news, *The Daily Show*. Increasing numbers of my students tell me that they rely on the show for their knowledge of the news, though of course they realize it is a comedy. *The Daily Show* website states, "The Emmy and Peabody Award–winning Daily Show takes a reality-based look at news, trends, pop culture, current events, politics, sports and entertainment with an alternative point of view. . . . *The Daily Show with*

Jon Stewart—it's even better than being informed." How is it "better" than simply being informed? Do *The Daily Show*'s viewers feel politically disempowered, and therefore cannot swallow the bitter pill of the news and our world's tragedies without Stewart's coating of laughter-as-resistance?

15. Nietzsche, *Human, All Too Human,* 28.

16. Unamuno, *Tragic Sense of Life,* 140.

17. James Cone, *My Soul Looks Back* (Nashville: Abingdon, 1982), 63.

18. Moltmann, *Theology of Play,* 31.

19. John K. Roth, "A Theodicy of Protest," in *Encountering Evil: Life Options in Theodicy,* ed. Stephen Davis (Atlanta: John Knox Press, 1981), 15, 17.

Bibliography

Adams, Hazard, ed. *Critical Theory Since Plato*. New York: Harcourt Brace, 1992.

Adorno, Theodor. *Aesthetic Theory*. Edited by Gretal Adorno and Rolf Tiedemann. Translated by C. Lenhardt. Boston: Routledge and Kegan Paul, 1984.

_____. *Negative Dialectics*. Translated by E. B. Ashton. New York: Continuum, 1966.

Arendt, Hannah. *Eichmann in Jerusalem: A Report on the Banality of Evil*. New York: Penguin, 1994.

Augustine. *Confessions*. Translated by Henry Chadwick. Oxford: Oxford University Press, 1991.

Bakhtin, Mikhail. *Rabelais and His World*. Translated by Helene Iswolsky. Bloomington: Indiana University Press, 1984.

Barth, Karl. *Church Dogmatics*. Vol. 3. 1. Edinburgh: T & T Clark, 1958.

Bascio, Patrick. *The Failure of White Theology: A Black Theological Perspective*. New York: Peter Lang, 1994.

Berenbaum, Michael. *The Vision of the Void, Theological Reflections on the Works of Elie Wiesel*. Middletown, CT: Wesleyan, 1979.

Berger, Peter. *Redeeming Laughter: The Comic Dimension of the Human Experience*. New York: Walter de Gruyter, 1997.

Bergson, Henri. *Laughter: An Essay on the Meaning of the Comic.* New York: Macmillan, 1913.

Bloch, Ernst. *The Principle of Hope.* 3 vols. Cambridge, MA: MIT Press, 1986.

Bonhoeffer, Dietrich. *Letters and Papers from Prison.* Edited by Eberhard Bethge. New York: Collier, 1972.

Bouchard, Larry D. "In Front of the Mask: The Priest in Contemporary Dramas of Integrity." *Word and World* 9, no. 4 (1989): 372–81.

_____. *Tragic Method and Tragic Theology: Evil in Contemporary Drama and Religious Thought.* University Park, PA: Penn State University Press, 1989.

Buber, Martin. *The Origin and Meaning of Hasidism.* Edited and translated by Maurice Friedman. New York: Harper and Row, 1960.

Buechner, Frederick. *The Book of Bebb.* San Francisco: Harper and Row, 1971.

Camus, Albert. *The Fall.* Translated by Justin O'Brien. New York: Modern Library, 1956.

Capps, Donald. *A Time to Laugh: The Religion of Humor.* New York: Continuum, 2005.

Cargas, Harry James. *Henry James Cargas in Conversation with Elie Wiesel.* New York: Paulist Press, 1976.

Cheek, William F. *Black Resistance before the Civil War.* Beverly Hills, CA: Glencoe Press, 1970.

Collins, Patricia Hill. *Black Feminist Thought: Knowledge, Consciousness and the Politics of Empowerment.* New York: Routledge, 1991.

Cone, James. *A Black Theology of Liberation.* Maryknoll, NY: Orbis, 1986.

_____. *God of the Oppressed.* Minneapolis: Seabury Press, 1975.

_____. *My Soul Looks Back.* Nashville: Abingdon, 1982.

_____. *The Spirituals and the Blues.* Maryknoll, NY: Orbis, 1972.

Corey, Susan. "The Religious Dimensions of the Grotesque in Literature: Toni Morrison's *Beloved.*" In *The Grotesque in Art and Literature,* edited by James Luther Adams and William Yates, 227–42. Grand Rapids: Eerdmans, 1997.

Cousar, Charles B. *A Theology of the Cross.* Minneapolis: Fortress, 1990.

Cox, Harvey. *The Feast of Fools: A Theological Essay on Festivity and Fantasy.* New York: Harper and Row, 1969.

Des Pres, Terrence. *Writing Into the World: Essays: 1973–1987*. New York: Viking, 1991.

Dostoevksy, Fyodor. *The Brothers Karamazov*. Translated by Richard Pevear and Larissa Volokhonsky. New York: Vintage, 1990.

Douglas, Kelly Brown. *The Black Christ*. Maryknoll, NY: Orbis, 1994.

_____. *Sexuality and the Black Church*. Maryknoll, NY: Orbis, 1999.

Endo, Shusaku. *The Life of Jesus*. Translated by Richard A. Schuchert. New York: Paulist Press, 1978.

_____. *Silence*. Translated by William Johnston. New York: Taplinger, 1969.

Fackenheim, Emil. "Midrashic Existence after the Holocaust: Reflections Occasioned by the Work of Elie Wiesel." In *Confronting the Holocaust: The Impact of Elie Wiesel*, edited by Alvin H. Rosenfeld and Irving Greenberg. Bloomington: Indiana University Press, 1978, 99–116.

Ford, David, ed. *The Modern Theologians*. Vol. 2. Oxford: Basil Blackwell, 1989.

Freud, Sigmund. *Jokes and Their Relation to the Unconscious*. Trans. James Strachey. New York: Norton, 1960.

Friedemann, Joe. *Le Rire dans l'Univers Tragique d'Elie Wiesel*. Paris: Librairie A.-G. Nizet, 1981.

Fry, Timothy, ed. *The Rule of St. Benedict in English*. Collegeville, MN: Liturgical Press, 1982.

Gilhus, Ingvild Soelid. *Laughing Gods, Weeping Virgins: Laughter in the History of Religions*. New York: Routledge, 1997.

Gilkes, Cheryl Townsend. *If It Wasn't for the Women: Black Women's Experience and Womanist Culture in Church and Community*. Maryknoll, NY: Orbis, 2001.

Goldman, Peter. *The Death and Life of Malcolm X*. Urbana: University of Illinois, 1973.

Gray, Frances. *Women and Laughter*. Charlottesville: University of Virginia Press, 1994.

Grewal, Gurleen. *Circles of Sorrow, Lines of Struggle: The Novels of Toni Morrison*. Baton Rouge: Louisiana State University Press, 1998.

Gritsch, Eric W. *Martin—God's Court Jester: Luther in Retrospect*. Philadelphia: Fortress Press, 1983.

Hopkins, Dwight. *Down, Up and Over: Slave Religion and Black Theology.* Minneapolis: Fortress Press, 2000.

_____. *Shoes That Fit Our Feet: Sources for a Constructive Black Theology.* Maryknoll, NY: Orbis, 1993.

Hopkins, Dwight, and George Cummings, eds. *Cut Loose Your Stammering Tongue: Black Theology in Slave Narratives.* Maryknoll, NY: Orbis, 1991.

Hyers, M. Conrad. *The Comic Vision and the Christian Faith: A Celebration of Life and Laughter.* New York: Pilgrim Press, 1981.

_____. *Holy Laughter: Essays on Religion in the Comic Perspective.* New York: Seabury Press, 1969.

Jones, Major. *Black Awareness: A Theology of Hope.* Nashville: Abingdon, 1971.

King, Martin Luther, Jr. *Strength to Love.* Philadelphia: Fortress Press, 1963.

Kitamori, Kazoh. *Theology and the Pain of God.* London: SCM Press, 1965.

Kuschel, Josef. *Laughter: A Theological Reflection.* New York: Continuum, 1994.

Langer, Lawrence. *The Holocaust and the Literary Imagination.* New Haven, CT: Yale, 1975.

_____. *Versions of Survival: The Holocaust and the Human Spirit.* Albany, NY: SUNY Press, 1982.

Levine, Lawrence W. *Black Culture and Black Consciousness: Afro-American Folk Thought From Slavery to Freedom.* Oxford: Oxford University Press, 1977.

Lipman, Steve. *Laughter in Hell: The Use of Humor during the Holocaust.* Northvale, NJ: Jason Aronson, 1991.

Loeb, Paul Rogat, ed. *The Impossible Will Take a Little While: A Citizen's Guide to Hope in a Time of Fear.* New York: Basic Books, 2004.

Lull, Timothy F., ed. *Martin Luther's Basic Theological Writings.* Minneapolis: Fortress Press, 1989.

Moltmann, Jürgen. *The Crucified God: The Cross of Christ as the Foundation and Criticism of Christian Theology.* Minneapolis: Fortress Press, 1993.

_____. *Theology of Hope.* Minneapolis: Fortress Press, 1967.

_____. *Theology of Play.* New York: Harper and Row, 1972.

Morreal, John, ed. *The Philosophy of Laughter and Humor*. Albany, NY: SUNY Press, 1987.

Morreal, John. *Comedy, Tragedy and Religion*. Albany, NY: SUNY Press, 1999.

_____. "Humor in the Holocaust: Its Critical, Cohesive, and Coping Functions." *Holocaust Teaching Resource Center*. November 22, 2001. http://www. holocaust-trc.org/holocaust_humor. htm.

_____. *Taking Laughter Seriously*. Albany, NY: SUNY Press, 1983.

Morrison, Toni. *Beloved*. New York: Plume, 1987.

_____. *Playing in the Dark: Whiteness and the Literary Imagination*. Cambridge, MA: Harvard University Press, 1992.

Niebuhr, Reinhold. "Humor and Faith." In *Holy Laughter*, edited by Conrad Hyers. New York: Seabury Press, 1969, 134–49.

Nietzsche, Friedrich. *Human, All Too Human: A Book for Free Spirits*. Cambridge: Cambridge University Press, 1986.

_____. *Thus Spoke Zarathustra*. New York: Penguin, 1954.

Nussbaum, Martha. "Tragedy and Cost Benefit Analysis." University of Virginia Lecture, Charlottesville, September 13, 2000.

Ostrower, Chaya. "Humor as a Defense Mechanism in the Holocaust." PhD diss., Tel-Aviv University, 2000. http://remember.org/humor/abstractn.html

Patterson, David. *In Dialogue and Dilemma with Elie Wiesel*. Wakefield, NH: Longwood, 1991.

Peterson, Michael L., ed. *The Problem of Evil: Selected Readings*. Notre Dame, IN: University of Notre Dame Press, 1992.

Raboteau, Albert J. *Slave Religion: The "Invisible Institution" in the Antebellum South*. Oxford: Oxford University Press, 1978.

Ricoeur, Paul. *Figuring the Sacred: Religion, Narrative, and Imagination*. Edited by Mark I. Wallace. Translated by David Pellauer. Minneapolis: Augsburg, 1995.

_____. *The Symbolism of Evil*. Translated by Emerson Buchanan. Boston: Beacon, 1967.

Rittner, Carol, and John K. Roth, eds. *Different Voices: Women and the Holocaust*. St. Paul, MN: Paragon, 1993.

Rosenfeld, Alvin H., and Irving Greenberg, eds. *Confronting the Holocaust*. Bloomington: Indiana University Press, 1978.

Rotenberg, Mordechai. *Dialogue with Deviance: The Hasidic Ethic and the Theory of Social Construction*. Lanham, MD: University Press of America, 1993.

Roth, John K. "A Theodicy of Protest." In *Encountering Evil: Life Options in Theodicy*, Edited by Stephen Davis. Atlanta: John Knox Press, 1981, 7–22.

Roth, John K., and Michael Berenbaum, eds. *Holocaust: Religious and Philosophical Implications*. St. Paul: Paragon, 1989.

Sanders, Barry. *Sudden Glory: Laughter as Subversive History*. Boston: Beacon, 1995.

Sanders, Cheryl, ed. *Living the Intersection: Womanism and Afrocentrism in Theology*. Minneapolis: Fortress, 1995.

Schindler, Pesach. *Hasidic Responses to the Holocaust*. Hoboken, NJ: KTAV Publishing, 1990.

Schuster, Ekkehard, and Reinhold Boscher-Kimmig. *Hope Against Hope: Johann Baptist Metz and Elie Wiesel Speak Out on the Holocaust*. Translated by J. Matthew Ashley. New York: Paulist Press, 1962.

Scott, James C. *Domination and the Arts of Resistance: Hidden Transcripts*. New Haven, CT: Yale University Press, 1990.

Scott, Nathan. *The Broken Center*. New Haven, CT: Yale University Press, 1966.

Screech, M. A. *Laughter at the Foot of the Cross*. New York: Penguin, 1997.

Shapiro, Susan. "Hearing the Testimony of Radical Negation." *Concilium* 175 (1984): 3–10.

Steiner, George. *Language and Silence*. New York: Atheneum, 1966.

Surin, Kenneth. "Taking Suffering Seriously." In *The Problem of Evil: Selected Readings*, edited by Michael L. Peterson, 339–49. Notre Dame, IN: University of Notre Dame Press, 1992.

Taylor, Carole Ann. *The Tragedy and Comedy of Resistance: Reading Modernity Through Black Women's Fiction*. Philadelphia: Pennsylvania Press, 2000.

Taylor-Guthrie, Danille, ed. *Conversations with Toni Morrison*. Jackson: Mississippi University Press, 1994.

Tillich, Paul. *Dynamics of Faith*. New York: Harper and Row, 1957.

Unamuno, Miguel de. *Tragic Sense of Life*. New York: Dover Publications, 1954.

Waite, Robert. *The Psychopathic God: Adolf Hitler*. New York: Basic Books, 1977.

West, Cornel. *Prophesy Deliverance! An Afro-American Revolutionary Christianity*. Philadelphia: Westminster, 1982.

West, Traci. *Wounds of the Spirit: Black Women, Violence, and Resistance Ethics*. New York: NYU Press, 1999.

Wiesel, Elie. *A Beggar in Jerusalem*. New York: Avon, 1970.

_____. *Ethics and Memory*. New York: Walter de Gruyter, 1977.

_____. *Four Hasidic Masters and Their Struggle with Melancholy*. Notre Dame, IN: University of Notre Dame Press, 1978.

_____. *From the Kingdom of Memory*. New York: Summit, 1990.

_____. *Gates of the Forest*. New York: Schocken, 1966.

_____. "The Holocaust as Literary Inspiration." In *Dimensions of the Holocaust*, edited by Lacey Baldwin Smith. Evanston, IL: Northwestern University Press, 1978, 4–19.

_____. *A Journey of Faith*. New York: Donald I. Fine, 1990.

_____. *Messengers of God: Biblical Portraits and Legends*. Translated by Marion Wiesel. New York: Random House, 1976.

_____. *The Oath*. New York: Random House, 1973.

_____. *Souls on Fire: Portraits and Legends of Hasidic Masters*. Translated by Marion Wiesel. New York: Random House, 1972.

Wiesel, Elie, and Albert H. Friedlander. *The Six Days of Destruction: Meditations Toward Hope*. New York: Paulist Press, 1988.

Wiesel, Elie, and Michael de Saint Cheron. *Evil and Exile*. Notre Dame, IN: University of Notre Dame Press, 1990.

Williams, Delores. *Sisters in the Wilderness: The Challenge of Womanist God-Talk*. Maryknoll, NY: Orbis, 1993.

Williams, Mark. *Endo Shusaku: A Literature of Reconciliation*. New York: Routledge, 1999.

Zwart, Hub. *Ethical Consensus and the Truth about Laughter: The Structure of Moral Transformations*. Kampen, The Netherlands: Kok Pharos Publishing House, 1996.

Index